THE
BIG BOOK OF
RECIPES FOR
BABIES,
TODDLERS,
& CHILDREN

BRIDGET WARDLEY
AND JUDY MORE

THE BIG BOOK OF RECIPES FOR BABIES, TODDLERS, & CHILDREN

365 QUICK, EASY, AND HEALTHY DISHES

DUNCAN BAIRD PUBLISHERS

LONDON

To our children Elliott, Henry, Lucy, and Sylvie

The Big Book of Recipes for Babies, Toddlers, & Children
Bridget Wardley and Judy More

Distributed in the USA and Canada by
Sterling Publishing Co., Inc.
387 Park Avenue South
New York, NY 10016-8810

This edition first published in the UK and USA in 2004 by
Duncan Baird Publishers Ltd
Sixth Floor, Castle House
75–76 Wells Street
London W1T 3QH

Managing Editor: Julia Charles
Editors: Ingrid Court-Jones with Becky Miles
Managing Designer: Manisha Patel
Designers: Rachel Cross with Sailesh Patel (food photography)
Commissioned photography: William Lingwood (food) and
    Vanessa Davies (children)
Photography Assistant: Estelle Cuthbert
Stylists: Joss Herd (food) and Helen Trent

Library of Congress Cataloging-in-Publication Data available

ISBN: 978-1-84483-106-7

10 9 8 7

Typeset in Frutiger and Helvetica
Color reproduction by Scanhouse, Malaysia
Printed in China by Imago

Publisher's Notes
This book has been written using the latest UK guidelines for weaning.
As these may differ from those used in the US, please follow US
guidelines or consult your pediatrician for further information.

In order to avoid gender bias, the use of "he" and "she",
when referring to a baby, alternates section by section
through this book.

For information about custom editions, special sales, premium
and corporate purchases, please contact Sterling Special Sales
Department at 800-805-5489 or specialsales@sterlingpub.com.

contents

INTRODUCTION

Choosing the right foods for your child when he is very young will help him to grow and develop. And by feeding him delicious and nutritious food while he is keen to follow your example, you will be instilling in him a knowledge of healthy eating for life. Using our experiences as dietitians and mothers we have written this book to help you to enjoy feeding your children as much as we have enjoyed feeding ours. Family meals are important and the recipes we have chosen are quick and easy, use nutritious ingredients, and, when combined with other foods, will give your children a healthy, immunity-boosting, growth-promoting diet.

As many parents find the different stages of feeding babies and young children daunting, we give clear recommendations through the stages of weaning and beyond with recipes and menu planners to help you to provide all the nutrients your child needs in the correct amounts. Busy lifestyles often leave little time for cooking, so we have devised recipes that use a wide range of cooking methods – from quick stir-frying to baking to slow casseroling. We have also included some recipes for foods that can be made in advance and frozen, as well as some that simply involve combining different foods on a plate in the right proportions.

Healthy eating does not have to mean depriving your child of their favorite foods. By using quality ingredients you can make delicious burgers, nuggets, pizzas, fries, and kebabs that are far more nutritious than the commercial varieties, which usually contain additives and an excess of salt, sugars, and fats. Research has shown that most children today eat far too much sugar, fat, and salt – mainly in the form of highly-processed snacks – and as a result, many of them are becoming overweight. By encouraging your child to be active, and above all by developing healthy eating patterns from an early age, you can prevent your child from developing such weight problems. Most parents – understandably – also worry when their child seems to lose his appetite. But most children go off their food from time to time. Bear in mind that your child doesn't need to eat well at every meal, or even every day. As long as he consumes a good balance of foods over a period of a week or so he will obtain all the nutrients he needs.

Finally, we'd like to share with you our three golden rules for happy and healthy eating:
• Eat together as a family as often as possible.
• Show your baby or child that you enjoy eating the foods that you want him to eat.
• Praise your child when he eats well and never indicate that you are anxious or upset when he doesn't.

HOW TO USE THIS BOOK

In Part 1 we give you all the information you require to put together a healthy diet for your child. There is everything you need to know about essential nutrients and food-combining, as well as strategies for preventing feeding problems and advice on how to deal with problems if they do occur. You will also find out how to shop wisely, how to make informed choices about the foods your family eats, and how to feed children who have food allergies.

In Parts 2 and 3 we guide you through the different stages of your child learning to eat, from when he begins solids to when he becomes a self-feeding two year old. In Part 4 there are recipes for 3–6 year olds based around the family meals of breakfast, lunch, and dinner, as well as snacks and drinks. We also offer ideas for nutritious party food and recipes that you can cook with your child.

The menu planners in Part 5 will help you to organize healthy menus; and we also include information on store-cupboard essentials and food hygiene.

We have devised a series of symbols to accompany each recipe which show, at a glance, whether it is suitable for vegetarians; whether it is gluten-, wheat-, or dairy-free; whether it contains eggs or peanuts; and whether it is a good source of iron, calcium, or omega-3 fats.

Key to symbols used in the recipes

V **Suitable for vegetarians** This recipe contains no meat or fish (although sometimes these will be offered as an optional addition).

Ⓖ **Gluten-free** This recipe contains no gluten.

Ⓦ **Wheat-free** This recipe contains no wheat, but may contain gluten. (Note that it is important also to check any ready-made ingredients included in any of the recipes to ensure that they are gluten- or wheat-free.)

Ⓓ **Dairy-free** This recipe contains no milk or products made from milk, such as cheese, yogurt, butter, or cream.

O **Contains eggs** Eggs are an ingredient in this recipe.

Ø **Contains peanuts** Peanuts are an ingredient in this recipe. (Note that if your child has an allergy to peanuts it is also vitally important to check any ready-made ingredients included in any of the recipes for added peanuts and for contamination with peanuts.)

Ⓘ **Good source of iron** This recipe contains an above-average amount of iron or a form of iron that we can absorb very easily.

Ⓒ **Good source of calcium** One serving of this recipe gives about one third of a young child's daily calcium requirement.

Ⓞ **High in omega-3s** This recipe contains an ingredient that is a rich source of omega-3 fats.

part one

the basics

Every parent wants the best for their child and giving
them a good start in life by feeding them nutritious
food is hugely important, not only because it maintains
good health in childhood, but also because it helps to
boost their immune systems. In turn, this can help to
protect them from disease and infection throughout
their adult lives.

In this section, we guide you through the principles
of healthy eating for young children and advise on
how best to provide them with a balanced diet. We
give practical information on teaching your baby and
toddler how to eat her first foods, offer strategies for
coping with feeding problems and food allergies and
suggest ways to shop wisely.

By educating children about delicious and nutritious
food while they are young, you will be teaching them
good habits and laying the foundations for a healthy
attitude towards food and eating for life.

HEALTHY EATING

Combining foods in the right proportions gives children the healthy balanced diet they need to thrive (see p.12–13). Their nutritional needs are different to those of adults and their intake of various nutrients should differ accordingly. Children under five are usually very active – growing and changing rapidly. They still have very small stomachs, but they burn off a lot of calories so they need to obtain a higher proportion of calories from fat in their food than older children and adults. Babies nourished by breastmilk or formula get half their calories from fat whereas the healthy lower-fat adult diet should obtain no more than a third of calories from fat. Between the ages of one and five a gradual shift toward the healthy lower-fat diet recommended for older children and adults should occur.

During this period of accelerated growth (0–5 years), children also require higher amounts of other vital nutrients, particularly iron, zinc and calcium, than adults. Conversely, their intake of fiber should be less than the amount recommended for adults as this can fill them up too quickly and reduces their ability to absorb other nutrients.

In addition, it is very important to keep salt intake low in babies and young children. Young babies' kidneys are unable to get rid of excess salt and in older children salt has been linked to higher blood pressure. Salt should never be added to food for babies and should be kept to a minimum when cooking for young children. Seventy-five per cent of the salt we eat is found in processed food, especially in crisps, cookies and convenience meals. Clear recommendations for salt intake in children have been made (see p.29) and these are considerably lower than the amounts many now consume. It is a good idea to avoid having salt shakers on the table and to add little salt, if any, when cooking. Our recipes keep salt to a minimum and use herbs and spices for flavor.

What children drink also contributes greatly to their diet. Milk and water are best as they do not damage teeth. Although fruit juices provide nutrients, they can cause tooth decay so offer them well-diluted and only at meal times. Fizzy and sugary drinks that have no nutritional value and cause decay are best avoided. Don't give children tea with meals as the tannins hinder absorption of other nutrients. Drinks containing caffeine should also be avoided.

Establishing healthy eating habits in children is not just about what is eaten, but how much and when. Children's appetites vary from day to day depending on how they feel and how active they are, so don't worry if they seem to fluctuate. However, generally speaking, children eat better when they have a well-developed routine. This is ideally three small meals with one or two nutritious snacks per day. Avoid letting them graze throughout the day as this does not allow them to feel hungry before a meal and to learn the feeling of having had enough. Many overweight children have no way of recognizing when they feel truly hungry or comfortably full because they snack all day.

Children learn by watching others so, as parents, we need to set a good example by eating the foods we want our children to eat and talking about how much we enjoy them. Here are some tips to help you to encourage healthy eating in your child:

- Provide meals at regular times so that your child is not too hungry or too tired to eat.
- Eat together as a family often and make meals relaxed and enjoyable for your child. Food should be easy for them to eat so cut it up where necessary and give them cutlery they can manage.
- Offer a variety of foods of different colors, shapes, and textures.
- Offer small portions allowing for second helpings if desired.
- Give confectionery and candy as an occasional special treat and give them at the end of meals rather than in between.
- Praise your child for eating well and sitting at the table.
- Never insist they eat everything on their plate.

FOOD-COMBINING

Until the age of 6 months babies can obtain all the nutrients they require from breastmilk or formula. After this time a combination of different foods is required to supply their needs. Once they reach the age of one babies can join in with family meals, eating many of the same foods as the rest of the family. A healthy balanced diet for babies, children, and adults can be achieved by dividing the foods we eat into five groups and then combining them in certain proportions. Provided that the proportions of the different food groups are maintained, the serving sizes for children do not have to be defined as these will naturally start off quite small and increase in size as the children grow. The five groups are:

Bread, cereals, and potatoes
This group includes all types of bread, pasta, rice, couscous, potatoes, sweet potatoes, breakfast cereals, and any foods made from other cereal crops, or their flour, such as oats, rye, maize, millet, and sorghum. They provide the bulk of the complex carbohydrates that give your child energy.

Each meal should be based on foods from this group and they should also be included at snack times. As a proportion of the total meal, these foods should comprise about one third of the plate.

Fruit and vegetables
This group includes fruit and vegetables that are fresh, frozen, canned, and dried. As well as containing some carbohydrates, they provide your child with her main source of antioxidants and flavonoids and a range of vitamins and minerals. To instill healthy eating habits in your child, be sure to offer fruit and vegetables at each meal so that she learns that they are an integral part of a balanced meal. During the course of a day, aim to give around five small portions, preferably a selection of different ones. As the fiber found in the fruits and vegetables is an important nutrient, juices made from them (which have had the fiber removed), can only be counted as one portion per day.

Milk and dairy
This includes milk, cheese, and yogurt – the dairy foods which are rich in protein, calcium, and other vitamins and minerals. Butter and cream, which have no protein and little calcium, are found in the fifth group with other fatty foods.

Children over a year old need three servings from this group per day. The serving sizes should increase as your child grows and her appetite increases accordingly. A single serving size from this group would be a glass of milk of about 4fl oz for a 1–3yr old, and 5–9fl oz for older children. Always use full-fat milk, yogurt and fromage frais for children under 2 years. If they are eating well you can change to semi-skimmed milk after the age of 2 years and skimmed milk after 5 years.

Children on vegan diets exclude all foods of animal origin, including the milk and dairy products from this group and meat, fish, and eggs from the next group. Their diet is at risk from a lack of protein, iron, calcium, zinc, and vitamin B12. Ask a dietician to assess your child's diet and to suggest an appropriate supplement. Very restricted diets are unsuitable for young children.

Meat, fish, eggs, nuts, and pulses

The foods in this group provide your child with the bulk of her protein, iron, and zinc, as well as some other minerals and vitamins. Pulses include beans, lentils, and chickpeas, which is important if your child is a vegetarian. Children eating meat and fish need 1–2 servings from this group per day. Vegetarian children need 2–3 servings per day. These servings should be combined with foods from the starchy bread, cereals, and potato group in order for their bodies to obtain the essential amino acids needed for growth (see p.14). Vegetarian sources of iron in this group are not absorbed by the body as easily as iron from meat and fish and need to be served with a good source of vitamin C to boost absorption.

Foods high in fat and sugar

Young, active children need some of these foods in order to provide them with calories, omega-3 and omega-6 fats and vitamins A, D, and E. However, only relatively small quantities are advised, as fatty foods provide a high ratio of calories to nutrients, and excess amounts can cause obesity.

Use a mixture of the different oils, butter, and margarine (see pp.14–15) in your cooking so that you can create an appropriate combination of fats in your child's diet.

Sugar, candy, sweetened drinks, crisps, cookies, cakes, and ice cream are also in this group. They can be eaten with, but not instead of, foods from the other, more nutritious, groups.

ESSENTIAL NUTRIENTS

Giving your child a healthy balanced diet based on the principle of
food-combining (see pp.12–13) will provide her with all the essential
nutrients she requires in the amounts she needs. Here, we expand on
the roles played by the various nutrients in the body, and describe
some of the best food sources containing them.

Carbohydrates

Carbohydrates provide your child with energy. They are made up of
starches and sugars . The body transforms them into glucose, the fuel
for the brain. They are found in foods from the cereal group, fruits,
vegetables, and lactose, the milk sugar present in milk and yogurt.
Combinations of cereals, vegetables, and fruits will also provide
different types of fiber (soluble and insoluble) which helps the
digestive system to work properly by encouraging the growth of
good bacteria and preventing constipation and diarrhea.

Proteins

Proteins are required to build and maintain all cells in the body.
Babies and children require a higher proportion of them in their diet
because of the vast number of new cells their bodies are creating as
they grow. Proteins are made up of long chains of amino acids linked
together. Some amino acids are made by our bodies and others come
from the food we eat. Those derived from diet are called essential
amino acids and these are found in the best combinations in milk,
meat, fish, and eggs. Vegetarian children should always eat protein
foods with a starchy food (see p.13) to ensure a similar combination
of amino acids.

Fats

There are many different types of fat, all of which provide the body
with energy. Some are much healthier than others, but there is no
single, ideal variety, so it is best to give your child a balance of
different fats – a mixture of monounsaturated and polyunsaturated
fats – limiting the amounts of saturated and trans fats in her diet.

Most of the fat in meat, butter, cream, wholemilk, cheese, coconut,
and palm oil is saturated fat. Large amounts are also present in many
processed foods, in particular commercially-baked cookies and cakes.
Trans fats are formed in the processing of food and are high in hard
margarines and foods that are made with hydrogenated vegetable oils.

Monounsaturated and polyunsaturated fats are found in vegetable
oils, nuts, and seeds. To utilize these fats the body converts them into
fatty acids, but there are two types of key polyunsaturated fatty acids

that cannot be made by our bodies. These are omega-3 and omega-6 essential fatty acids. They are known as essential as they can only be obtained through diet. A good balance of these two fats is vital for your growing child. They are used by your child's body to make LCPs or LCPUFAs (long chain polyunsaturated fatty acids), which play a crucial role in the development and maintenance of a healthy brain and nervous system, and good vision. They also help to prevent allergies, and some respiratory and skin conditions.

Newborn babies cannot make enough LCPs themselves, but there are plenty in breastmilk if the mother has a good diet herself. They are now also added to some formula milks. There is usually enough omega-6 in our diets, although research now suggests that some older babies and young children may not be making enough omega-3 LCPs duc to a deficiency of omega-3 fats in their diet. The best source of omega-3 LCPs is oily fish (salmon, fresh tuna, mackerel, and herring) and this should be included in your child's diet once a week. Other rich sources of omega-3 include walnuts and walnut oil, rapeseed oil, linseeds and linseed oil. Other seeds, nuts, and oils are rich in omega-6 fats, but very low in omega-3. Good combinations of omega-3 and omega-6 fats can be found in olive and soya oils, meat and milk products from animals grazed on grass, and eggs from hens fed on an omega-3 enriched diet.

Vitamins

Vitamin A
Important for growth, preventing infections, healthy skin, and good night vision, vitamin A can be found in liver, kidney, oily fish, and eggs. Carotenes, which are found in orange, red, and dark green fruit and vegetables (especially carrots, red bell peppers, spinach, broccoli, and tomatoes) are converted to vitamin A in the body. Deficiency causes night blindness, skin problems, and greater risk of infections.

B-complex vitamins
This group includes thiamine (B1), riboflavin (B2), niacin (B3), pantothenic acid (B5), pyridoxine (B6), biotin, vitamin B12, and folate (folic acid). They are all important for growth and the development of a healthy nervous system, and are needed to convert food into energy. They also help to prevent heart disease and cancer. Vitamin B12 and folate are important in preventing anemia. B-vitamins are found in many foods but no foods except liver and yeast extract contain them all. Good sources include meat, milk products, fish, eggs, cereals, seeds and vegetables. Dark green vegetables are very high in folate.

Vitamin C

This is essential for protecting cells from damage, for good iron absorption, and for maintaining blood vessels, cartilage, muscle, and bone. Vitamin C is also involved in wound healing. Rich sources are blackcurrants, kiwi fruit, citrus fruits, tomatoes, green bell peppers, and strawberries. A severe deficiency of vitamin C causes scurvy.

Vitamin D

Needed for the proper absorption of calcium by the body, our main source of vitamin D comes from the effect of sunlight or daylight on the skin during summer months. We build up a reserve when we are outside in summer to supply us during winter. The few food sources of vitamin D are oily fish, margarines, and fortified breakfast cereals. Babies and children with dark skins make less vitamin D than those with white skins. Breastmilk is low in vitamin D, but babies whose mothers were in good health during pregnancy are born with enough to last them for about 6 months. Vitamin D, along with vitamin A, is added to formula milks. From 6 months of age breastfed babies and those drinking less than 18fl oz of formula a day need a supplement of vitamins until they are 5 years old. Inadequate intake of vitamin D causes rickets, a disease that, unfortunately, is on the increase.

Vitamin E

Found in fatty foods such as vegetable oils, margarines, avocados, walnuts, meat, fish, and eggs, this is an important antioxidant that protects cell structures in all parts of the body.

Vitamin K

Needed to ensure normal blood clotting, this vitamin is supplied mostly by bacteria in the intestine. Green leafy vegetables are a good food source.

Minerals

Calcium

This is vital to build strong healthy bones and teeth. Good sources include milk, cheese, and yogurt, fortified soya milk and yogurt, almonds, and canned fish with edible bones, such as sardines.

Copper and Magnesium

Generally found in all foods in tiny amounts, these are involved in energy and protein production.

Fluoride

Using a smear of fluoride toothpaste twice a day when cleaning teeth will provide enough to help protect your child against dental decay.

Iodine

This is found in fish, milk, and eggs. It is part of the thyroid hormone thyroxine, which regulates the conversion of food into energy and assists general mental and physical development.

Iron

Iron is involved in carrying oxygen around the body in the red blood cells and also energy production. Too little causes anemia and this is very common in toddlers. Anemia causes tiredness and delayed growth and development. Good food sources of haem iron (iron which is absorbed easily by the body) are red meat, liver, and oily fish. Good food sources of non haem iron (which needs vitamin C to help absorption) are pulses, fortified breakfast cereals, nuts, seeds, and some vegetables.

Potassium

This is important for fluid balance in the body, muscle contractions and proper nerve function. Rich food sources of potassium include fruit, vegetables, wholegrains, cocoa, and chocolate.

Selenium

This is involved in hormone and energy production and the protection of cells. Rich food sources are fish, meat, cereals, Brazil nuts, cashew nuts, and vegetables grown on soils high in selenium.

Sodium/salt

This is important for fluid balance in the body and for maintaining blood pressure. Enough sodium is present in bread, cereals, milk, and meat for our needs. Excessive sodium can cause high blood pressure in adolescents and adults. Generally we eat too much sodium. See p.29 for guidelines on recommended sodium intake for children.

Zinc

This mineral aids wound healing, immune function, growth, energy metabolism as well as hormone production. Good food sources of zinc are meat, seafood, egg yolk, milk, wholegrain cereals, and peanut butter. Zinc deficiency can cause skin problems and growth impairment.

Phytochemicals

Nutrition is a constantly evolving science and recent developments have discovered a range of substances known as phytochemicals, which are found in plant foods and which play protective roles against various diseases including heart disease and cancer. One particular group of phytochemicals has become quite well known – the flavonoid group. Flavonoids are found in plant pigments and give fruits and vegetables their bright colors. They reduce inflammation and boost immunity. Lycopene in tomatoes and quercetin in apples, onions, and red wine are reasonably well-known but there are many hundreds of others. All flavonoids are important antioxidants. Eating a variety of fruits and vegetables gives a good mix of flavonoids and other phytochemicals. They are not generally included in vitamin and mineral supplements.

Antioxidants

These are a group of nutrients that boost the immune system and redress imbalances caused by damaging chemicals produced by the body's own metabolism. They include vitamins A, C, and E; the minerals zinc, selenium, copper, and manganese and the flavonoids described under Phytochemicals above. Feeding your child a diet rich in foods containing antioxidants will provide a significant boost to her immune health.

Probiotics and Prebiotics

Probiotics are bacteria found in live yogurt and live yogurt drinks, which, once consumed, work beneficially in our intestines by aiding the absorption of some nutrients, helping to boost immunity and reducing constipation and diarrhea. Prebiotics are food fibers that stimulate the growth of these beneficial bacteria in our intestines.

Water

As well as eating the right foods, a good supply of fluids is also needed to keep your child fit and healthy. On average, children need 6–8 drinks each day to get enough fluid to keep them well-hydrated. In hot weather or after a lot of running about they may need more.

If children do not drink enough they may suffer from headaches, tiredness, loss of appetite, and, in the longer term, constipation and urinary tract infections. Encourage your child to drink water rather than sugary squashes, as these can reduce the appetite for more nutritious foods and can cause diarrhea in some toddlers.

FROM MILK TO FAMILY MEALS: LEARNING TO EAT

First feeds

Breast is best and for the first 6 months of their lives babies need
only breast milk to thrive. One of the key advantages to be gained
from breastfeeding is the protection it gives your baby against
infection and illness. Mothers produce antibodies to viruses in their
specific environment and pass these antibodies on to the baby in
their breast milk, thus preventing the baby from becoming ill with
the virus. Breastfed babies are less likely to get ear infections and
tummy upsets than non-breastfed babies. In the longer term, toddlers
and children who are exclusively breastfed for the first few months
of life will be less likely to suffer from allergies, asthma, and
diabetes. There may even be long-term advantages for health in later
life. Breastfeeding mothers should eat a balanced diet before and
during pregnancy and while breastfeeding in order to produce the
best quality breast milk for their babies.

Some mothers find that breastfeeding comes naturally and is
very easy and convenient for them. However many find it difficult,
especially in the early stages and, without good advice and support,
give up before they would have liked to. The advice and help available
to mothers who are finding breastfeeding difficult varies enormously.
There are several organizations with trained breastfeeding counsellors
(see p.221). Find out which of these agencies has a counsellor local to
you before giving birth, so that you can feel well prepared should
you struggle.

If you are unable to breastfeed, use an approved infant formula
milk. These are made according to strict manufacturing guidelines
in order to safeguard babies' nutrition. Research findings are
continually being used to improve infant formula so that it is as
close to breast milk as science and technology can make it. Always
make it up according to instructions to ensure the correct balance
of fluid and nutrients.

First-stage solids
When to begin

Start to introduce your baby to solid foods at six months or earlier,
but not before 4 months (17 weeks). At this stage babies are putting
toys into their mouths and many show an interest in other people
eating. By waiting until the age of at least four months you are
giving your baby's intestines plenty of time to develop and mature,
thereby reducing her chances of future allergies to food. If you delay

until after the age of six months your baby may become anemic as her body stores of iron begin to run out at this time and breast milk alone will not provide enough iron, zinc, and other nutrients to maintain healthy growth and development.

How to begin

Begin with a smile! No matter how anxious you may be feeling, you are about to teach your baby to eat and enjoy solid food, one of life's great pleasures. Try and make every meal enjoyable for both of you. Mealtimes are an opportunity for interaction with your baby and can be a lot of fun.

Your baby will have to learn certain skills in order to be able to manage solid food. The first of these is how to take food from a spoon. Some mothers give their baby the weaning spoon to play with for a few days before the first meal so that it does not feel strange in their mouth. When you feel that your baby is ready, mix a little of your chosen food (see recipes 001–012, pp.31–7) with some milk so that it is the consistency of runny yogurt. Half fill a plastic weaning spoon with the food and slightly tip it into your baby's mouth allowing her to suck the food from the spoon.

Once your baby has taken the food she will need to learn a second skill – how to get the food from the spoon to the back of her mouth using her tongue. When babies suck at the breast they push their tongue forward. So, when you first give solid food they will usually push the tongue forward and the food will come straight back out. This doesn't mean they don't like the food. It will take several attempts for them to realize that by not pushing the tongue forward the food will stay in the mouth. Eventually they will also learn how to co-ordinate the food to the back of the mouth to be swallowed. To learn these skills they need time, patience, and a smiling face to encourage them.

Don't worry how much your baby actually eats in the first week or two as she will still be getting almost all of her nutrients from milk. Keep trying solids once a day, every day, so that it becomes part of her routine. A good time to do this is halfway through a milk feed so that your baby is not starving hungry nor so full she doesn't want to open her mouth. She will soon learn how to co-ordinate the food in her mouth – it just takes a little practice.

Some babies master these skills very quickly, others take longer. Be guided by *your* baby and go at her pace. It is very important to try to read the signals your baby is giving you. If she opens her mouth she is ready for more food, if she closes it and turns her head away she has probably had enough. Generally, babies who begin weaning closer to 6 months than 4 months will progress much more quickly. Remember that they learn by watching others so make sure they see you and others eating.

Once your baby has learnt how to eat solid food she will begin to take a larger quantity and will realise that it satisfies her hunger. You can now give solids before the milk feed and make them a thicker consistency. Make sure that the food is ready for your baby when she re-opens her mouth. Hungry babies can get frustrated if they are fed slowly when they are used to drinking milk very quickly.

Certain foods are common allergy triggers and delaying their introduction to your child's diet is thought to reduce the risk of developing an allergy to them. These are cereals containing gluten (wheat, rye, barley, and oats), eggs, fish and shell fish, all of which should be introduced after the age of 6 months. Citrus fruits such as oranges, clementines, lemons, and limes are also usually introduced after 6 months. Honey should be avoided until 1 year because it can contain bacteria that causes severe food poisoning in babies. Salt and sugar should not be added to baby foods.

Second-stage solids

Introducing more nutritious foods

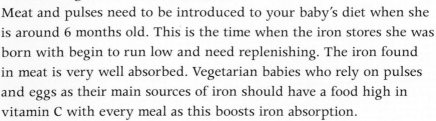

Meat and pulses need to be introduced to your baby's diet when she is around 6 months old. This is the time when the iron stores she was born with begin to run low and need replenishing. The iron found in meat is very well absorbed. Vegetarian babies who rely on pulses and eggs as their main sources of iron should have a food high in vitamin C with every meal as this boosts iron absorption.

Although full of vitamins and minerals, the vegetable and fruit purées that make up the bulk of your baby's first solids are very low in calories. As you increase her intake of solids and she drinks less milk you need to increase the calorie, protein, and nutrient content of your baby's solids. This is sometimes called increasing the nutrient density of solid foods.

Introducing different textures

From the age of 6½ months it is time to begin teaching your baby to enjoy a variety of foods with different textures and tastes. You do not have to wait for a mouth full of teeth to introduce lumpy food. Babies' gums are quite hard and can squash soft lumps very well. It takes a while to learn to control lumps in the mouth so don't be surprised if they come back out to begin with – it doesn't mean she doesn't like the food.

Start introducing lumpy food when your baby can sit upright and has good head control. This way, if a lump isn't chewed enough she can cough it back easily. Coughing back lumps is a normal part of learning how to eat, so don't feel you need to clap her on the back or tip her upside down every time. This will give her a fright and make her wary of eating foods with lumps. However, there is always the possibility of choking so never leave your baby unattended when she is eating. Babies who are not given the opportunity to learn to chew at this age may refuse lumpy food quite stubbornly when they get older.

Involving your baby

As meals get bigger, the time taken to eat them becomes longer. Some babies have a very short attention span and they may get bored quite quickly. Give them their own spoon, so that they can experiment, and expect a mess. Babies put their fingers in food to learn more about what they are eating, and you should allow them to do so.

At the same time that you begin to offer lumpy food to your baby give her some soft finger foods to feed herself with at each meal. Teaching a baby to eat and feed themselves is a very messy business and this is difficult for some new mothers to accept. However, trying to restrict the mess by not letting them be involved may result in them eating less. Equally, respect your baby's decision when she indicates she has had enough, as her appetite will vary from day to day. Take any uneaten food away with a smile and never try to force feed.

Introducing a cup or beaker
As your baby's intake of solids increases, offer her sips of water from a cup or beaker throughout the meal. Sipping rather than sucking fluid is another new skill to learn and it will take some practice before she can control the water flow herself. Encourage and help her to hold the cup or beaker herself. Once your baby has mastered this, you can let her use the cup or beaker instead of a bottle for milk feeds, aiming to discontinue bottles at around one year of age.

Moving on to family meals

Offering a wide a variety of foods and textures between 6 and 12 months will ensure that by 1 year babies will be enjoying family meals and eating many of the same foods as the rest of the family. You will need to cut up hard foods into bite-size pieces. Until babies are between 1½ and 2 years old, they are open to trying new foods, but as they get older they often become much choosier and you may have to offer new foods several times before they will eat them.

A toddler's appetite will be reduced if she is distracted by things around her, such as the TV. If she is tired or miserable because she has become overly hungry she may also have a reduced appetite. Feed your toddler when she is not too tired and avoid shouting at her or coercing her to eat. Eat with your child and include her at family mealtimes. Try to make these experiences happy ones, where she sits at a table and is free from distractions. Offer new foods alongside foods that you know she will like but do not fall into the trap of cooking different meals for every member of the family.

From one year onwards children continue to move forward, learning to cut up and chew harder foods. The pace of this development will vary with each child. By the time your child is an independent and assertive toddler your aim is to have developed a good pattern for lifetime eating. As your child grows, continue to eat together as a family and enjoy a variety of healthy foods. When children are old enough, include them in the preparation of food and discuss food selection and menus with them. As children get older mealtimes also become an important family focus for catching up on news, such as how their day at school went.

COPING WITH FEEDING PROBLEMS

From time to time, many children go through phases of eating very little. This is a normal part of their development and there are many possible explanations. It may be that they have a sore throat, cold or are fighting off an infection. Teething and sore gums are another possibility. Children who feel sad, lonely, anxious, or insecure for any reason may eat less. Some children realize that by refusing food they get their parents' attention: any attention, even if the parent is cross, is better than none. Whatever the reason, if a child goes off her food, parents usually find it exasperating and a cause for concern.

In some cases parents may have created the problem themselves because they expect their child to eat more than she needs to. Many children grow and develop quite normally even though they seem to eat much less than others of the same age. Ask your doctor to check your child's growth and development before worrying unnecessarily.

If your child is not eating well, stay calm and don't blame yourself. Make mealtimes pleasant, relaxed occasions with the family eating and chatting together. A child who is shouted at, coerced to eat more when she is full or dislikes the food, or continually offered food throughout the day can become upset and lose her appetite. If this becomes the pattern she will become anxious as mealtimes approach. Here are some suggestions to help you tackle eating problems:

- Offer food at regular mealtimes with one small nutritious snack halfway between meals. The rest of the time don't offer any food. Don't give candy and chocolates that you know she will take "just so that she has eaten something". Always include something you know she will eat at each meal and snack, in addition to new or less favored foods. Praise her for what she does eat and don't show you are anxious or upset when she doesn't eat.
- Make sure each meal is balanced and nutritious so that when she does eat well she is getting plenty of nutrients.
- Offer small portions so that your child does not feel overwhelmed by a large plate of food. Praise her when she finishes it and offer a second helping but don't insist on this.
- Try not to rush meals. Equally, do not extend the time of the meal in the hope your child will eat more. Limit meal times to 20–30 minutes and take away uneaten food without comment. Then wait for the next snack or mealtime when she may eat more.
- Don't let your child fill up on large quantities of fluid leaving no room for food in her small stomach. Limit drinks between meals to

water and keep milk and milk products to 3 servings per day.
- Involve your child when you are buying food – allow her to choose foods, put them in the trolley and unpack them when you get home. Let her help with meal preparation and cooking.
- Some children eat better in the company of other children so arrange for your child to have some meals with her friends.
- Change the venue of meals and have an impromptu picnic with everyone in the garden or on the playroom floor – make it fun!
- Don't use foods as a bribe or as a reward. If you offer Food B as a reward for eating up Food A then, in essence, you are telling your child that Food B is a desirable food and Food A is not – usually the opposite of the health message you have in mind.
- If one meal turns into a disaster, don't feel guilty. Put it behind you and approach the next meal positively.
- Make a list of all the food your child eats over a week. If there are foods from all the food groups (see p.12) and some variety within each group, you will be reassured that the problem may not be as bad as you thought. If you continue to be concerned about your child's eating talk to your pediatrician who may refer you to a specialist dietitian.

MANAGING ALLERGIES AND INTOLERANCES

Food allergies and intolerances are more common in young children than in older children and adults because, in most cases, children grow out of them by the time they are 5 years old. The most common foods that cause allergies and intolerances are cows' milk, eggs, peanuts, fish, shellfish, wheat, soy, and citrus fruits.

Adverse reactions to food can involve skin rashes, swelling of the lips, face, and eye areas, and wheezing. Belly aches, vomiting, diarrhea, constipation, and poor weight gain may also be indicators. Anaphylaxis is a rare but severe reaction in which the heart rate increases, blood pressure falls, widespread swelling occurs and breathing becomes difficult. If this occurs, medical attention must be sought immediately as the condition can be fatal.

If there is a known risk of food allergy in your family you should introduce the culprits to your child carefully after 6 months of age, noting any reactions and withdrawing a particular food if necessary. If you think that your child has a food allergy or intolerance, see a dietitian for advice on how to manage the condition and how to ensure that your child's diet provides her with all the nutrients she needs. You must also learn to read food labels so that you can check for offending foods and their derivatives in all packaged foods.

Many children do grow out of food allergies, so if your child is a sufferer it is important to have her retested for the allergy or intolerance around her fifth birthday so that you do not continue to avoid foods unnecessarily. The allergies that are most likely to persist beyond the age of five are those to nuts and fish.

Here is some more information regarding some of the most common food allergens and possible replacements for them:

Wheat and gluten
The cereal crop wheat contains many different proteins and children who are allergic or intolerant to wheat react to one or more of these specific proteins. A common offender is gluten, a protein not only found in wheat but also in rye, barley, and oats. Severe gluten intolerance is known as celiac disease and can cause permanent damage to the small intestine. If your child is diagnosed with celiac disease, the only treatment is to follow a diet free from gluten grains (wheat, barley, rye, and oats) and any products (such as bread and pasta, cookies and cakes) made from them. There are plenty of gluten-free alternatives to these staple foods, including potatoes, rice, maize, buckwheat, millet, and sorghum. This is an increasingly

common condition and many food manufacturers now make a range of clearly labeled gluten-free cereal products to choose from.

Cows' milk and cows' milk products
If your child exhibits a reaction to cows' milk you must exclude from her diet all cows' milk, cheese, yogurt, fromage frais, butter, cream, and any foods containing skimmed milk powder or the milk proteins casein and whey. Many children who are allergic to cows' milk are also allergic to other animal milks such as goat or sheep milk. Soy milk, soy yogurts and other soy desserts can be used in place of milk products and are increasingly widely available. If using soy products as a cows' milk substitute, buy those with added calcium to avoid your child becoming calcium deficient.

Soy and soy products
If your child reacts badly to soy you must read food labels with care as soy flour is used in a very wide range of foods. Many breads, commercial cookies, cakes, and foods made with pastry may contain it. Tofu, soy milk and soy yogurts must also be excluded.

Peanuts
Allergic reactions to peanuts can be severe and even a trace of them can trigger a response in sensitive children. Avoid peanut butter, satay sauce, and any foods containing peanuts. The peanut is more closely related to pulses than to other nuts which all grow on trees, so it is rare for a child who is allergic to peanuts to be allergic to other nuts as well. However, the processing and packaging of tree nuts and peanuts sometimes takes place in the same vicinity, leading to the risk of contamination, so treat all nuts and nut products with care.

Additives
Some children react to certain food additives, the most common being the colourings tartrazine (E102), sunset yellow (E110), carmoisine (E122), ponceau 4R (E124), and the preservative sodium benzoate (E211). Some hyperactive children may benefit from removal of these from their diet. Colorings are commonly used in yogurts and desserts, milkshakes, other flavored drinks, candy and ice lollies.

There are several agencies which offer parents with allergic children support and information (see p.221). Most large supermarkets also provide lists of suitable food alternatives – check their websites or with their customer service departments.

SENSIBLE SHOPPING

In the developed world we are able to buy a huge range of foods from all over the world all year round in our local supermarkets. Although this means we have a wide choice of produce, there are compromises to be made. Many of us no longer know when foods are in season which is when they are cheapest and have the best flavor and the maximum amount of nutrients, owing to their comparatively short storage time. Seasonal food is generally higher in vitamins, particularly folic acid and vitamin C, which deteriorate with storage. One antidote to this is to get to know which foods are in season and, where possible, to source them locally. Farmers' markets are appearing in more and more areas, selling locally produced foods in season.

Another shopping choice we have today is whether or not to buy organic food. This is produced without the use of most agrochemicals. Naturally occurring fertilizers and pesticides are allowed, but all other pesticides, herbicides, and genetically-modified organisms (most of which have been developed in the last 35 years) are banned. Organic food has a much shorter shelf life and can only be stored for short periods, but it does contain more folic acid and vitamin C than non-organic. Although each pesticide used in the food industry is checked for safety, the effects of ingesting combinations of different pesticide residues, such as a family might consume in a meal of several different foods, has not been assessed. This is of more concern for children who eat more food per unit of body weight than adults and are therefore more susceptible to any possible effects. Buying some organic foods will help reduce your child's intake of pesticides.

With the increasing number of food scares appearing in the media it is easy for parents to become confused about what they should and should not be feeding their children. It is important to remember that the media often sensationalize studies published in scientific journals, taking comments out of context and focusing only on a small part of the study. The United States National Agricultural Library has the latest up to date information and advice on these issues. Despite scare stories, advice on feeding children has remained virtually unchanged over the last 10 years.

In general, it is advisable to choose the freshest food available from known reliable suppliers. The section at the back of this book on Store Cupboard Essentials (see p.218) will help you to complete your healthy shopping list.

In addition to the above advice, there are a few ingredients that merit further discussion as a result of their inclusion in so many foods and their implications for your child's diet and health:

Sodium and salt

We all need small amounts of sodium in our diets and many foods naturally contain it. However, salt is about 40 per cent sodium and most of us eat too much salt. Three quarters of the salt we eat comes from processed food so it is important to read labels and choose foods with the lowest sodium/salt content. As a general rule, foods with 0.1g sodium/100g are low in salt while foods with 0.5g sodium/100g are high in salt. Use the following guide for recommended daily levels of salt intake for children:

- 7-12 months, 1 gram salt (0.4g sodium) per day
- 1-3 years, 2 grams salt (0.8g sodium) per day
- 4-6 years, 3 grams salt (1.2g sodium) per day
- 7-10 years, 5 grams salt (2g sodium) per day
- 11-14 years, 6 grams salt (2.4g sodium) per day

Sugar

This is added to improve flavor, but many processed foods contain very high amounts, often disguised in different forms, such as sucrose, dextrose, glucose syrup, fructose, golden syrup, honey, and fruit juice concentrate. Look carefully at the ingredients listed on food labels and choose lower sugar foods. Also check labels for the artificial sweeteners acesulfame k, aspartame, saccharin and sorbitol, which are unsuitable for children under three years but are often found in drinks, candy, ice lollies and yogurts.

Oils and Fats

Some oils and fats are far more beneficial for health than others (see p.14) and knowledge of this should inform your shopping accordingly. Butter and cream are high in saturated fat. Use them sparingly as children get older, and buy organic varieties made from cows fed on grass as these have higher levels of the desirable polyunsaturated omega-3 fats. Margarines have less saturated fat, but often contain trans fats, which can also block the production of LCPs (see p.15). Choose softer margarines rather than hard ones as these have lower levels of trans fats. Rapeseed oil and walnut oil are the best oil sources of omega-3 fats. Olive oil is mainly monounsaturated fat, but contains small amounts of omega-3 and omega-6 fats in good balance. Sunflower and safflower oils are high in omega-6 fats. For roasting or broiling use olive, rapeseed or soya oils. For salads use walnut, sesame oil or olive oil.

part two

weaning and first foods

From the time your baby first starts on solids sometime between four and six months of age, until he is ready to join in family meals at around the age of one, he will acquire many new skills. He will begin by learning how to take thin solids from a spoon. He will progress to eating thicker purées, and then master how to chew lumps, so that he can have the same foods as the rest of the family. We aim to help you make your baby's first experiences of food as enjoyable as possible, so that he forms a positive attitude toward eating, which he will keep throughout his toddler years and beyond.

In this section you'll find delicious recipes for weaning and first foods that will not only introduce your baby to a wide selection of fresh tastes and textures, but will also give him a firm basis for developing and growing in optimum health.

SMOOTH FIRST TASTES

Begin weaning by 6 months but not earlier than 4 months. Your baby will probably be exploring toys with his mouth and may be interested in your food. Start by offering  him half a spoon of solids once a day. The consistency should be slightly thicker than milk, so that he can suck it from the spoon. As he accepts the solids, slowly increase the quantity and add less milk. Then, introduce solids at a second feed. Give cereal or a vegetable purée at one feed and a fruit purée at the other. Finally, offer your baby solids at a third feed.

Use the cooking liquid to make the purées so that no nutrients are lost, and freeze them in ice-cube trays for future use. As some vegetable purées are low in calories, we always combine the vegetables with potato to increase the calorie content. At this stage you can sit your baby on your knee or in a bouncer to feed him.

001 first rice flakes

V ✗ ✗

Rice flakes make an excellent first solid food. They require a little cooking, but offer a good, homemade alternative to commercial baby rice.

PREPARATION
20 minutes

STORAGE
Suitable for
freezing; keeps
for up to 24 hours
in the fridge

2 tbsp rice flakes
⅔ cup water or formula milk

expressed breastmilk or formula
milk to thin

Place the rice and water or formula milk in a small saucepan and bring to the boil. Reduce heat and simmer for about 10 minutes until mixture thickens. Remove from heat and allow to cool and thicken further. Take out a portion and push through a sieve with the back of a spoon. Thin down with expressed breastmilk or formula milk. *Makes 8–10 servings*

002 first ground rice

V ✗ ✗

PREPARATION
15 minutes

STORAGE
Suitable for
freezing; keeps
for up to 24 hours
in the fridge

1 tbsp ground rice
⅔ cup water or formula milk

expressed breastmilk or formula
milk to thin

Place the ground rice in a small saucepan with the water or formula milk. Stir to disperse any lumps. Bring to the boil, reduce heat and simmer for 5–6 minutes until mixture thickens. Take out a portion and allow to cool and thicken further. Push mixture through a sieve with the back of a spoon to get a very smooth texture. Thin down to the required consistency with expressed breastmilk or formula milk. *Makes 6–8 servings*

003 millet porridge

V ✗ ✗

PREPARATION
15 minutes

STORAGE
Suitable for
freezing; keeps
for up to 24 hours
in the fridge

1 tbsp millet flakes
⅔ cup water or formula milk

expressed breastmilk or formula
milk to thin

Place the millet flakes in a small saucepan with the water or formula milk. Stir to disperse any lumps. Bring to the boil, reduce heat and simmer for 5–6 minutes until the mixture thickens. Take out a portion and allow to cool and thicken further. The porridge will be very smooth already, but you can push it through a sieve if you wish. Thin down to the required consistency with expressed breastmilk or formula milk. *Makes 6–8 servings*

004 potato purée

Potato makes an ideal first vegetable purée. It contains small amounts of iron and vitamin C, and when puréed it is very smooth and easy for your baby to suck from a spoon. Sweet potato works equally well.

PREPARATION
25 minutes

1 medium potato, peeled and diced
½ cup water
expressed breastmilk or formula milk to thin

STORAGE
Suitable for freezing; keeps for up to 24 hours in the fridge

Put the water into a small saucepan and bring to the boil. Add the potato and cover with a tight-fitting lid. Bring back to the boil and simmer for about 10 minutes until tender. Check to ensure that the water does not boil away, adding more if necessary. Purée the potato with the cooking water until smooth. Take out one portion to serve and add expressed breastmilk or formula milk to thin. *Makes 9–12 servings*

005 carrot and potato purée

Babies love the sweet taste of carrot. Here, we have combined it with potato to provide extra calories.

PREPARATION
25 minutes

1 medium carrot, peeled and diced
1 medium potato, peeled and diced
½ cup water
expressed breastmilk or formula milk to thin

STORAGE
Suitable for freezing; keeps for up to 24 hours in the fridge

Put the water into a small pan and bring to the boil. Add the vegetables and cover. Bring back to the boil and simmer for about 10 minutes until tender. Purée the vegetables with the cooking water. Take out one portion to serve and thin with expressed breastmilk or formula milk. *Makes 12–14 servings*

006 pea and potato purée

PREPARATION
25 minutes

1 medium potato, peeled and diced
½ cup water
½ cup frozen peas
expressed breastmilk or formula milk to thin

STORAGE
Suitable for freezing; keeps for up to 24 hours in the fridge

Put the water into a small pan and bring to the boil. Add the potato and cover with a tight-fitting lid. Bring back to the boil and simmer for about 10 minutes until tender. Add the peas, bring back to the boil again and simmer for a further 2 minutes until they are tender. Check to make sure that the water does not boil away, adding a little more if necessary. Purée the potato and peas with the cooking water until smooth. Take out a portion to serve and add expressed breastmilk or formula milk to thin. *Makes 12–14 servings*

007 parsnip purée
V ✖ ✖

Parsnip is another sweet vegetable popular with babies. It is a good source of calories and can be combined with broccoli, carrot, or other soft vegetables.

PREPARATION
30 minutes

1 medium parsnip, peeled and diced
½ cup water
expressed breastmilk or formula milk to thin

STORAGE
Suitable for freezing; keeps for up to 24 hours in the fridge

Put the water into a saucepan and bring to the boil. Add the parsnip and cover with a tight-fitting lid. Bring back to the boil and simmer for 15 minutes until parsnip is tender. Add more water, if necessary. Purée the parsnip with the cooking water until smooth. Take out one portion to serve and thin with expressed breastmilk or formula milk. *Makes 2–3 servings*

008 sweet potato and cauliflower purée *(below)*
V ✖ ✖

Orange-fleshed sweet potatoes are rich in beta-carotene. Combining them with broccoli or courgette also works well.

PREPARATION
10 minutes

6oz sweet potato, peeled and diced
4oz cauliflower florets
½ cup water

expressed breastmilk or formula milk to thin

STORAGE
Suitable for freezing; keeps for up to 24 hours in the fridge

Put the water into a saucepan and bring to the boil. Add the sweet potato and place the cauliflower florets on top. Cover with a tight-fitting lid and bring back to the boil. Simmer gently for about 10 minutes until both vegetables are tender. Check to ensure that the water does not boil away, adding a little more if necessary. Purée the vegetables until smooth. Take out one portion to serve and add expressed breastmilk or formula milk to thin. *Makes 12–14 servings*

009 avocado purée (below)

V ✗ ✗

The great thing about avocado pears is that they don't need to be cooked, so it only takes a few minutes to make this highly nutritious purée. Serve immediately after preparing, as it discolors quickly.

PREPARATION
10 minutes

1 small ripe avocado, peeled and pitted
expressed breastmilk or formula milk to thin

STORAGE
Use within ½ hour

Mash the fruit with a fork until it forms a purée. For a very smooth texture, push through a sieve with the back of a spoon. Add expressed breastmilk or formula milk to thin to the required consistency. *Makes 1–2 servings*

010   apple purée

Use juicy eating apples to give this first fruit purée the sweetness that babies find so appealing.

PREPARATION
25 minutes

STORAGE
Suitable for
freezing; keeps
for up to 24 hours
in the fridge

1 sweet eating apple, peeled, cored, and diced
1 tbsp water
expressed breastmilk or formula milk to thin

Place the apple and the water in a saucepan, cover with a tight-fitting lid, and bring to the boil. Reduce heat and simmer for 6–8 minutes until tender. Purée the fruit with the cooking water and press through a sieve. Take out one portion to serve. Add expressed breastmilk or formula milk to make a thinner consistency. *Makes 4–6 servings*

011   pear and apple purée

Combining fruits will add variety to your baby's first meals, but you can also use pears on their own.

PREPARATION
30 minutes

STORAGE
Suitable for
freezing; keeps
for up to 24 hours
in the fridge

1 very ripe medium pear, peeled, cored, and diced
1 sweet eating apple, peeled, cored, and diced
2 tbsp water
expressed breastmilk or formula milk to thin

Place the pear and the apple in a small saucepan with the water. Cover with a tight-fitting lid and bring to the boil. Reduce the heat and simmer for 10–12 minutes until very soft. Purée the fruits with the cooking water. Press through a sieve. Take out one portion to serve. Add expressed breastmilk or formula milk to thin. *Makes 6–8 servings*

012   peach and mango purée

PREPARATION
25 minutes

STORAGE
Suitable for
freezing; keeps
for up to 24 hours
in the fridge

1 ripe peach, peeled, pitted, and diced
½ ripe mango, peeled, pitted, and diced
1 tbsp water
expressed breastmilk or formula milk to thin

Place the peach and mango in a small saucepan with the water. Cover with a tight-fitting lid and bring to the boil. Reduce heat and simmer for 5 minutes until tender. Purée the fruits with the cooking water. Press through a sieve. Take out one portion to serve. Add expressed breastmilk or formula milk to thin. *Makes 4–6 servings*

MOVING ON

From 6 months of age onward your baby needs more nutritious foods, such as oats, meat, and pulses, which are high in iron and/or rich in zinc and B vitamins. He can now start to have eggs, fish and cereals containing gluten. You can use cows' milk in his food (but continue with breastmilk or formula for feeds until he is one).

For breakfast, give your baby oats and cereals that soften with milk. For lunch and dinner, offer meals made up of one third meat or pulses, one third starchy food, and one third vegetables. Begin with one ice-cube-size portion of each and increase this to two or more per meal as his appetite grows. Start with smooth purées, but gradually thicken them and introduce lumps to prepare him to chew.

013 creamy first porridge

V ✂ ▣

Giving your baby porridge will increase his iron intake, as oats contain more iron than rice. This can be made in a microwave or conventionally.

PREPARATION
5 minutes/
10 minutes

STORAGE
Suitable for
freezing; keeps
for 1 hour covered

2 tbsp porridge oats
⅔ cup expressed breastmilk,

formula milk, or cows' milk
more milk, as above, to thin

Place the oats and milk in a wide bowl. Microwave on full power, uncovered, for about 3 minutes. Allow to stand for about 2 minutes to thicken. The first few times purée the porridge and/or push through a sieve to make it very smooth, but thereafter let your baby try it with fine, soft lumps. Take out one portion. Thin down with more milk to the required consistency. If you don't have a microwave, put the oats and milk in a saucepan and stir well. Bring to the boil, reduce heat and simmer for 5–7 minutes until a soft, thick mixture forms. *Makes 3–4 servings*

014 porridge with puréed fruit

V ✂ ▣

Mixing fruit with porridge adds vitamin C, which will improve your baby's absorption of iron from the porridge.

PREPARATION
10 minutes

STORAGE
Suitable for
freezing; keeps
for 1 hour covered

4 tbsp creamy porridge, cooked (recipe 013, above)
2 tbsp puréed fruit (recipes 010, 011, and 012, or use any of your baby's favourite fruit purées)
expressed breastmilk, formula milk, or cows' milk to thin

Place the cooked porridge in a bowl. Stir in the fruit and mix. Thin with expressed breastmilk, formula milk, or cows' milk, if necessary. *Makes 1–2 servings*

015 lentils with carrot and coriander

V ✂ ✂ 🥜 🌿

Lentils are a good source of vegetable protein and iron. The vitamin C in the orange juice will help your baby to absorb the iron they contain.

PREPARATION
40 minutes

STORAGE
Suitable for
freezing; keeps
for up to 24 hours
in the fridge

4 tbsp red lentils
1 medium potato, peeled and diced
1 large carrot, peeled and diced
½ tsp ground coriander

1 cup water
½ orange, squeezed
cooled, boiled water to thin

Put the lentils in a sieve. Immerse in a bowl of water and rinse thoroughly. Remove from the water and drain. Place the lentils, vegetables, coriander, and water in a saucepan and cover with a tight-fitting lid. Bring to the boil. Reduce heat and simmer for 30 minutes until vegetables are tender and lentils soft. Purée until smooth. Add the orange juice. If the purée is too thick, add cool, boiled water to thin. *Makes 8–12 servings*

016 creamy tofu and parsnip

Tofu is another excellent source of vegetable protein and it also contains the essential minerals calcium and magnesium.

PREPARATION
25 minutes

STORAGE
Suitable for freezing; keeps for up to 24 hours in the fridge

½ cup water
1 medium parsnip, peeled and diced
1 medium potato, peeled and diced
2¾oz tofu, drained and crumbled

juice of ½ orange
expressed breastmilk, formula milk, or cows' milk to thin

Put the water into a small saucepan and bring to the boil. Add the parsnip and potato and cover with a tight-fitting lid. Bring back to the boil and simmer for about 10 minutes until tender. Purée the vegetables, tofu, and orange juice together until smooth. Take out one portion to serve. Thin with the milk, if necessary. *Makes 4–8 servings*

---

017 poached haddock with vegetables

PREPARATION
40 minutes

STORAGE
Suitable for freezing; keeps for up to 24 hours in the fridge

⅓ cup water
1 small sweet potato, peeled and diced
10 small broccoli florets

½ cup milk
3½oz fresh haddock fillet, skinned and boned
cooled, boiled water or milk to thin

Put the water into a small saucepan and bring to the boil. Add the sweet potato and broccoli and cover with a tight-fitting lid. Bring back to the boil and simmer for about 10 minutes until tender. While the vegetables are cooking, pour the milk into a small frying pan. Add the haddock fillet and heat. Simmer uncovered for 7–8 minutes, until haddock turns white. Mash haddock in the cooking milk, removing any bones. Mash the vegetables and mix with the fish. Purée until smooth. Take out one portion to serve. Add cooled, boiled water or milk to thin, if necessary. *Makes 8–12 servings*

---

018 chicken with rice and leeks

PREPARATION
40 minutes

STORAGE
Suitable for freezing; keeps for up to 24 hours in the fridge

3 tbsp white basmati or long grain rice
1¼ cups water
½ small chicken breast, skinned and

cut into small pieces
1 small leek, washed and thinly sliced
water to thin

Put the rice in a sieve. Wash and drain it. Place in a small saucepan and add the water. Bring to the boil and reduce heat. Cover with a tight-fitting lid and simmer for 5 minutes. Add the chicken and the leek and continue to simmer for another 20 minutes until the chicken is cooked right through, and the rice and leeks are tender. Add a little more water, if necessary. Purée the mixture until smooth. Take out one portion to serve. Add cooled, boiled water to thin, if necessary. *Makes 6–8 servings*

019 beef with zucchini and red bell pepper

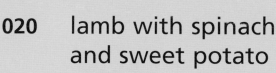

Red meat is very rich in iron, zinc, and protein.

PREPARATION
40 minutes

STORAGE
Suitable for freezing; keeps for up to 24 hours in the fridge

½ cup water
3oz lean braising beef, diced
1 medium potato, peeled and diced

½ small zucchini, diced
½ red bell pepper, diced
cooled, boiled water to thin

Put the water in a small saucepan. Bring to the boil and add in the beef and diced vegetables. Cover with a tight-fitting lid and simmer for at least 15 minutes until meat is cooked right through and the vegetables are very soft. Purée with the cooking water until smooth. Take out one portion to serve and add cooled, boiled water to thin, if necessary.
Makes 6–10 servings

020 lamb with spinach and sweet potato

PREPARATION
40 minutes

STORAGE
Suitable for freezing; keeps for up to 24 hours in the fridge

½ cup water
3oz lean lamb loin or chump chop, diced
½ medium sweet potato, peeled and

diced
1¾oz spinach, washed thoroughly and chopped
cooled, boiled water to thin

Put the water into a small saucepan and bring to the boil. Add the lamb and sweet potato. Cover with a tight-fitting lid, reduce heat and simmer for 5 minutes. Remove the lid and add the spinach. Replace the lid when the spinach wilts. Continue simmering for about 15 minutes until the meat is cooked right through and the vegetables are soft. Purée with the cooking water until smooth. Take out one portion to serve and add cooled, boiled water to thin, if necessary. *Makes 6–10 servings*

021 pork with apple, parsnip, and rutabaga

PREPARATION
40 minutes

STORAGE
Suitable for freezing; keeps for up to 24 hours in the fridge

½ eating apple, peeled, cored, and diced
½ cup water
3oz lean pork loin chop, diced

1 medium parsnip, peeled and cut into thin slices
3½oz rutabaga, peeled and diced
cooled, boiled water to thin

Put the water into a small saucepan and bring to the boil. Add in the pork, apple and vegetables. Cover with a tight-fitting lid and simmer for at least 15 minutes until the meat is cooked through and the vegetables are soft. Purée with the cooking water. Take out one portion to serve, and add cooled, boiled water to thin, if necessary. *Makes 6–10 servings*

022 creamy egg custard

V ✗ ✗ O ▣

Making this creamy custard with an egg to thicken it gives a nutritious milk pudding with plenty of protein and a liitle iron.

PREPARATION
45 minutes–1 hour

STORAGE
Keeps for up
to 24 hours in
the fridge

1¼ cups milk
2 tsp superfine sugar
2 eggs
1 tsp vanilla extract

Preheat the oven to 150°C/300°F/gas mark 2. Heat the milk in a small saucepan. Beat the sugar and eggs together in a bowl until the sugar dissolves. Whisk in the hot milk and vanilla extract and pour into a small ovenproof dish. Bake for 30–45 minutes until set. *Makes 6–8 servings*

023 fruity milk pudding

V ✗ ✗ ▣

PREPARATION
1¾–2¼ hours

STORAGE
Keeps for up
to 24 hours in
the fridge

1¼ cups milk
1½ tbsp sago or tapioca
3 tbsp puréed fruit (recipes 010, 011, and 012)

Preheat the oven to 150°C/300°F/gas mark 2. Wash the sago or tapioca in a sieve and drain. Place in an ovenproof dish and pour on the milk. Bake in the oven for 1½–2 hours. Stir the pudding 2 or 3 times during the first 25 minutes to mix in any skin that forms. Mix equal quantities of pudding and puréed fruit to serve. *Makes 6–8 servings of milk pudding*

024 avocado and banana yogurt

V ✗ ✗ ▣

Both these fruits are easy to purée when ripe and require no cooking. Make this purée just before serving, as the fruit will discolor if left to stand.

PREPARATION
10 minutes

STORAGE
Keeps for ½ hour
in the fridge

½ ripe banana, peeled and sliced
½ small ripe avocado, peeled and stoned
4 tbsp full-fat, natural bio-yogurt

Mash the fruit together well with a fork or purée in a blender. Stir in the yogurt and mix thoroughly. *Makes 2–4 servings*

025 fresh peach yogurt *(below)*

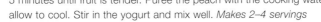

The combination of juicy, fresh fruit and natural, full-fat yogurt makes a quick, nutritious pudding. Using bio-yogurt will provide your baby with small doses of healthy probiotics. For variation, you can try other fruits, such as nectarines, apricots, mangoes, apples, or pears.

PREPARATION
10 minutes

1 ripe peach, peeled, pitted, and diced
1 tbsp water
4 tbsp natural bio-yogurt

STORAGE
Keeps for up
to 24 hours in
the fridge

Place the peach and the water in a small saucepan, cover with a tight-fitting lid and bring to the boil. Reduce heat and simmer for about 5 minutes until fruit is tender. Purée the peach with the cooking water and allow to cool. Stir in the yogurt and mix well. *Makes 2–4 servings*

MEALS WITH SOFT LUMPS AND FIRST FINGER FOODS

Between 6½ and 9 months of age, when your baby is able to sit upright and he can manage quite thick purées, you can begin to give food with soft lumps. The simplest way to do this is by mashing it. Fine finger control also develops at around seven months, so soft finger foods make interesting objects for babies to explore with their hands and mouths. Begin with toasted bread crusts, breadsticks, and soft fruits and vegetables. Eating thicker solids will make your baby more thirsty so offer a beaker of water with meals. Finish meals with a milk pudding, or a breast- or formula feed. Sitting your baby in a high chair at this age will make it easier for him to feed himself with finger foods.

026 banana porridge

This porridge is a perfect introduction to foods with soft lumps. You can make it either in a microwave or conventionally.

PREPARATION
10 minutes /
15 minutes

2 tbsp porridge oats
⅔ cup milk or water
½ ripe banana

STORAGE
Serve immediately

Place the oats and milk or water in a wide bowl. Microwave on full power, uncovered, for 3 minutes. Leave the porridge on one side to cool and thicken. Mash the banana. Mix the banana with a portion of porridge. If you don't have a microwave, place the oats and milk or water together in a saucepan, stir, and bring to the boil. Reduce heat and simmer for about 5 minutes until a soft, thick mixture forms. *Makes 2–4 servings*

027 porridge with apple

PREPARATION
10 minutes /
15 minutes

2 tbsp porridge oats
½ small eating apple, peeled, cored, and finely diced
⅔ cup milk or water

STORAGE
Serve immediately

Place the oats, diced apple, and milk or water in a wide bowl. Microwave on full power, uncovered, for 3 minutes. Leave the porridge to cool and thicken. Mash the apple into the oats with a fork. Alternatively, place the oats, apple, and milk or water in a saucepan, stir, and bring to the boil. Reduce heat and simmer for 5 minutes until a soft, thick mixture forms. *Makes 2–4 servings*

028 scrambled egg

PREPARATION
10 minutes

1 egg
1 tbsp milk
1 tsp butter

STORAGE
Serve immediately

Beat the egg with the milk in a small bowl. Melt the butter over a gentle heat in a small frying pan and pour in the egg mixture. Stir until the egg is cooked through, but still soft. Remove from the heat, allow to cool, and serve immediately. Serve with crusts from lightly toasted bread or soft vegetable fingers (see recipe 031; p.47). *Makes 1–2 servings*

029 spinach dhal

The combination of lentils and rice in this tasty vegetarian dish will provide your baby with good quality protein, as in meat.

PREPARATION
45 minutes

STORAGE
Suitable for freezing; keeps for up to 24 hours in the fridge

¼ cup red lentils, rinsed and drained
2 tbsp basmati or long grain rice, rinsed and drained
½ red bell pepper, cored, deseeded, and sliced
1 tsp olive oil

pinch ground cumin
pinch ground coriander
pinch mixed herbs
1¼ cups water
1 cup chopped spinach
2 tbsp canned tomatoes, chopped

Place the lentils, rice, red bell pepper, oil, spices, herbs, and water in a saucepan and bring to the boil. Cover and simmer for about 25 minutes until rice is tender. Take out 2 slices of red bell pepper. Stir in the spinach and tomatoes and cook for a further 2–3 minutes, until the spinach has wilted. Mash with a fork. Serve with the 2 slices of bell pepper as finger food. *Makes 3–4 servings*

030 sweet potato, chickpea, and cauliflower mash

This veggie mash makes a delicious meat-free meal that contains lots of iron and protein in the chickpeas. You can either cook your own chickpeas or use precooked, canned ones that have no added salt.

PREPARATION
1–1¼ hours

STORAGE
Suitable for freezing; keeps for up to 24 hours in the fridge

3 tbsp chickpeas
1 small sweet potato
8 small cauliflower florets

If cooking your own chickpeas, soak them overnight in cold water. Drain and rinse them with fresh water. Place them in a saucepan, cover with water, and bring to the boil. Reduce the heat and simmer for about 1 hour until the chickpeas are soft. If using canned chickpeas, drain them well. Purée with a little water as needed. Meanwhile, steam the sweet potato and cauliflower for about 15 minutes until tender. Mash the vegetables and mix in with the puréed chickpeas. Take out one portion to serve.
Makes 6 servings

031   soft vegetable fingers

These vegetables make a great accompaniment to savory dishes. They will help your baby to feel involved with his food and to develop dexterity. Steaming is the best way to cook them as this retains shape and nutrients.

PREPARATION
20 minutes

STORAGE
Keep in the fridge
for up to
24 hours

2 broccoli florets
2 cauliflower florets
1 small sweet potato
4 green beans

other suitable vegetables:
small tender string beans
potato
zucchini

Cut or break the broccoli and cauliflower florets into pieces small enough for your baby to handle. Top and tail the green beans and cut them in half. Peel the sweet potato and cut it into small fingers about 2in long. Place the vegetables in an electric steamer and steam them according to the instructions that come with the machine. Alternatively, place the vegetables in a steaming basket or pan over a large saucepan with enough water to reach just under the bottom of the basket and steam for about 10 minutes, until the vegetables are tender but not soft.
Makes 2–4 servings

032   soft summer fruit sticks

Choose soft, ripe fruits that are nutrient-rich and easy to chew. Giving fruit will help your baby learn to chew well. Cooked fruit loses some of its nutrients.

PREPARATION
20 minutes

STORAGE
Serve immediately

1 kiwi
¼ melon
½ peach
½ banana

other suitable fruits:
mango
papaya
nectarine
pear

Peel the kiwi fruit. Cut the rind from the melon and remove the seeds. Peel the peach and remove the stone. Cut all the fruit into pieces about 1–1½in long, and just thick enough for your baby to grasp. Arrange the fruit attractively on a plate and let your baby choose what he would like to try.
Makes 6–8 servings

033   pasta with sweet pepper sauce *(below)*

Pasta is a quick and easy food to prepare for your baby. Experiment with different shapes and sizes, but it is best to use small pasta, such as shells, bows, or macaroni, which you can easily break up into even smaller pieces, if necessary.

PREPARATION
25 minutes

STORAGE
Suitable for
freezing; keeps
for up to 24 hours
in the fridge

½ cup pasta shapes
2 tsp olive oil
½ small leek, washed and chopped
1 red bell pepper, seeded and
   chopped
½ small zucchini, chopped
4 tbsp chopped tomatoes, canned

without added salt
¼ clove garlic, finely chopped
1 tsp chopped parsley
½ tsp dried oregano or basil
1 tbsp grated mild, hard cheese,
   such as Cheddar

Cook the pasta in the water until soft, according to the instructions on the packet. Drain well. Heat the oil in a small skillet. Add the leek and bell pepper and cook for 5 minutes to soften. Add the zucchini, canned tomatoes, garlic, and dried herbs, and simmer gently for 15 minutes. Blend to a smooth sauce with a hand blender or in a food processor. Stir in the cooked pasta shapes and mash with a fork to break the pasta into smaller pieces. Stir in the grated cheese until it melts. Serve. *Makes 6–8 servings*

034 first spaghetti bolognaise

*As your baby grows you will no longer need to purée the mince. You can
also use turkey instead of beef, but this provides less iron.*

PREPARATION
30–40 minutes

STORAGE
Suitable for
freezing; keeps
for up to 24 hours
in the fridge

1 tbsp vegetable oil
½ small onion, peeled and
  finely chopped
2 celery sticks, finely chopped
1 carrot, grated

4½oz lean ground beef
3 tbsp tomato purée (without salt)
½ cup vegetable stock
½ tsp dried oregano
spaghetti or small pasta shapes

Heat the oil in a small skillet. Add the onion and sauté until transparent and
soft. Add the celery, carrot, and the ground beef and cook until browned.
Stir in the tomato purée, vegetable stock, and oregano. Bring to the boil,
reduce the heat, and simmer for 15–20 minutes until the meat and
vegetables are fully cooked. Purée. Cook the pasta (if using spaghetti,
break into small pieces) in the water according to the instructions on the
packet. Serve the puréed meat sauce with the small pieces of pasta.
Makes 6–8 servings

035 fish kedgeree

PREPARATION
30 minutes

STORAGE
Suitable for
freezing; keeps
for up to 24 hours
in the fridge

3 tbsp basmati or long grain rice
1¼ cups water
4 tbsp frozen peas
½ carrot cut into sticks
½ cup milk
3½oz white fish fillet, skinned

Put the rice in a sieve and wash well with water. Drain. Place the rice in
a small saucepan and add the water. Cover with a tight-fitting lid and bring
to the boil. Reduce heat and simmer for 10 minutes. Add the peas and
carrots. Continue cooking for about 15 minutes until the rice and carrots
are tender. Add a little more water, if necessary. Meanwhile, pour the milk
into a small frying pan and add the fish fillet. Bring to the boil and simmer
for 7–8 minutes until the fish is cooked through. Flake the fish, checking
carefully for and removing any bones. Remove 2 or 3 carrot sticks from
the rice mixture to use as finger food. Add the flaked fish to the rice and
vegetables, mixing well, then mash together. Serve. *Makes 6–10 servings*

036 mackerel and vegetable mash

Unlike the smoked variety, fresh mackerel has a delicate flavor that babies like. Fresh mackerel is also a great source of those all-important LCPs and contains more iron than white fish.

PREPARATION
25 minutes

STORAGE
Suitable for freezing; keeps for up to 24 hours in the fridge

½ cup water
1 small potato, peeled and diced
4 cauliflower florets
3 tbsp frozen peas

⅛ cup milk
1 fresh mackerel fillet, skinned and washed

Put the water in a small saucepan and bring to the boil. Add the potato and place the cauliflower florets on top. Bring back to the boil, reduce heat and simmer for 5 minutes. Add the frozen peas and simmer for a further 5–8 minutes until the potato is soft and the peas cooked. Meanwhile, put the milk in a frying pan, bring to the boil, and add the mackerel fillet. Reduce heat and simmer uncovered for 7–8 minutes until the mackerel is cooked right through. Flake the fish into the milk, removing any bones. Add vegetables to the fish and mash together with a fork. *Makes 4–6 servings*

037 lamb casserole with tomatoes and potatoes

Lamb cooked slowly in a casserole is a favorite with babies because it is so tender and succulent. It is a good source of B-vitamins, iron, and zinc.

PREPARATION
1¼–1½ hours

STORAGE
Suitable for freezing; keeps for up to 24 hours in the fridge

1 lamb cutlet, diced
2 scallions, thinly sliced
1 medium potato, peeled and cut in half
1 medium carrot, peeled and cut into fingers

¼ red bell pepper, chopped
1 tomato, chopped
½ cup water or vegetable stock (recipe 252; page 151)
pinch dried rosemary

Preheat the oven to 180°C/350°F/gas mark 4. Place all the ingredients in a small casserole dish. Cook in the oven for 10–15 minutes until bubbling then turn the temperature down to 150°C/300°F/gas mark 2. Continue to cook for a further 30–40 minutes until the lamb is very soft—when you can break it apart with a fork. Remove from the oven and reserve one or two pieces of carrot to give as finger food. Mash the potatoes and vegetables into the meat juices and break up the pieces of lamb. Remove the tomato skin. Serve. *Makes 2–3 servings*

038 chicken with leeks

If you are not confident that your baby will be able to cope with the mashed chicken in this recipe, take it out when cooked, and purée it the first few times you make it.

PREPARATION
50 minutes

STORAGE
Suitable for freezing; keeps for up to 24 hours in the fridge

white part of 1 leek, sliced thinly
½ tbsp oil
1 chicken breast, diced
2 carrots, peeled and chopped
2 medium potatoes, peeled and chopped

½ cup chicken stock or water
1 sprig thyme
1 bay leaf
1 sprig parsley
2 tbsp crème fraîche

In a saucepan, sauté the leek in the oil until soft. Add the chicken, vegetables, stock, and herbs. Bring to the boil, reduce heat, cover, and simmer for 30–40 minutes. Mash the vegetables into the juices and break the chicken into small pieces with a fork. Stir in the crème fraîche. *Makes 2–4 servings*

039 beef stew

If you can, prepare this dish early in the day, as beef needs long, slow cooking to make it really tender. Casseroling the meat in this way should make it soft enough to mash with the vegetables, but you can purée it the first time you try this recipe, if you prefer.

PREPARATION
2½–3½ hours

STORAGE
Suitable for freezing; keeps for up to 24 hours in the fridge

1 tbsp flour
1 tsp paprika
2 tsp olive oil
8oz lean braising steak, diced
½ small onion, thinly sliced
⅔ cup vegetable stock or water
1 small carrot, peeled and sliced

2 medium potatoes, peeled and diced
½ stick celery, sliced
¼ small rutabaga or ½ small parsnip, peeled and diced
6 small button mushrooms
1 tsp mixed herbs

Preheat the oven to 150°C/300°F/gas mark 2. Mix the flour and paprika together in a small bowl and toss the meat in this to coat it. Heat the oil in a skillet, add the onions, and stir-fry for 2–3 minutes. Then add the floured meat. Keep stirring for about 2–3 minutes until the meat is browned on the outside. Add the stock or water and stir for 1 minute to incorporate all the flour and juices. Remove from the heat and transfer to a small casserole dish. Add the vegetables and herbs, then cover and cook in the oven for 2–3 hours. Purée or mash with a fork and serve with some steamed carrot or sweet potato as finger food. *Makes 8–10 servings*

MASHED OR CHOPPED MEALS AND FINGER FOODS

From 9 to 12 months of age your baby takes the final step in weaning. If you use the recipes in this section, by the time he is one your baby will have tasted a variety of foods and explored many different textures at the crucial stage when he is still open to trying new foods. Our recipes contain no added salt—we use herbs and mild spices to give flavor. It is vital now to include the foods, herbs, and spices that you eat as a family so that your baby can get used to them. He may not yet be able to eat very chewy or crunchy foods but he can still enjoy them if you cut them into small pieces or soften them by cooking.

If your baby cries during feeding it may be because he is thirsty, so always include a drink of water or very diluted fruit juice. Finish each meal either with a milk pudding, breastmilk, or formula milk.

040 first muesli

PREPARATION
10 minutes

1 tbsp rolled oats
½ tbsp sultanas
1 tbsp dried apricot or peach, finely
  chopped

1 tbsp wheatgerm
1 tbsp ground almonds
3 tbsp unsweetened apple, orange,
  or pineapple juice

STORAGE
Dry mixture keeps
for a few days
in an airtight
container

Mix the oats, sultanas, and dried fruit together in a bowl. Put them in a food processor and chop them finely for about 30 seconds. Transfer them to the serving bowl and add in the wheatgerm and ground almonds. Pour in the fruit juice and leave to soak for about 5 minutes to soften. Serve with milk or yogurt and offer apple sticks or orange segments as finger food.
Makes 1–2 servings

041 eggy toast fingers

These make a delicious breakfast or lunch. You can use either white or wholewheat bread, or one slice of each.

PREPARATION
10 minutes

1 large egg
2 tbsp milk
2 tsp butter
2 slices white or wholewheat bread, crusts removed

STORAGE
Serve immediately

Beat the egg and milk together in a shallow dish. Melt the butter in a skillet. Dip each slice of bread into the egg mixture and make sure that both sides are fully coated. Place the bread into the melted butter and fry over a gentle heat for 2–3 minutes until golden brown. Turn and fry the other side. Cut into fingers and serve. *Makes 3–4 servings*

042 macaroni cheese

This traditional dish makes a tasty, calcium-packed meal for your baby that is guaranteed to become a firm favorite. You can use any small pasta shapes in place of the macaroni.

PREPARATION
20 minutes

¾ cup macaroni
1oz butter
2 tbsp all-purpose flour

1¼ cups milk
1 cup strong cheese, grated

STORAGE
Suitable for
freezing; keeps
for up to 24 hours
in the fridge

Cook the macaroni until soft or according to instructions on the packet. Drain. Melt the butter in a saucepan and add in the flour. Cook for about 2 minutes over a low heat—don't let the flour turn brown. Pour the milk in slowly while stirring with a wooden spoon or balloon whisk. Keep stirring until you have a smooth sauce. Bring to the boil, reduce heat, and simmer gently for 2–3 minutes until the sauce thickens. Remove from the heat and stir in the grated cheese and cooked macaroni. Cut the macaroni into smaller pieces with a fork, if necessary. Serve with peas and green beans.
Makes 4–6 servings

043 roasted vegetable sticks *(below)*

Roasting intensifies flavors and gives vegetables a sweeter taste that will encourage your baby to eat them.

PREPARATION
45 minutes

STORAGE
Suitable for freezing, but best made just before serving

1 small beet
1 medium carrot
¼ celeriac
1 small parsnip
1 small potato

½ red or yellow bell pepper
½ small sweet potato
1 tsp ground cumin
2–3 tbsp olive oil for brushing

Preheat the oven to 180°C/350°F/gas mark 4. Peel all the vegetables (except the bell peppers) and cut all except the parsnip and sweet potato into the size of thick fries about 2in long. Make the parsnip and sweet potato slightly larger. Wash the bell peppers well, deseed them, and cut them into strips about ½in wide. Stir the ground cumin into the oil. Brush some oil onto a baking sheet and heat in the oven for 2–3 minutes until hot. Place the vegetable sticks on the baking sheet and brush each all over with oil. Return to the oven and bake for 20–30 minutes until tender. When cooked, place sticks on paper towels to cool and absorb any excess oil. Beware of beet juice stains to fingers and clothes. *Makes 4–6 servings*

044 pasta with lentils

This lentil sauce contains plenty of vegetarian protein as well as nutrients from the vegetables. Add a topping of grated cheese for extra flavor.

PREPARATION
45 minutes

STORAGE
Suitable for freezing; keeps for up to 24 hours in the fridge

½ cup Puy lentils, rinsed
1 tbsp olive oil
½ small onion, finely sliced
1 garlic clove, crushed
½ small zucchini, diced
½ orange or green bell pepper, cored, deseeded, and diced
4 small button mushrooms, well

washed and chopped
7oz canned, chopped tomatoes
2 tbsp tomato purée
1 tsp dried mixed herbs
black pepper to taste
1 cup pasta spirals
grated cheese for topping (optional)

Place the lentils in a saucepan and add water to cover them. Bring to the boil, reduce heat, and simmer for 25 minutes. Heat the oil in a skillet and add the onion, garlic, zucchini, bell pepper, and mushrooms. Stir-fry for 5–10 minutes. Add the chopped tomatoes, purée, herbs, and pepper. Cover and cook for about 5 minutes. Drain the lentils and purée or mash them. Stir into the sauce. Cook pasta according to instructions on the packet. Keep a few pasta spirals as finger food and mash rest into the lentil sauce. Serve sprinkled with grated cheese (if using). *Makes 4–6 servings*

045 zucchini, cauliflower, and chickpea curry

This is a mild and creamy first curry, which is an ideal introduction to the taste for your baby. The chickpeas and optional peanut butter contain vegetable protein, while the tomato purée has vitamin C, which will boost your baby's iron absorption.

PREPARATION
45 minutes

STORAGE
Suitable for freezing; keeps for up to 24 hours in the fridge

1 tbsp olive oil
1 small onion, finely chopped
½ medium cauliflower, cut into florets
2 medium zucchini, diced
2 tsp mild curry paste
1 tbsp tomato purée

2 tbsp smooth peanut butter (optional)
14oz can chickpeas, rinsed and drained
1¼ cups vegetable stock or water
1 cup natural bio-yogurt

Place the onion in a skillet with the oil. Fry over a gentle heat until softened. Add the cauliflower and zucchini and cook for a further 2 minutes. Stir in the curry paste, tomato purée, peanut butter (if using), chickpeas, and vegetable stock or water. Cover and simmer for 20 minutes. Remove from the heat and allow to stand for 10 minutes before stirring in the yogurt. Take out a portion and mash or chop. Serve with rice and sliced bananas. *Makes 6–10 servings*

046   lemony fish

Whether broiled or fried, fish cooks so quickly it really is "fast food". It is also versatile, combining well with potatoes, rice, or pasta. Serve with one or two vegetables to complete the meal.

PREPARATION
10 minutes

STORAGE
Keeps for up
to 24 hours
in the fridge

1 fillet of fresh white fish, such as haddock, sea bass, or cod,
    skinned and boned (about 5oz)
juice of 1 lemon
1 tbsp olive oil or butter

Melt the oil or butter in a skillet. Drizzle half the lemon juice over one side of the fish and put it into the pan with the lemony side down. Drizzle the rest of the lemon juice onto the upturned side. Allow to cook over a gentle heat for about 2 minutes and then turn over and cook the other side. Flake the fish with a fork and remove any bones. Serve with mashed potatoes, rice, or pasta, and vegetables, such as carrots and peas. *Makes 3–6 servings*

047   pork with apples

You can make this recipe for your baby when you are preparing pork tenderloin for other members of the family. If you are very busy, why not make double portions so that you have some left over to serve for lunch the next day?

PREPARATION
1 hour 15
minutes–1 hour
30 minutes

STORAGE
Suitable for
freezing; keeps
for up to 24 hours
in the fridge

¼ onion, chopped
2 tsp olive oil
2 slices pork tenderloin
    (1in thick), finely diced
2 tsp plain flour
¼ cup unsweetened apple juice
¼–½ cup water

½ eating apple, peeled, cored, and
    chopped
pinch dried thyme
½ carrot, peeled and cut into strips
½ small parsnip, peeled and cut into
    strips
1 small potato, peeled and quartered

Preheat the oven to 150°C/300F°/gas mark 2. In a skillet, sauté the onion in the oil, add the pork, and cook a little longer. Sprinkle on the flour and gradually add the apple juice and water. Add the apple and thyme. Bring to the boil, stirring continually while the sauce thickens. Add a little extra water if sauce is too thick. Place in an ovenproof dish with a lid and cook in the oven for 30 minutes. Add the vegetables and potatoes, return to the oven, and cook for a further 30 minutes until the vegetables are soft. The meat will be very tender and can be mashed a little with the potatoes, if needed. The vegetable pieces can be removed from the sauce and eaten with the fingers. This dish contains everything your baby needs for a complete meal, but if you wish you could serve it with a green vegetable, such as broccoli. *Makes 2–4 servings*

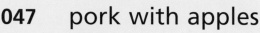

048 chicken and vegetable stir-fry

Stir-fried chicken breast is soft enough for infants to chew, but note that other meats cooked in this way may be too tough.

PREPARATION
30 minutes

STORAGE
Keeps for up
to 24 hours in
the fridge

1 tbsp olive oil
½ chicken breast, thinly sliced
½ tsp dried tarragon
½ red bell pepper, deseeded and thinly sliced
6 baby corn, sliced lengthways
3 tbsp frozen peas

Heat the oil in a skillet. Add the chicken slices and tarragon, and stir-fry for a few minutes. Add the red bell pepper and baby corn and continue to stir-fry over a gentle heat for 10–15 minutes until the chicken has cooked right through. Meanwhile, bring a small saucepan of water to the boil and add the frozen peas. Reduce heat and simmer for 3–4 minutes until peas are hot right through. Lift out with a slotted spoon and add to the stir-fry. Serve with rice, pasta, or steamed potatoes. Cut the chicken into small pieces. *Makes 2–3 servings*

049 Moroccan lamb with couscous

A mildly spiced lamb dish to introduce your baby to a more exotic taste to stimulate his palate.

PREPARATION
1–1½ hours

STORAGE
Suitable for
freezing; keeps
for up to 24 hours
in the fridge

¼ tsp ground cumin
¼ tsp ground coriander
pinch nutmeg
4oz lean lamb neck fillet, trimmed
  and diced
1 tbsp olive oil
2 tbsp diced eggplant

1 tsp grated fresh ginger or
  ½ tsp ground ginger
½ clove garlic, crushed
7oz canned, chopped
  tomatoes
6 tbsp couscous
1 cup boiling water

Mix the ground spices together in a bowl. Toss the cubes of lamb into the mixed spices and stir well until the lamb is well-coated. Heat the oil in a skillet and fry the lamb until browned. Add the diced eggplant and continue to fry, stirring for 2 minutes. Add in the ginger and garlic, and fry for another minute. Add the chopped tomatoes, cover tightly with a lid, and simmer gently for about 1 hour until the lamb is tender. Put the couscous in a bowl and pour over the boiling water. Leave to stand for 5 minutes until the water is all absorbed. Fluff up the couscous with a fork and mix into the lamb dish. Take out one portion and cut the lamb into small bite-size pieces. Serve with steamed carrot sticks and broccoli florets. *Makes 4–6 servings*

050   ready-to-go fruit fingers

The following fruits are the perfect size for little hands to grasp. You can give those in the left-hand column to your baby without peeling them. It is advisable to stay close by when he is eating any of these fruits, as choking is always a potential hazard.

PREPARATION
5–10 minutes

STORAGE
Serve immediately

fruits that need to be washed:
- 4 cherries
- 4 grapes
- 3 strawberries
- 4 raspberries

other suitable fruits that need to be peeled and pips removed:
- clementines
- oranges
- satsumas

Wash the fruit well and place on a paper towel to dry. Cut the cherries in half and remove the stones and stalks. Cut the grapes in half and remove any pips with the tip of a knife. Hull the strawberries. Cut any very large strawberries in half. Arrange attractively on a plate and serve on its own or with fruit yogurt as a dip. *Makes 2–3 servings*

051   fruity rice pudding with cinnamon

By adding fruit and cinnamon to this traditional milk pudding, you will be exposing your baby to a wider range of flavors at a critical time in his development. Use other seasonal fruit if sweet apples are not available.

PREPARATION
1 hour 40 minutes

STORAGE
Keeps for up
to 24 hours in
the fridge

- ¼ cup pudding rice
- 1 tbsp superfine sugar
- 1 eating apple, peeled and chopped
- 2 tbsp golden raisins
- 1½ cups milk
- ½ tsp ground cinnamon

Preheat the oven to 150°C/300°F/gas mark 2. Rinse the rice and drain. Place all the ingredients in a shallow ovenproof dish and stir well. Place in the oven and bake for 1½ hours until the rice is soft. It is also delicious when eaten cold. *Makes 2–4 servings*

052 first chocolate pudding with fruit fingers *(below)*

 Ⓥ ⊗ ⊗ ▣

The combination of cocoa and milk makes this first chocolate pudding very nutritious. Strawberries, or peach and pear fingers go well with this.

PREPARATION
15 minutes

STORAGE
Keeps for up to 24 hours in the fridge

1 tbsp cocoa powder
2 tsp sugar
1 tbsp cornstarch
1¼ cups milk

2 strawberries, halved
½ peach, peeled and cut into fingers
½ pear, peeled and cut into fingers

Put the cocoa powder, sugar, and cornstarch in a jug and stir in just enough milk (about ¼ cup) to dissolve them. Meanwhile, pour the rest of the milk into a saucepan and bring to the boil. Pour onto the cocoa paste and stir well. Return the mixture to the pan, put back on the heat, and stir continuously until the mixture thickens. Remove from the heat, pour into a serving bowl, and allow to cool. Serve warm or chilled, with the fruit fingers, which can be dipped into the pudding or eaten with it. *Makes 2–4 servings*

part three

1-2 year olds

During your toddler's second year she will start to become more independent, and her physical, intellectual, and social abilities will develop rapidly. Children of this age increasingly want (and are able) to assert themselves, often saying "no" to requests and enjoying doing so! Parents tend to worry more when their child refuses food than when she won't wear a hat or socks. But to the child it is all just part of the same game. If you do find yourself battling with her at mealtimes, try to keep calm. Bear in mind that, while it is your responsibility as a parent to provide good, nutritious food for your child, you should let her choose how much she eats and you shouldn't ever force her to eat. Rest assured that most children's appetites vary somewhat from day to day and week to week, but even out over the longer term.

SELF-FEEDING AND FINGER FOODS

Between the ages of one and two, toddlers develop definite food likes and dislikes and often become wary of new tastes. To counteract this tendency eat with your child as often as possible and show her you enjoy foods—after all, she learns by copying you.

Choose foods suitable for your toddler's ability. Although your child can probably use cutlery, she may find it difficult to eat quickly enough to satisfy her hunger, so she will need help at times. We have included recipes that can be eaten easily with fingers to allow your child to enjoy her new-found independence at feeding and nourishing herself. For more ideas see the meal planner for 1–2 year olds on p.214. Most of the recipes for 3–6 year olds can also be adapted for this age group by reducing quantities and cutting food up.

053   sandwich shapes

Use cookie-cutters, if you have them, to cut these sandwiches into shapes. If not, use a sharp knife. Try other simple fillings such as cream cheese or half a teaspoonful of yeast spread mixed with half a teaspoonful of butter.

PREPARATION
10 minutes

STORAGE
Best made just
before serving

1 tsp butter (optional)
1 slice white bread
1 slice brown or wholewheat bread
1 tbsp smooth peanut butter
1 tbsp mashed banana

If using, spread the butter on the bread very thinly. Spread the peanut butter on one slice of bread and the banana on the other. Sandwich the two slices together. Cut off the crusts and cut into shapes, such as stars or hearts. Serve with sticks of cucumber and carrot. *Makes 1–2 servings*

054   houmous and red bell pepper triangles

PREPARATION
10 minutes

STORAGE
Best made just
before serving

2 slices brown or wholewheat bread
1 tsp butter (optional)
2 tbsp houmous
1 tbsp red bell pepper, diced very small

Spread the butter on the bread very thinly (if using). Spread the houmous on both slices of bread. Sprinkle the bell pepper over one of the slices and sandwich the other one on top. Cut into 8 small triangles. Serve with fresh vegetable sticks, such as cucumber and carrot. *Makes 1–2 servings*

055   crackers with cream cheese and pineapple

Low-salt crackers, crispbreads or rice cakes make a change from bread. Cream cheese goes especially well with crackers, but you can use any filling.

PREPARATION
10 minutes

STORAGE
Best made just
before serving

2 crackers or crispbreads, or 1 plain rice cake
1 tsp butter, optional
1 tbsp cream cheese
1 tbsp finely chopped fresh pineapple or
 canned, crushed pineapple (well drained)

Spread the crackers, crispbreads, or rice cake thinly with the butter (if using). Mix the cream cheese and pineapple together and spread over both crackers cr crispbreads. Rice cakes are thick and they only need a topping. Sandwich the crackers or crispbreads together. *Makes 1 serving*

056 fish-shaped sandwiches *(below)*

○●

*You can easily create these fun sandwiches using a fish-shaped
cookie-cutter or a knife. Tuna is very popular with children, but you
can also try substituting other canned fish, such as sardines or pilchards,
as these are an even richer source of iron and omega-3 LCPs.*

PREPARATION
10 minutes

STORAGE
Best made just
before serving

2 tbsp well drained, canned tuna

2 tsp mayonnaise or natural bio-yogurt

½ tsp finely chopped, fresh chives or parsley (optional)

2 slices white or wholewheat bread

1 tsp butter

Mash the tuna, herbs and mayonnaise/yogurt together using a fork.
Butter the two slices of bread. Spread the tuna mayonnaise mixture on one
slice of bread and sandwich the other slice on top. Cut off the crusts and
cut into fish shapes. Serve with cherry tomatoes and cucumber slices.
Makes 1–2 servings

057   fishy toast fingers

Smoked or canned varieties of oily fish are already cooked and make a quick and iron-rich toast topping for toddlers. They are an excellent source of vitamins A and D, as well as omega-3 LCPs.

PREPARATION
15 minutes

⅛ cup smoked mackerel or sardines canned in oil, and well drained
1 tbsp natural bio-yogurt
½ tsp lemon juice

1 tsp tomato purée (optional)
4 slices thick white or wholewheat bread

STORAGE
Fish mixture will keep for up to 2 days in the fridge

Mash the fish with the yogurt and lemon juice. Stir in the tomato purée (if using). Toast the bread and spread with the fish mixture. If you wish to serve warm, place under a preheated broiler for 1–2 minutes. Cut into fingers and serve with cherry tomatoes or carrot sticks. *Makes 2–4 servings*

058   toast fingers with chicken liver pâté

Chicken liver pâté has a surprisingly delicate flavor that toddlers love. Besides tasting good it is a great source of iron and vitamin A.

PREPARATION
30 minutes

4oz chicken livers
2oz butter
½ small onion, chopped
2 tsp mixed herbs

½ celery stick, chopped
1 tbsp unsweetened apple juice
4 slices thick white bread

STORAGE
Pâté will keep for up to 2 days in the fridge

Melt the butter in a skillet. Add the chopped onion and cook for 5–7 minutes until soft and golden. Trim and chop the chicken livers and add to the skillet, along with the herbs, celery, and apple juice. Cook for a further 10–12 minutes, stirring often—the livers should be cooked right through and the vegetables soft. Remove from the heat and mash together with a fork, or use a blender if you prefer a smoother texture. Toast the bread and spread with the pâté. Cut into fingers and serve with cherry tomatoes or slices of cucumber. *Makes 2–4 servings*

059   tuna pasta bake

PREPARATION
45 minutes

¾ cup penne pasta
2oz canned tuna, drained
½ cup frozen peas, defrosted

1 egg
⅔ cup milk
4 tbsp Cheddar, grated

STORAGE
Keeps for up to 2 days in the fridge

Preheat the oven to 190°C/375°F/gas mark 5. Cook the pasta as directed on the packet. Stir the tuna and peas into the pasta and place in a small, greased ovenproof dish. Beat together the eggs and milk and half the Cheddar. Pour over the pasta. Sprinkle the rest of the cheese on top and bake for 20–30 minutes until golden. Serve with an extra vegetable, such as carrots. *Makes 2–4 servings*

060 mini falafels

These mildly spiced finger foods are a good source of vegetarian protein. Serve them with pasta shapes to provide your child with a protein source as rich as meat. Ideally, allow these to chill for 30 minutes before frying.

PREPARATION
1 hour–1 hour 15 minutes

STORAGE
Keep for up to 24 hours in the fridge, uncooked

14oz canned chickpeas, rinsed and drained
1 small onion, finely chopped
1 clove garlic, peeled and chopped
1 tbsp fresh coriander chopped

1 tsp ground coriander
1 tsp ground cumin
2–4 tbsp flour
1–2 tbsp olive oil

Place the chickpeas in a food processor with the onion, garlic, cumin, and both types of coriander. Blend until you have a smooth purée. Let the mixture rest for at least 30 minutes. Take walnut-sized portions and shape them into small, flat rounds ⅛in thick. Roll the falafels lightly in the flour and chill for 15–30 minutes. Heat the oil in a skillet and fry the falafels over a medium heat for about 10 minutes, turning frequently. Serve with Mint and Cucumber Yoghurt Dip (recipe 245; p.147), pasta shapes, and slices of cucumber and red bell pepper. *Makes 4–6 servings*

061 butternut squash gnocchi

PREPARATION
25 minutes

STORAGE
Best made just before serving

4oz potatoes, peeled and diced
6oz butternut squash, peeled, deseeded, and diced
1 egg yolk
5 tbsp flour

pinch nutmeg
pinch black pepper
1oz butter
½ tsp cumin seeds
4–5 tbsp grated, mild cheese to serve

Steam the potatoes and squash for 10–15 minutes until tender. Meanwhile, bring a large saucepan of water to the boil. Mash the potato and squash together in a bowl. Beat in the egg yolk, flour, nutmeg, and black pepper to form a soft moist dough. If it seems too moist, add a little extra flour. Drop about 8 heaped teaspoonfuls of the dough into the saucepan of boiling water, keeping them well apart. Boil for 1–2 minutes—the gnocchi will rise to the surface. Lift out with a slotted spoon and place in a serving bowl. Continue cooking the rest of the dough mixture in batches, in the same way. Melt the butter in a skillet and add the cumin seeds and the gnocchi. Toss them carefully in the butter to heat through and then tip them back into the serving bowl. Before serving sprinkle the grated cheese over the gnocchi. Serve with roasted vegetables or raw vegetable sticks. *Makes 4–6 servings*

062 toddler's tortilla *(above)*

This delicious tortilla is quick to make and highly nutritious, containing lots of protein and calcium as well as a wide range of vitamins and flavonoids.

PREPARATION
30 minutes

STORAGE
Keeps for 2 days
in the fridge

2 tsp olive oil
½ scallion, finely chopped
1 medium potato, peeled, diced, and
    steamed
2 tbsp cooked, diced fresh

vegetables, or frozen mixed
    vegetables
2 large eggs, beaten
2 tbsp cheese, grated

Heat the oil in a small skillet. Add the scallion, potato, and vegetables and fry for 6–8 minutes over a gentle heat, stirring occasionally, until the potatoes are slightly brown and the vegetables are hot. Sprinkle on the grated cheese and then pour in the beaten eggs. Leave to cook without stirring until the underside is set. Place the pan under a preheated broiler until the top is golden brown and the eggs are cooked all the way through. Slide the tortilla onto a chopping board and slice into fingers or triangles to serve.
Makes 2–4 servings

063 mini monkfish kebabs *(below)*

Monkfish is the ideal fish for kebabs as it is soft and easy to push onto a skewer, but it doesn't fall to pieces when cooked. It is full of protein and iodine and low in fat, making it a very healthy choice.

PREPARATION
20 minutes

STORAGE
Best made just
before serving

1 medium tomato, cut into 6 wedges
12 small cubes of monkfish tail
½ small red bell pepper, deseeded and cut into 6 squares
½ small yellow bell pepper, deseeded and cut into 6 squares
3 button mushrooms, washed, but not peeled
½ tbsp olive oil
juice of ½ lemon
pinch of black pepper

Preheat the broiler. Take six wooden cocktail sticks and wet them slightly before use (to prevent them from burning under the broiler). Make up 6 very small kebabs by threading a piece of tomato, a cube of monkfish, a red bell pepper square, a second cube of monkfish, 1 yellow bell pepper square, and a button mushroom onto each stick. Mix the olive oil, lemon juice, and pepper together to make a dressing. Place the kebabs on a broiler lined with foil and brush with the olive oil dressing. Broil for about 6 minutes, then turn, brush the other side with the dressing and broil for a further 5 minutes until the fish is cooked right through. Serve with cooked pasta shapes.
Makes 3–4 servings

064 home-made fish fingers

⊜O

These are quick and easy to make and contain more fish and less fat and salt than commercially produced frozen fish fingers.

PREPARATION
15 minutes

STORAGE
Best made just
before serving

4oz cod fillet, skin and bones removed
1 egg, beaten
4 tbsp dried breadcrumbs
1 tbsp olive oil

Cut the cod fillet into four pieces. Put the beaten egg in a bowl, sprinkle the breadcrumbs on a flat plate, and gently heat the oil in a skillet. Dip the fish pieces in the egg and roll them in the breadcrumbs until coated. Fry them for 4–5 minutes each until the fish is cooked right through and the breadcrumbs are golden brown, turning them once. Serve with mashed potato and Soft Vegetable Fingers (recipe 031; p.47). *Makes 2–4 servings*

065 baby fish cakes

⊗⊗⊗⊜O⊘

Smoked mackerel flesh is a good, safe choice for babies because it is easy to flake. You can use smoked trout or smoked eel as an alternative.

PREPARATION
30 minutes

STORAGE
Suitable for
freezing. Keep
for up to 24 hours
in the fridge,
uncooked

2 cups potatoes, peeled and cut into pieces
1 cup fillets of smoked mackerel, trout or eel
2 tbsp finely chopped fresh chives or parsley
juice of 1 lemon
1 egg, beaten

Put 1in water in a saucepan and bring to the boil. Add the potatoes, reduce the heat, and simmer for about 10 minutes until tender. Place the smoked fish in a bowl and flake it with a fork. Tip in the cooked potatoes and chives. Mash the potatoes and fish together until well mixed. Add in half the lemon juice and just enough whisked egg to make a mixture that binds well but isn't too runny. Shape heaped dessertspoonfuls of mixture into balls with your fingers and put them on a broiler lined with a sheet of aluminium foil. Cook under a hot broiler for about 5 minutes until golden brown on each side, turning once. Drizzle with the remaining lemon juice and serve with roasted tomatoes or stir-fried vegetable sticks. *Makes 4–6 servings*

066 first chicken nuggets

PREPARATION
25 minutes

1 chicken breast, cut into small strips
2–3 tbsp dried breadcrumbs
1 egg, beaten

STORAGE
Suitable for
freezing; keep
for up to 24 hours
in the fridge

Preheat the oven to 200°C/400°F/gas mark 6. Lightly grease an oven pan by brushing with olive oil. Dip the chicken breast strips in the egg and then in the breadcrumbs. Place each nugget on the baking pan. Cook in the oven for 10–15 minutes until golden on both sides, turning once. Serve with Roasted Vegetable Sticks (recipe 043; p.54). *Makes 2–4 servings*

067 glazed chicken drumsticks

PREPARATION
1 hour

4 chicken drumsticks
1 tbsp honey
juice of 1 lemon
1 tsp grated lemon rind

juice of 1 orange
1 tsp grated orange rind
1 tbsp Worcester sauce
1 tbsp tomato ketchup

STORAGE
Keep for up
to 24 hours in
the fridge

Preheat the oven to 180°C/350°F/gas mark 4. Score the fleshy part of the drumsticks. Place them in a shallow ovenproof dish. Mix together the remaining ingredients in a bowl and spoon over the chicken. Place in the oven and cook for 45 minutes turning a few times to continue coating the drumsticks with the sticky glaze. Allow to cool. Serve with oven fries and roasted vegetables. *Makes 4 servings*

068 meat loaf with tomato and bell pepper sauce

PREPARATION
1 hour

1 small onion, peeled and cut into
  quarters
1 medium carrot, finely grated
2 tbsp breadcrumbs
1 tbsp tomato paste
1 tsp dried oregano or mixed herbs

pinch of ground black pepper
1 egg, beaten
7oz lean ground beef
tomato and bell pepper sauce
  (recipe 070; opposite page)

STORAGE
Suitable for
freezing; keeps
for 2 days in
the fridge

Preheat the oven to 180°C/350°F/gas mark 4. Place the onion pieces in a food processor and chop until finely ground. Add in the carrot, breadcrumbs, tomato paste, mixed herbs, and egg. Process for 5–10 seconds. Add in the ground beef and process for a further 5–10 seconds to make a finer mince and to mix well. Shape the mixture into a loaf in a baking pan and bake uncovered for 45 minutes. Serve the meat loaf in slices and cover with the Tomato and Bell Pepper Sauce (recipe 070; opposite page). For finger food, cut each slice into 4 cubes. Serve with small boiled potatoes and broccoli florets to complete the meal. *Makes 6–8 servings*

069   mini meatballs

*Try making these mini meatballs using the same ingredients as recipe 068
(opposite page)—they are a quicker option than the meat loaf.*

PREPARATION
30–45 minutes

STORAGE
Suitable for
freezing; keep for
2 days in the fridge

Preheat the broiler or oven to 180°C/350°F/gas mark 4. Follow the
instructions for the meat loaf in recipe 068, but process the meat mixture
for an extra 1–2 minutes to make a smoother texture. Form meat balls
about the size of a walnut and place in a baking pan. Broil them for about
15 minutes under a preheated broiler, turning once, or bake them in the
oven for 25–30 minutes. Serve with the Tomato and Bell Pepper Sauce in
recipe 070 and potato wedges or pasta shapes to make a finger-food meal.
Makes 16 meatballs

070   tomato and bell pepper sauce

*Bursting with immune-boosting vitamin C and lycopene, this tasty sauce
makes an ideal accompaniment for recipes 068 (opposite page) and 069.*

PREPARATION
20 minutes

1 tbsp olive oil
½ onion, finely sliced
1 red or green bell pepper, deseeded
  and diced

1 clove garlic, crushed
14 oz canned, chopped tomatoes
1 tsp dried oregano
pinch black pepper

STORAGE
Suitable for
freezing; keeps
for 2 days in
the fridge

Put the oil in a skillet and heat. Add the onion. Sauté gently until it turns
transparent, then add the diced bell pepper and garlic. Continue to sauté
for another 5 minutes. Add the tomatoes, herbs, and black pepper and
simmer until the onions and bell pepper are completely soft. Purée in a
blender or food processor to make a smooth sauce. Keep warm to serve
with the meat loaf or mini meatballs.

071   mini pitta pizzas

*Your toddler can help you to put these quick pizzas together. For added fun
you can make the topping into faces by using a crescent-shaped piece of red
bell pepper for the mouth and two pieces of green bell pepper for the eyes.*

PREPARATION
10 minutes

1 tbsp tomato paste
2 mini pitta breads
1 tsp dried oregano
2 tbsp chopped ham (optional)

4 thin slices zucchini, diced
½ red bell pepper, diced
1 tbsp grated Cheddar
1 tbsp grated Parmesan

STORAGE
Best made just
before serving

Preheat the broiler. Spread the tomato paste over one side of the pitta
breads. Sprinkle over the oregano and then scatter the ham (if using),
zucchini and bell pepper pieces evenly over the top. Sprinkle on the two
types of cheese. Broil for 5 minutes or until the cheese melts and is just
beginning to brown. Leave to cool. Cut into slices or triangles and serve
with carrot and cucumber sticks. *Makes 2 servings*

072 stir-fried vegetable sticks

PREPARATION
15 minutes

1 tbsp olive oil
6 small cauliflower florets
6 cobs of baby corn, halved (or left
    whole if they are very small)

6 mangetout, topped and tailed
1 red bell pepper, cored, deseeded,
    and sliced lengthwise

STORAGE
Best made just
before serving

Heat the oil in a skillet or wok. Add the cauliflower and cook for
2 minutes. Then add the baby corn, mangetout and bell pepper. Stir the
vegetables from time to time to stop them burning. Continue cooking for
3–4 minutes until slightly soft, but still *al dente*. Serve with baby fish cakes
(recipe 065; p.69) or mini meatballs (recipe 069; p.71). *Makes 3–6 servings*

073 honey-glazed mini corn cobs

PREPARATION
15–20 minutes

1 corn cob
1 tbsp butter
2 tsps runny honey

STORAGE
Best made just
before serving

Cut the corn cobs crosswise into 2in sections. Steam or cook in boiling
water for 10–15 minutes until tender. Drain. Melt the butter in a small skillet
over a low heat. Add the honey and then the corn, and cook gently for
about 5 minutes, turning frequently to prevent burning the honey. Serve
with First Chicken Nuggets (recipe 066; p.70). *Makes 3–6 servings*

074 drop scones

*The eggs and milk make these a high protein snack. They are delicious
on their own or served topped with a fruit purée and yogurt mix.*

PREPARATION
20 minutes

2 cups all-purpose flour
1 tsp baking soda
2 tsp cream of tartar
1 tbsp superfine sugar

2 eggs
1 tsp soy oil
1¼ cups milk
butter (for frying)

STORAGE
Keeps for up
to 1 hour in
the fridge

Mix the flour, baking soda, and cream of tartar together in a large bowl.
Make a well in the center, add the eggs and oil, and whisk them with a
balloon whisk, gradually incorporating some of the flour. Remake the well
and this time add in ½ cup milk at a time, again whisking and incorporating
the flour. Keep whisking until you have a smooth batter. Let this stand
overnight if possible, or for at least 30 minutes before using. Melt a little
butter in a large skillet. Drop heaped tablespoonfuls of batter into the skillet
to make small rounds well-spaced apart. Allow them to cook until bubbles
appear on the surface and burst. Turn them over and cook for a further
1–2 minutes until they are golden brown on both sides. Make several
batches to use up all the mixture. *Makes 20 scones*

075 tropical fruit salad

As well as being a real taste sensation, this fruit salad provides a great boost of vitamin C and beta-carotene.

PREPARATION
10 minutes

1 small ripe mango
1 ripe kiwi
1 slice fresh pineapple
½ small ripe banana

STORAGE
Best made just before serving, but keeps for up to 4 hours in the fridge

Peel the mango. Carefully slice the flesh off the stone and cut it into small bite-sized pieces. Peel the kiwi fruit and cut this into 6 wedges. Cut away the rind and hard core from the pineapple and slice into batons. Slice the banana. Mix all of the fruit together and serve. *Makes 2–4 servings*

076 warming winter fruit salad

PREPARATION
20 minutes

½ cup dried peaches or pears
¾ cup dried apple rings
¼ cup dried banana chips
½ cup dried mango
⅔ cup (5fl oz) orange juice

⅔ cup water
1 clove
1 cinnamon stick
1 tbsp grated orange rind

STORAGE
Keeps for up to 2 days in the fridge

Cut all of the dried fruit into small pieces and put it in a pan along with the orange juice, water, clove, cinnamon stick, and grated orange zest. Simmer gently for about 10 minutes until the fruit is tender, adding extra water if necessary. Allow to cool and test the temperature before serving. Serve with custard or a non-dairy alternative. *Makes 4–6 servings*

077 autumn fruit salad

PREPARATION
5–10 minutes

1 satsuma or clementine
½ eating apple
½ ripe pear
4 blackberries or loganberries
4 small seedless grapes

STORAGE
Best made just before serving but keeps for up to 4 hours in the fridge

Peel the satsuma or clementine and divide into segments. If there are pips, remove them by cutting the segments in half. Wash the rest of the fruit well. Core the apple and pear and cut them into bite-sized cubes. Mix all the fruits together in a bowl. If you are not going to serve the fruit salad immediately, sprinkle some orange juice over the apple and pear to stop them from discoloring. Serve with natural bio-yogurt or vanilla ice-cream, or a non-dairy alternative. *Makes 2–4 servings*

078 summer fruit salad *(below)*

A refreshing, healthy treat on a hot summer's day!

PREPARATION
15 minutes

STORAGE
Best made just
before serving,
but keeps for
up to 4 hours
in the fridge

1 ripe peach or nectarine
1 ripe apricot
6 strawberries
6 raspberries
1 wedge of watermelon

Wash the peach, apricot, and berries. Cut the peach and apricot in half
and remove the stones. (Most toddlers will be happy eating these two fruits
with the skin left on, but some do prefer them peeled.) Hull the strawberries.
Cut the rind from the watermelon and remove the seeds. Cut all the fruit into
bite-sized pieces and mix the fruits together. Serve the salad on its own or
with a fruit sorbet or some ice cream. *Makes 2–4 servings*

079   mixed fruit jello

Choose soft fruits in season to maximize the nutrients in this jello, but don't use fresh kiwi, pineapple, or papaya as these prevent jello from setting.

PREPARATION
2 hours 15 minutes
–3 hours 15 minutes

STORAGE
Keeps for up to 2
days in the fridge

1 packet jello
½ cup boiling water
1 cup cold water
¾ cup unsweetened fruit juice, such
   as orange, apple, grape, or

blackcurrant
1½ cups finely chopped fresh fruit,
   such as peaches, strawberries,
   pears, or bananas

Place the jello in a large jug and pour in the boiling water. Stir to dissolve. Add the cold water and then the fruit juice. Take one large jello mold or several small molds or dishes and place the fruit in the bottom. Pour the jello mixture over the fruit. Stir to distribute the fruit throughout the jello and place in the fridge. Leave for 2–3 hours to set. *Makes 4–6 servings*

080   custard tarts

PREPARATION
40 minutes

STORAGE
Suitable for
freezing; keep
for up to 24 hours
in the fridge

1 cup flour
2oz butter
1 tbsp cold water
2 large eggs

1 tbsp sugar
1¼ cups milk, hot
1 tsp vanilla extract
ground nutmeg (optional)

Preheat the oven to 200°C/400°F/gas mark 6. Process the flour and butter together in a food processor until crumbly. Pour in the water and process again until a stiff dough forms. If you have time, wrap it in a cloth and leave it in the fridge for 30 minutes. Roll out the dough on a floured board and cut into rounds to line the bottom and sides of 12 foil tart cases. Whisk the eggs with the sugar in a jug. Add the hot milk and vanilla extract and mix well. Pour the milk mixture into the pastry cases until three-quarters full. Sprinkle a pinch of nutmeg on top (if using). Bake for about 20 minutes until the custard is set. Serve with fruit fingers. *Makes 12 tarts*

081   banana custard

PREPARATION
10 minutes

STORAGE
Keeps for up
to 1 hour in
the fridge

1¼ cups milk
1 tbsp custard powder
1 banana, sliced

Put the custard powder in a bowl, add about 2–3 tablespoonfuls of the milk and stir to dissolve. Put the remainder of the milk in a small saucepan and bring to the boil. Pour the boiling milk into the bowl with the dissolved custard powder mix and stir to mix thoroughly. Pour the contents of the bowl back into the saucepan and put back onto the heat. Stir continuously until the custard thickens. Put the sliced banana in a serving dish. Pour the custard over the banana. Make sure the custard has cooled sufficiently before serving. *Makes 2–4 servings*

part four

3-6 year olds

Between the ages of three and six your child changes dramatically from a toddler into a pre-schooler and then a schoolchild. In this crucial period during which he is expected to learn so much, he needs optimum nutrition to boost his brainpower. As we've previously mentioned, one of the best ways to ensure that he eats well and learns to enjoy his food is to eat together as a family. Eating regular, nutritious meals will ensure that he gets all the nourishment he needs.

In this section we offer a wide range of delicious, healthy recipes for your growing child. Included are breakfasts, lunches, and dinners, plus soups, side dishes, and desserts. We also give some great ideas for drinks, snacks, and nutritious party foods. Finally, we have offered a selection of recipes that are easy and fun to cook with your child.

BREAKFASTS

After the overnight fast our brains need fuel to kick-start them into action, so it is vital that your child learns to eat breakfast, which is the most important meal of the day. Children who start the day with a nutritious breakfast are better behaved, have longer attention spans, and perform better at school.

This collection of recipes uses basic, healthy ingredients. Many can be prepared quickly, especially if you measure out the ingredients the night before. If you have more time at the weekends, why not try something more adventurous than usual. Or plan ahead and make, say, muffins or English scones to freeze for use as quick and easy breakfasts during the following week.

082 tropical muesli

Making your own muesli gives you control over what goes in it. This one is milk- and wheat-free, but you can add skimmed milk powder and use wheat flakes instead of cornflakes, if you wish.

PREPARATION
5 minutes

STORAGE
Keeps for up to
1 week in an
airtight container

2 tbsp rolled oats
1 tbsp wheatgerm
1 tbsp cornflakes, crushed
1 tbsp ground almonds/hazelnuts

2 tbsp dried fruit, such as chopped
   papayas, mangoes, or apricots
1 tbsp shredded coconut
1 tsp brown sugar

Mix all the ingredients together in a bowl. Serve with milk, or natural bio-yogurt and fresh fruit. *Makes 1–2 servings*

083 muesli bars

These muesli bars are sweet and filling, but they are also packed full of nutrients. They will tempt even the most reluctant breakfast-eater!

PREPARATION
30–35 minutes

STORAGE
Wrap bars
individually in
cling film. Keep
for up to 4 days
in the fridge or
in an airtight tin

3½ cups unsweetened muesli
   (without whole nuts)
3 tbsp ground pumpkin seeds
½ cup dried, chopped apricots
½ cup chopped dates

4½oz butter
¼ cup raw brown sugar
4 tbsp honey
2 ripe bananas, mashed

Preheat the oven to 180°C/350°F/gas mark 4. Lightly grease a baking pan. Mix together the muesli, pumpkin seeds, and dried fruit in a large bowl. Place the butter with the sugar and honey in a small saucepan and allow to melt. Add the bananas. Pour this mixture onto the muesli and stir well. Transfer the muesli mixture into the prepared pan. Press down using the back of a spoon. Bake in the oven for 20–25 minutes until golden brown. Allow to cool before cutting into bars. Serve with a glass of milk. *Makes 10–12 bars*

084 microwaved porridge with apricots

PREPARATION
5 minutes

STORAGE
Best made just
before serving

6 tbsp rolled oats
6 dried apricots, diced
½ cup milk
½ cup water

Put the oats and chopped apricots in a wide bowl. Pour the milk and water in and mix well. Microwave on full power, uncovered for 3 minutes. Serve with extra milk or natural bio-yogurt. *Makes 1–3 servings*

085   blueberry yogurt delight

Ⓥ Ⓢ

This quick breakfast is delicious and nutritionally complete. For variation, try using other soft fruits, such as strawberries, raspberries, or peaches.

PREPARATION

5 minutes

1 small carton natural bio-yogurt
1–2 tsp maple syrup/runny honey
2 tbsp blueberries
2–3 tbsp muesli

STORAGE
Best made just
before serving

Place the yogurt in a bowl. Gradually mix in the maple syrup/honey and the blueberries, squashing the berries a little with the back of a spoon. Sprinkle the yogurt mixture with muesli. *Makes 1–2 servings*

086   breakfast in a glass

Ⓥ Ⓢ

This is great for children who find eating breakfast a struggle.

PREPARATION

10 minutes

1 banana, peeled and chopped
½ mango, peeled, pitted, and
  chopped
⅔ cup milk

⅔ cup natural bio-yogurt
1 tbsp wheatgerm
1 tbsp maple syrup (optional)

STORAGE
Best made just
before serving

Place all the ingredients in a blender or food processor. Whizz until smooth. *Makes 1–2 servings*

087   soy yogurt shake

Ⓥ 🚫 Ⓞ Ⓢ

PREPARATION
10 minutes

⅔ cup strawberry-flavored soy yogurt
⅔ cup soy milk fortified with calcium
8–10 strawberries, washed and hulled
½ banana, peeled and chopped
1 tbsp wheatgerm

STORAGE
Best made just
before serving

Place all the ingredients in a blender or food processor. Whizz until smooth. *Makes 1–2 servings*

088 mini blueberry pancakes

V O ▣

PREPARATION
30 minutes

1 egg
¾ cup natural bio-yogurt
½ cup milk
1 tbsp vegetable oil

1 cup all-purpose flour
½ tsp baking soda
10–12 tbsp blueberries

STORAGE
Suitable for
freezing; best
made just before
serving, but batter
can be made the
night before and
kept in the fridge

Place the egg, yogurt, milk, and oil in a bowl and mix together. Add the flour and baking soda. Mix well with a fork. Add a little extra milk if batter is too thick. Heat up a large skillet or griddle, adding a little oil if necessary. Drop spoonfuls of the batter in the skillet/onto the griddle, allowing room for each pancake to spread. Place a few blueberries on top of each one. Cook on medium heat until bubbles appear and the undersides are golden brown. Turn and cook other sides until golden. Serve immediately or keep warm in oven until all are cooked. Serve with yogurt, or blueberries and maple syrup. *Makes 12 pancakes*

089 chocolate banana pancakes *(below)*

V O ▣

PREPARATION
20 minutes

1 cup all-purpose flour
1 tsp baking powder
1 egg
1 cup milk

1 tbsp vegetable oil
¼ banana, chopped
2 tbsp chocolate chips

STORAGE
Suitable for
freezing; best
made just before
serving, but batter
can be made the
night before and
kept in the fridge

Place the flour and baking powder in a bowl, and add the egg, milk, and oil. Mix until almost smooth. Stir in the banana and chocolate chips. Heat up a large skillet/griddle, adding a little oil if needed. Drop spoonfuls of the batter in the skillet/on to the griddle, allowing room for each pancake to spread. Cook on a medium heat until bubbles appear and undersides are golden brown. Turn and cook the other sides until golden. Serve immediately or keep warm in oven until all are cooked. Serve with sliced banana and maple syrup. *Makes 8–10 pancakes*

090 oaty breakfast pancakes

V O (icons)

PREPARATION
30 minutes

1¼ cups all-purpose flour
1 cup oats
2 tbsp baking powder

2 eggs, beaten
2 cups milk
4 tbsp vegetable oil

STORAGE
Suitable for freezing; best made just before serving, but batter can be made the night before and kept in the fridge

Place the flour, oats, and baking powder in a bowl. Add the egg, milk, and oil and mix well. Heat up a large skillet/griddle, adding oil if needed. Drop spoonfuls of the batter into the skillet/onto the griddle, allowing room for each pancake to spread. Cook on medium heat until bubbles appear and undersides are golden brown. Turn and cook the other sides. Serve immediately or keep warm until rest are cooked. Top with berries and maple syrup. *Makes 16–20 pancakes*

091 pecan pancakes

V O (icons)

PREPARATION
20 minutes

3 cups mixed flours and fine grains, such as buckwheat, maize meal, brown rice flour, and quinoa
1 tbsp baking powder
1½ tsp baking soda
3 eggs

⅔ cup natural bio-yogurt
2½ cups milk
4 tbsp runny honey
4 tbsp vegetable oil
1 cup toasted pecan nuts, chopped

STORAGE
Suitable for freezing; best made just before serving, but batter can be made the night before and kept in the fridge

Mix the flours, baking powder, and baking soda together. In a separate bowl whisk the eggs, yogurt, milk, honey, and oil together. Add the wet ingredients to the dry ingredients and mix. Stir in the chopped pecans. Heat up a large skillet/griddle, adding oil if needed. Drop spoonfuls of the batter into the skillet/onto the griddle, allowing room for each pancake to spread. Cook on medium heat until bubbles appear and undersides are golden brown. Turn and cook the other sides. Serve immediately or keep warm until rest are cooked. Serve with slices of banana and extra honey. *Makes 18–20 pancakes*

092 wholewheat raisin muffins

V O (icons)

PREPARATION
10 minutes

¼ cup wholewheat flour
1 cup all-purpose white flour
⅓ cup wheatgerm
½ cup raisins
3 tsp baking powder

¼ cup soft dark brown sugar
1 egg, beaten
1½oz unsalted butter, melted
1¼ cups milk

STORAGE
Suitable for freezing, but best served immediately

Preheat the oven to 200°C/400°F/gas mark 6. Mix together all the dry ingredients in a bowl. Beat the egg and add the butter and the milk. Pour the wet ingredients onto the dry ingredients and mix lightly until combined. Spoon into muffin cases. Bake for 10–15 minutes until firm to touch and lightly browned. Serve immediately with sliced banana and a glass of milk. *Makes 10–12 muffins*

093 apple and oat muffins

PREPARATION
35 minutes

STORAGE
Suitable for
freezing, but
best served
immediately

1 cup all-purpose white flour
2 tsp baking powder
1½oz oatmeal/rolled oats
2oz light muscovado sugar
2 eating apples, peeled, cored,
  and diced

3 tbsp golden raisins/raisins
1½oz butter, softened or melted
4½oz natural bio-yogurt
4fl oz milk
1 egg

Preheat the oven to 200°C/400°F/gas mark 6. Line a muffin pan with
paper cases. Mix the flour, baking powder, oatmeal, and sugar in a bowl.
Stir in the apples and raisins. In another bowl beat together the butter,
yogurt, milk, and egg. Add this wet mixture to the dry ingredients, stirring
quickly and briefly, until just incorporated. Do not overmix. Spoon the
mixture into the cases and sprinkle with a little oatmeal. Bake for
15 minutes until just firm to touch. Cool on a wire rack. Serve with
a glass of milk or hot chocolate. *Makes 10–12 large muffins*

094 blueberry muffins

PREPARATION
35–40 minutes

STORAGE
Suitable for
freezing, but
best served
immediately

2¾oz unsalted butter
½ cup natural bio-yogurt
½ cup milk
1 egg
½ cup all-purpose flour

50g (2oz) sugar
½ tsp baking soda
2 tsp baking powder
1 cup blueberries

Preheat the oven to 200°C/400°F/gas mark 6. Line a muffin pan with paper
cases. Melt the butter in a small saucepan and allow to cool slightly. Mix
together the yogurt, milk, and egg in a bowl, and add the melted butter. In
another bowl mix together all the dry ingredients. Add the egg mixture and
mix lightly. Fold in blueberries. Spoon mixture into muffin cases. Bake for
20–25 minutes until golden brown and firm to touch. Cool on a wire rack.
Serve with a glass of milk. *Makes 10–12 small muffins*

095 banana oat muffins

PREPARATION
35–40 minutes

STORAGE
Suitable for
freezing, but
best served
immediately

1oz unsalted butter
3 tsp runny honey
2 large ripe bananas
1 cup all-purpose flour
⅔ cup oatmeal/rolled oats

1 heaped tsp baking powder
½ tsp baking soda
½ tsp cinnamon
⅓ cup milk

Preheat the oven to 190°C/375°F/gas mark 5. Line a muffin pan with
paper cases. Melt the butter and honey in a skillet. Mix together all the
dry ingredients in a bowl. Mash the bananas and mix with the honey and
butter. Add this mixture and the milk to the dry ingredients, stirring until
mixed lightly. Spoon into the muffin cases. Bake for 25 minutes until golden
brown and firm to touch. Serve with slices of banana and a glass of milk.
Makes 8–10 small muffins

096 cinnamon French toast fingers
Ⓥ Ⓞ ✎

🕐 **PREPARATION**
10 minutes

❄ **STORAGE**
Suitable for
freezing, but
best served
immediately

1 egg
1 tbsp milk
cinnamon (to taste)
2 slices wholewheat bread, cut into

fingers
1 tbsp oil
maple syrup (to serve)

Mix the egg, milk, and cinnamon in a flat dish. Coat the bread fingers in the egg mixture on both sides. Heat the oil in a skillet over a medium heat. Add the bread fingers and fry until golden on both sides. Serve with maple syrup in an eggcup to dip the toast fingers in. *Makes 2 servings*

097 vanilla honey French toast shapes
Ⓥ Ⓞ ✎

🕐 **PREPARATION**
10 minutes

❄ **STORAGE**
Suitable for
freezing, but
best served
immediately

1 egg
1 tbsp milk
2–3 drops of vanilla essence
1 tsp runny honey
2 slices wholewheat bread, cut into

shapes, such as stars or triangles
1 tbsp oil
3–4 strawberries, hulled and sliced
  (to serve)

Mix together the egg, milk, vanilla essence, and honey in a flat dish. Cut the bread into shapes using cookie-cutters or a sharp knife. Coat the bread shapes in the egg mixture on both sides. Heat the oil in a skillet over a medium heat. Add the bread shapes and fry until golden on both sides. Serve with sliced strawberries and a little extra honey. *Makes 2 servings*

098 English breakfast scones

PREPARATION
15–20 minutes

STORAGE
Suitable for
freezing, but
best served
immediately

2 cups all-purpose flour, plus extra
   for rolling out
1 tbsp baking powder
pinch of salt

2oz butter, cut into small pieces
1 tbsp sugar
⅔ cup semi-skimmed milk

Preheat oven to 220°C/425°F/gas mark 7. Sift the flour, baking powder,
and salt into a bowl. Add the butter and rub in until the mixture resembles
breadcrumbs. Add the sugar, then pour in the milk. Mix together with a
metal spoon to form a dough. Place on a floured surface and knead lightly.
Roll out to a thickness of 1in. Cut into circles with a cutter. Place in a
baking pan and sprinkle with flour. Bake for 7–10 minutes until risen and
golden. Allow to cool. Serve with butter and jam. *Makes 4–6 scones*

099 fruity English scones

PREPARATION
15–20 minutes

STORAGE
Suitable for
freezing, but
best served
immediately

1¼ cups all-purpose flour plus extra
   for rolling out
½ cup wholewheat flour
1½ tbsp baking powder
pinch of salt

2oz butter, cut into small pieces
1 tbsp sugar
1 tbsp raisins
1 tbsp chopped dates
⅔ cup milk

Preheat oven to 220°C/425°F/gas mark 7. Sift flour, baking powder,
and salt into a bowl. Add butter and rub in until the mixture resembles
breadcrumbs. Add sugar, raisins, and dates and then pour in milk and mix
together gently with a metal spoon to form a dough. Place onto a floured
surface and knead very lightly. Roll out to a thickness of 1in. Cut into circles
using a cutter. Place on baking pan. Sprinkle tops with a little flour. Bake for
7–10 minutes until well risen and lightly brown. Allow to cool slightly before
serving with butter and jam. *Makes 4–6 scones*

100 English muffin breakfast pizzas

PREPARATION
10 minutes

STORAGE
Best made just
before serving

2 English muffins
4–5 tbsp Quick Tomato Sauce
   (recipe 157; p.111)
4 tbsp grated mild Cheddar
4 tbsp grated mozzarella

Split the muffins in half and toast them. Spread with tomato sauce and
sprinkle evenly with the two cheeses. Broil for a few minutes until the
cheese is bubbling. Serve with a glass of fruit juice. *Makes 1–2 servings*

101   corn and bacon muffins

PREPARATION
40 minutes

STORAGE
Suitable for
freezing; keep
for up to 24 hours
in an airtight
container

6 slices lean back bacon
1 medium onion, peeled and diced
1½ cups self-rising flour
½ tsp baking powder
½ cup Cheddar, grated

12oz canned corn, drained
⅔ cup milk
2 eggs
5 tbsp olive oil

Preheat the oven to 200°C/400°F/gas mark 6. Line a muffin pan with
paper muffin cases. Trim any fat off the bacon slices and then cut into
squares. Place in a small skillet, add the onion, and gently fry for 5–10
minutes until well cooked. Place the flour and baking powder in a bowl
and mix. Stir in the cheese and corn. In another bowl whisk the milk,
eggs, and oil together. Add this mixture to the flour mixture, then add the
onion and bacon. Stir to combine but do not overmix. Spoon into the
muffin cases and bake for 15 minutes until firm to touch. Cool on a wire
rack. *Makes 12 muffins*

102   bacon and tomato bagel sandwich

PREPARATION
15 minutes

STORAGE
Best made just
before serving

2 slices lean back bacon
½ large tomato, cut into 2 slices
1 bagel, split in half and lightly toasted

Put the bacon and tomato slices under the broiler and cook for 10 minutes,
turning the bacon to do both sides. Place one slice of the broiled tomato
on each side of the bagel. Squash the tomato and spread to cover each
side of the bagel fully. Place the bacon on top and sandwich together. Cut
in half or into quarters. *Makes 1–2 servings*

103   omelet in a pitta pocket

PREPARATION
15 minutes

STORAGE
Best made just
before serving

1 egg
pinch of black pepper
1 tsp butter/olive oil

1 tbsp grated cheese
½ large pitta bread

Put the egg and black pepper in a bowl and beat using a fork. Melt the
butter/oil in a small skillet and turn up the heat. Once sizzling, pour in the
egg mixture and allow to set a little before adding the cheese. Cook over
a medium to high heat until the omelet is completely set. Fold it over
and cut it in half. Lightly toast the pitta bread. Then split the pitta bread
lengthwise and put the omelet inside. Serve with a glass of fruit juice.
Makes 1 serving

104 mushroom omelet
V Ⓧ Ⓧ Ⓞ Ⓟ

PREPARATION
15 minutes

2 eggs
pinch of salt
pinch of black pepper

1–2 tsp butter/olive oil
2–3 button mushrooms, thinly sliced

STORAGE
Best made just
before serving

Place the eggs, salt, and black pepper in a bowl, and beat with a fork. Melt
the butter/olive oil in a medium-size skillet, add the sliced mushrooms, and
sauté until softened. Remove mushrooms from the skillet and put to one
side. Put a little more butter/olive oil in the skillet and allow it to melt—it
should cover the base and a little way up the sides. Turn up the heat.
When the butter/olive oil is sizzling, pour in the egg mixture and add the
mushrooms. Mix a little with the fork. Cook over a medium to high heat
until the omelet is completely set. Remove from the heat. Fold it over and
cut it in half. Serve with toast. *Makes 2 servings*

105 tomato and basil omelet
V Ⓧ Ⓧ Ⓞ Ⓟ

PREPARATION
10–15 minutes

2 eggs
pinch of salt
pinch of pepper

1 tsp butter/olive oil
½ tomato, finely chopped
1 tbsp chopped fresh basil

STORAGE
Best made just
before serving

Place the eggs, salt and black pepper in a bowl, and beat with a fork.
Melt the butter/olive oil in a medium-size skillet, and turn up the heat. Once
sizzling, pour in the egg mixture and add the tomato and the basil. Mix a little with the fork. Cook over a medium to high heat until the omelet is completely set. Remove from the heat. Fold it over and cut it in half.
Serve with toast. *Makes 2 servings*

106 scrambled eggs with smoked salmon
Ⓧ Ⓧ Ⓞ Ⓟ Ⓐ

PREPARATION
10 minutes

2 eggs
2 tbsp milk
pinch of black pepper
1 tsp butter/olive oil

1oz smoked salmon, cut into thin
    strips
2 tbsp chopped fresh parsley

STORAGE
Best made just
before serving

Place the eggs and black pepper in a bowl, and beat with a fork. Melt the
butter/olive oil over a gentle heat in a skillet. Pour in the egg mixture. After
about 30 seconds stir in the smoked salmon strips and one tablespoonful
of parsley. Continue stirring over the gentle heat until the egg is cooked
right through. Remove from the heat and sprinkle with the remaining
parsley. Fold it over and cut it into portions. Serve with toast fingers.
Makes 2–3 servings

LUNCHES

Lunch is important because it boosts your child's energy levels in the middle of the day. It is also a good time to get your child to eat fruit and vegetables, and to try new foods. At the weekend lunch might be the main family meal, while during the week it might be a light or portable meal—for example, a packed lunch to take to school.

To reflect this diversity, we include delicious recipes suitable for lunch boxes and picnics (anything that can be kept in the fridge can also be kept in a cool bag), as well as some to enjoy at home. The recipes are all quick and easy to make, and some use up leftovers from main meals. You can use food-combining (see pp.12–13) to put together nutritionally complete lunches by making sure you base them on a starchy food served with a high-protein food, vegetables, and fruit.

107 basic baked potatoes

Rich in fiber and vitamin C, baked potatoes are very versatile and they can form the basis of a variety of quick and healthy meals. The best potatoes to bake are the floury (rather than waxy) varieties.

PREPARATION
1–1½ hours

2 medium potatoes
olive oil for brushing (optional)

STORAGE
Best made just
before serving

Preheat the oven to 190°C/375°F/gas mark 5. Wash and scrub the potatoes thoroughly. Prick the potato skins several times with a fork. Place in a baking pan and brush all over with oil (if using). Put in the oven and cook for about 1 hour until potatoes feel soft when pressed. Cut in half lengthwise and serve with a simple topping, such as grated cheese or preheated baked beans. *Makes 2–4 servings*

108 baked potato with cauliflower cheese

This delicious, creamy topping is packed with calcium for strong bones and teeth.

PREPARATION
15–20 minutes

½ medium cauliflower, cut into florets
1oz butter
2 tbsp flour

1¼ cups milk
2 medium potatoes, baked
1 cup grated Cheddar

STORAGE
Best made just
before serving

Boil or steam the cauliflower until soft. Meanwhile, melt the butter in a large saucepan and add in the flour. Cook for about 2 minutes on a low heat—the flour should not turn brown. Pour the milk in slowly while stirring with a wooden spoon or a balloon whisk. Keep stirring until you have a smooth sauce. Bring to the boil, reduce heat, and simmer for 2–3 minutes until the sauce thickens. Remove from the heat and stir in the cooked cauliflower florets and three quarters of the grated cheese. Preheat the broiler. Cut the baked potatoes in half lengthwise and scoop out about half of the flesh from the middle. Fill the potato skins with the cauliflower cheese mixture and sprinkle the remaining grated cheese over the top. Place under the broiler for about 3 minutes until the cheese on top has melted and turned golden. *Makes 2–4 servings*

109 baked potato with pizza topping *(below)*

Ⓥ ⊗ ⊗ ▯

PREPARATION
15 minutes/
20 minutes

STORAGE
Best made just
before serving

2 medium potatoes, baked
4 tbsp Quick Tomato Sauce
  (recipe 157; p.111)
½ green/red bell pepper, deseeded
  and chopped

1 large field mushroom, chopped
pinch of dried oregano
2 tbsp grated mozzarella
2 tbsp grated Cheddar

Cut open the potatoes lengthwise. Spoon half the tomato sauce onto each potato and add the green/red bell pepper and the mushroom. Sprinkle on the oregano. Heat for 1–1½ minutes in the microwave until the vegetables soften. Add the grated cheese and either microwave for 30 seconds or melt the cheese under the broiler. *Makes 2–4 servings*

110 baked potato with roasted vegetables

Ⓥ Ⓧ Ⓧ ⊟

PREPARATION
5–10 minutes

2 medium potatoes, baked
6 tbsp Roasted Autumn Vegetables
  (recipe 221; p.138)

2 tbsp grated mozzarella
2 tbsp grated Cheddar
1 tbsp grated Parmesan (optional)

STORAGE
Best made just
before serving

Cut open the potatoes lengthwise. Spoon half the roasted vegetables into each potato. Heat for 1 minute in the microwave until the vegetables are hot. Add the grated Cheddar and Parmesan (if using) and either microwave for 30 seconds or melt the cheese under the broiler. *Makes 2–4 servings*

111 tuna baked potato

Ⓧ Ⓧ ⊟

PREPARATION
5–10 minutes

2 medium potatoes, baked
2 tsp butter
4 tbsp canned tuna, drained

2 tbsp grated mozzarella
2 tbsp grated Cheddar

STORAGE
Best made just
before serving

Cut open the potatoes lengthwise. Spread butter onto each half. Spoon half the tuna onto each potato. Add the cheese and heat for 1 minute in the microwave or melt cheese under the broiler. *Makes 2–4* servings

112 twice-baked potato

Ⓥ Ⓧ Ⓧ ⊟

PREPARATION
1¼–1½ hours

1 large baking potato, scrubbed clean
1 tsp butter
3 tbsp natural bio-yogurt

2 tbsp chopped chives
3 tbsp grated Cheddar

STORAGE
Best made just
before serving

Preheat the oven to 200°C/400°F/gas mark 6. Prick the potato skin several times with a fork, place in a baking pan, and put in the oven. Cook for 1 hour until soft. Cut the potato in half lengthwise. Scoop out most of the flesh, leaving the potato skins intact. Put the flesh in a bowl and add the butter, yogurt, chives, and 2 tablespoonfuls of grated cheese. Beat to make a light, fluffy mixture and pile back into the potato skins. Top with the rest of the grated cheese and put back in the oven until the cheese melts. *Makes 2 servings*

113 Italian frittata
V ⊗ ⊗ ⊗ ◐ ♪ ▣

Frittata makes a quick and healthy meal in minutes. The eggs and cheese are full of protein and the vegetables are rich in flavonoids and vitamins.

PREPARATION
20 minutes

STORAGE
Best made just
before serving

1 tbsp olive oil
½ small leek, washed and sliced
1 stick celery, washed and chopped
½ red bell pepper, deseeded and
    chopped

4oz baby spinach, washed and
    chopped
3 eggs
pinch of black pepper (optional)
⅓ cup Cheddar, grated

Put the oil in a medium-size skillet and heat. Add the leek, celery, and red bell pepper and cook for about 5 minutes until soft. Add the spinach and cook for a further 2–3 minutes until it wilts. In a bowl, beat the eggs with the black pepper (if using). Pour the eggs over the vegetables in the skillet. Cook over a medium heat until the base sets. Sprinkle on the grated cheese and place under the broiler until the cheese melts and the top is set. Serve with crusty bread or breadsticks. *Makes 2–4 servings*

114 spinach soufflé
V ◐ ♪ ▣

This is another good way to get children to eat spinach. You can use frozen spinach to make this recipe even quicker.

PREPARATION
1–1¼ hours

STORAGE
Best made just
before serving

1 tsp butter (for frying)
7oz spinach, washed and finely
    chopped
1oz butter
2 tbsp flour

1¼ cups milk
4 large eggs, separated
1 cup Cheddar, grated
pinch of black pepper
pinch of ground nutmeg

Preheat the oven to 190°C/375°F/gas mark 5. Melt a teaspoonful of butter in a small skillet and add the spinach. Stir over a gentle heat for about 5 minutes until it wilts. Leave to stand. Grease a medium-size soufflé dish. Melt the remaining butter in a small saucepan and then add in the flour. Cook for about 2 minutes on a low heat—it should not turn brown. Stir in the milk with a wooden spoon or balloon whisk. Keep stirring until you have a smooth sauce. Bring to the boil and simmer gently for 2–3 minutes until the sauce thickens. Remove from the heat and stir in the spinach, pepper, and nutmeg. Then add the 4 egg yolks and mix thoroughly. In a separate bowl, whisk the egg whites until stiff and fold them in with the grated cheese. Pour into the greased soufflé dish and bake for 30–40 minutes in the oven until set and golden brown on top. *Makes 6–8 servings*

115 corn fritters

Corn is popular with most children and these fritters make excellent, nutritious finger food. They have even more flavor cold the next day. You can substitute ordinary wheat flour for cornstarch and polenta flour, but then the recipe will no longer be gluten-free.

PREPARATION
35 minutes

STORAGE
Suitable for
freezing; keeps
for up to 2 days
in the fridge

2 tbsp cornstarch
2 tbsp polenta flour
pinch of black pepper
pinch of ground coriander seeds
2 large eggs, beaten
3 tbsp finely chopped scallions

2 tbsp finely chopped chives
1 tbsp finely chopped
  fresh coriander
12oz canned corn, well drained
olive oil (for frying)

Put the cornstarch, polenta flour, black pepper, and ground coriander in a bowl and mix together. Add the beaten eggs and keep stirring to form a smooth batter. Add the scallions, chives, and fresh coriander. Then stir in the corn until evenly distributed in the batter. Heat some oil in a large skillet. Ladle about 2 heaped tablespoonfuls of corn batter into the pan. You will get several fritters in the skillet at the same time. Cook the fritters for a few minutes on one side and then turn and cook for a few minutes on the other side. Drain the fritters on paper towels and keep warm while cooking the rest. Serve with vegetable soup or a salad. *Makes 12 fritters*

116 tuna and pesto pasta

Tuna is usually a hit with children. Use fresh fish if you can as it contains more of those vital LCPs, but the canned variety is a good second best.

PREPARATION
25 minutes

STORAGE
Keeps for up
to 24 hours in
the fridge

1 cup dry pasta shapes
1 tbsp olive oil/oil from canned tuna
1 tbsp tomato paste

1 tbsp pesto sauce/
  3 tbsp finely chopped fresh basil
4oz cooked fresh tuna

Cook the pasta according to instructions on the packet. Heat the oil in a large saucepan and stir in the tomato paste and pesto sauce/fresh basil. Flake the tuna and add, stirring until well combined. Add the pasta and continue cooking over a gentle heat until heated right through. Keep stirring to prevent the pasta from sticking. Serve with salad. *Makes 4 servings*

117   Chinese egg-fried rice *(above)*

ⓋⓍⓍⓈⓄ◯🖉

The rice, egg, and vegetables make this a nutritionally balanced meal.

PREPARATION
40 minutes

STORAGE
Keeps
for up to
24 hours in
the fridge

1 cup long grain or basmati rice
3 tbsp vegetable oil
3 eggs, lightly beaten
1 small onion, peeled and chopped
2 medium carrots, peeled and
   chopped
½ red bell pepper, deseeded and

   chopped
½ green bell pepper, deseeded and
   chopped
6 tbsp frozen peas
1 scallion, sliced
2 tbsp soy sauce

Cook the rice according to instructions on the packet. Put a little of the oil
in a small skillet and heat. Add the eggs and cook until set. Cut into strips. In
a large skillet/wok, heat the remaining oil and sauté the onion, carrots, and
bell peppers until soft. Add the peas and cook for 1 minute more. Add the
rice and continue to cook, stirring for 2–3 minutes. Then add the cooked egg
strips and scallion, and cook for a further 1–2 minutes. Remove from the
heat, sprinkle with soy sauce, and serve. *Makes 3–4 servings*

118 spinach and ricotta pancakes

Ⓥ Ⓞ ◉ Ⓞ

This tasty and filling vegetarian lunch contains beta-carotene, iron, and plenty of protein. For very young children you can finely chop or grind the the pine nuts, and add extra sliced celery.

PREPARATION
40 minutes

STORAGE
Keep for up
to 24 hours
in the fridge

4 tbsp all-purpose flour
1 egg, beaten
½ tbsp olive oil
⅔ cup milk
3½oz frozen spinach

3 tbsp pine nuts
⅔ cup ricotta
2 tbsp grated Parmesan
1 stick celery, finely sliced

Place the flour in a bowl and make a well in the middle. Add the egg and stir into the flour to form a batter. Add the oil and mix well. Gradually stir in the milk. Leave to stand. Put the spinach in a small saucepan and thaw over a gentle heat, stirring occasionally until all the liquid has evaporated. Stir into the batter. Heat a small, greased skillet and pour in a small ladleful of batter. Allow to spread and cook for a few minutes on either side until golden brown. Next, make the filling. Place the pine nuts in a small skillet and stir over a gentle heat until golden brown. In a bowl, beat the ricotta and the Parmesan together and then add the pine nuts and celery. Divide the filling between the pancakes and spread evenly. Roll up. Place all the filled crêpes in an ovenproof dish, cover with kitchen foil, and bake for 15 minutes at 190°C/375°F/gas mark 5. Serve with Tomato and Basil Sauce (recipe 161; p.112) and extra celery sticks. *Makes 2–4 servings*

119 double-cheese pitta pizza

Ⓥ ◉

PREPARATION
5 minutes

STORAGE
Best made just
before serving

1½–2 tbsp pasta sauce (recipes 157; p.111 and 161; p.112)
1 small pitta bread
1 tbsp grated Cheddar
1 tbsp grated mozzarella
pinch of dried oregano

Spread the sauce on one side of the pitta bread. Sprinkle on the cheese and the oregano. Cook under the broiler for 2–3 minutes until the cheese is bubbling. *Makes 1 serving*

120 mushroom and bell pepper pitta pizza

PREPARATION
5 minutes

STORAGE
Best made just
before serving

1 small pitta bread
1½–2 tbsp pasta sauce (recipes 157;
    p.111 and 161; p.112)
1 small button mushroom, sliced

1 tsp chopped red/green bell pepper
1 tbsp grated Cheddar/mozzarella
pinch of oregano

Spread the sauce on one side of the pitta bread. Sprinkle on the mushroom and bell pepper, followed by the cheese and the oregano. Cook under the broiler for 2–3 minutes until the cheese is bubbling. *Makes 1 serving*

121 ham and pineapple pitta pizza

PREPARATION
5 minutes

STORAGE
Best made just
before serving

1 small pitta bread
1½–2 tbsp pasta sauce (recipes 157;
    p.111 and 161; p.112)
1 slice ham, cut into strips
1 tsp fresh/canned pineapple,

chopped
1 tbsp grated Cheddar/
    mozzarella
pinch of oregano

Spread the sauce on one side of the pitta bread. Sprinkle on the ham and pineapple, followed by the cheese and the oregano. Cook under the broiler for 2–3 minutes until the cheese is bubbling. *Makes 1 serving*

122 French bread pizza

This is a very quick way to make a tasty pizza and a good way to use up a baguette that is past its best.

PREPARATION
5 minutes

STORAGE
Best made just
before serving

1 piece of baguette about 5in
    in length
2 tsps tomato paste
½ tsp dried oregano

½ slice ham, cut into small squares
1 medium tomato, thinly sliced
2 tbsp grated Cheddar/
    mozzarella

Split the baguette lengthwise and place in a broiler-proof dish with cut sides facing upward. Spread with tomato paste and sprinkle on the oregano. Top with the pieces of ham and the tomato slices. Cover with the grated cheese and broil for 2–3 minutes until the cheese is bubbling. *Makes 1–2 servings*

123 bacon and zucchini scone-based pizza

○ ∅ ⊟

PREPARATION
20 minutes

STORAGE
Suitable for freezing, but best made just before serving

1¾ cups self-rising flour, plus extra
   for rolling out
2oz butter
1 egg
½ cup milk
4 tbsp passata/Quick Tomato Sauce
   (recipe 157; p.111)
2 tbsp chopped fresh basil

4 slices lean back bacon
½ zucchini, diced
1 red/green bell pepper, deseeded
   and diced
6 black olives, pitted and halved
   (optional)
½ cup Cheddar/mozzarella,
   grated

Preheat the oven to 200°C/400°F/gas mark 6. Put the flour in a bowl and rub in the butter, or process in a food processor until mixture resembles breadcrumbs. Stir in the egg and enough milk to mix to a smooth, soft dough. Knead lightly on a floured surface and roll out until dough is about ½in thick. Place in a baking pan. Spread the passata over the top and sprinkle on the basil. Cut fat from the bacon, dice the remaining flesh, and sprinkle over the pizza. Top with the diced zucchini and bell pepper. Add the olives (if using) and sprinkle on the grated cheese. Bake for 10–15 minutes until the base is well risen, the bacon cooked through, and the cheese bubbling. Serve with salad. *Makes 4–6 servings*

124 chicken and corn pizza

∅ ⊟

The delicious taste of the freshly-baked pizza dough in this recipe is guaranteed to activate your child's taste buds.

PREPARATION
2 hours

STORAGE
Suitable for freezing, but best made just before serving

1¾ cup all-purpose white flour
½ tsp superfine sugar
½ sachet active dried yeast
1 tbsp olive oil
1½ tbsp milk
½ cup hand-hot water
4 tbsp tomato paste

2 tbsp chopped fresh thyme
½ boneless cooked chicken breast,
   diced
3½oz canned corn, drained
¾ cup Cheddar/mozzarella,
   grated

Put the flour in a bowl and stir in the sugar and the yeast. Make a well in the center and add the oil, milk, and water. Mix to a smooth dough that forms a ball and leaves the sides of the bowl clean. Knead for 5 minutes, then place in a clean bowl, cover with a tea towel, and leave to rise in a warm place for 1 hour. Knead the risen dough a little, then break into two pieces. Press each into a thin round and transfer them to an oiled baking pan. Prick the pizza bases all over with a fork. Cover each with half the tomato paste and sprinkle on the thyme. Preheat the oven to 200°C/400°F/gas mark 6. Meanwhile, leave the pizzas to stand for 20 minutes to allow them to rise a little more. Place in the oven and bake for 15 minutes. Sprinkle on the chicken and the corn, and cover with the grated cheese. Bake in the oven for a further 10 minutes until the cheese has melted. Serve with a salad. *Makes 2–4 servings*

125 houmous

This delicious spread is full of vital minerals, such as iron and magnesium.

PREPARATION
10 minutes

STORAGE
Suitable for freezing; keeps for up to 2 days in the fridge

14oz canned chickpeas, drained and
  rinsed well
juice of ½ lemon
juice of 1 lime
2 cloves garlic, peeled
½ tsp ground cumin

pinch of salt
1 tbsp tahini paste
3 tbsp walnut oil
1–2 tsp chopped fresh parsley
  (to garnish)

Put all the ingredients except the oil in a food processor or a blender. Process until smooth, gradually adding the oil through a funnel. Transfer into a serving bowl. Sprinkle with chopped parsley to garnish. Serve on toast triangles or as a sandwich filling. *Makes 6–7 servings*

126 tofu and avocado dip

This is a lovely, pale green vegetarian dip, which is also delicious spread on toast or in sandwiches.

PREPARATION
5 minutes

STORAGE
Keeps for up to 2 hours in the fridge, but best served immediately

1 ripe avocado, peeled and pitted
⅔ cup tofu, broken into pieces
juice of ½ lemon
1 clove garlic
dash of Tabasco/hot pepper sauce

1 tbsp chopped fresh parsley
1 tbsp olive oil
pinch of salt
slice of lemon (to garnish)

Put all the ingredients in a food processor and whizz for 1–2 minutes until the mixture is smooth. Spoon into a bowl and garnish with a slice of lemon. Serve with Pitta Bread Chips (recipe 333; p.187). *Makes 4–6 servings*

127 black-eye pea spread

PREPARATION
10 minutes

STORAGE
Suitable for freezing; keeps for up to 2 days in the fridge

14oz black-eye peas, drained and
  rinsed well
4 tbsp Spicy Tomato Salsa (recipe
  243; p.147)
2 tbsp chopped fresh coriander
pinch of ground cumin

juice ½ lemon
1 tsp olive oil
pinch of salt
pinch of pepper
chopped fresh parsley (to garnish)

Place all the ingredients together in a food processor or blender and whizz until smooth. Spoon into a serving bow and garnish with a little chopped parsley sprinkled on the top. Serve as a dip with Pitta Bread Chips (recipe 333; p.187) or vegetable sticks, or spread on toast. *Makes 6–7 servings*

128 guacamole

*This traditional Mexican dip is not only delicious but also full of
nutrients—particularly vitamin E and healthy monounsaturated fats.*

PREPARATION
10 minutes

STORAGE
Best made just
before serving

2 ripe avocados, halved and pitted
juice of ½ lime
2–3 tbsp lemon juice
1 large tomato, deseeded and
  finely chopped

1 tbsp finely chopped scallion
1 tsp finely chopped fresh coriander
dash of Tabasco/hot pepper sauce
  (optional)

In a bowl, mash the avocado, then add the other ingredients, and mix well.
Serve with Pitta Bread Chips (recipe 333; p.187), corn chips, or vegetable
sticks, or use as a sandwich filling. *Makes 4–6 servings*

129 chicken guacamole sandwiches

PREPARATION
5 minutes

STORAGE
Best made just
before serving

2 slices wholewheat bread
2 tbsp Guacamole
2–3 thin slices chicken breast
3 slices tomato (optional)

Spread the Guacamole on the bread. On one slice, place the chicken
breast slices on top of the Guacamole, and cover with the tomato (if using).
Sandwich together. Cut into 4 triangles or squares. *Makes 1–2 servings*

130 potted beef spread

PREPARATION
1 hour 45
minutes–2 hours

STORAGE
Suitable for
freezing; keeps
for up to 2 days
in the fridge

½ cup very lean ground beef
¼ small onion
1 bay leaf

pinch of salt
½oz butter, melted

Preheat the oven to 150°C/300°F/gas mark 2. Place the ground beef,
onion, and bay leaf in a small ovenproof dish. Add enough water just to
cover the meat. Bring to the boil on the hob, stirring as necessary. Cover
the dish with a lid and place in the oven to cook for about 1½ hours,
checking occasionally to see whether or not you need to add more water.
Remove from oven and allow to cool. Take out the bay leaf. Using a slatted
spoon, place the meat and onion in a food processor. Whizz until you have
a smooth thick paste, gradually adding a little of the meat water. Add the
butter, and a little salt if necessary, and process for a few more seconds.
Spoon the mixture into a small bowl and press down using the back of a
spoon. Place in the fridge to set. Serve spread on bread or toast, or in
sandwiches with cucumber. *Makes 4–6 servings*

131 potted chicken spread

This tasty spread makes a healthy and nutritious sandwich filling, ideal for a packed lunch. It contains lots of protein, but no additives or preservatives. Try making it with chicken thigh or leg meat to increase the iron content.

PREPARATION
1 hour–1 hour 30 minutes

STORAGE
Suitable for freezing; keeps for up to 2 days in the fridge

1 chicken breast
pinch of dried sage
pinch of dried thyme
1 tsp melted butter

Preheat the oven to 150°C/300°F/gas mark 2. Put the chicken breast in a small ovenproof dish, sprinkle on the herbs, and add enough water just to cover the meat. Put the lid on and cook in the oven for 50 minutes to 1 hour until the chicken is tender, checking occasionally to see whether or not you need to add more water. Remove from the oven and allow to cool. Put the chicken and a little of the cooking water in a food processor. Whizz until beginning to become smooth, add the melted butter, and process until you have a smooth paste. Add more of the extra cooking water, if necessary. Spoon into a small pot, cover, and place in the fridge to set. Serve in a baguette with salad. *Makes 2–4 servings*

132 potted chicken toast triangles

PREPARATION
5–10 minutes

STORAGE
Best made just before serving

2 slices wholewheat toast
3–4 tbsp Potted Chicken Spread (recipe 131; above)
4 cherry tomatoes, sliced

Spread the potted chicken on the toast. Cut into triangles and arrange small slices of tomato on top. *Makes 2 servings*

133 salmon and shrimp spread

PREPARATION
15 minutes

STORAGE
Suitable for freezing; keeps for up to 2 days in the fridge

1 small skinless salmon fillet
⅓ cup milk
1 bay leaf
pinch of freshly grated nutmeg

½ cup frozen pre-cooked shrimps, defrosted
1 tbsp reduced-fat mayonnaise
a few drops of lemon juice

Place the salmon, milk, bay leaf, and nutmeg in a skillet. Poach the salmon in the milk over a medium heat for 3–4 minutes. Leave to cool. When cool, lift the salmon from the milk and put in a food processor with the shrimps, mayonnaise, and lemon juice. Process until smooth. Spoon into a small dish, cover, and refrigerate. Serve in sandwiches, or on toast or pitta bread with cucumber and cress. *Makes 4–6 servings*

134 fishy dipping plate

To add variation here you can include different vegetables, and use bagel chips or wedges of pitta bread instead of tortilla chips.

PREPARATION
5–10 minutes

STORAGE
Best made just before serving

2 tbsp Salmon and Shrimp Spread (recipe 133; opposite page)
2 tbsp Tomato and Avocado Salsa (recipe 241; p.146)
1 small carrot, cut into sticks

4–5 sugarsnap peas, trimmed and strings removed
¼ red bell pepper, cut into strips
3–4 Tortilla Chips (recipe 334; p.188)

Put the spread and the salsa into eggcups or small bowls. Place in the center of a large plate and arrange the vegetables and tortilla chips around them to serve. *Makes 1 serving*

135 veggie dipping plate

PREPARATION
5–10 minutes

STORAGE
Best made just before serving

2 tbsp houmous (recipe 125; p.98)
2 tbsp Mint and Cucumber Yogurt Dip (recipe 245; p.147)
1 small carrot, cut into sticks
1 stick celery, cut into strips

1 piece cucumber, about 1¼in in length, cut into sticks
2–3 Breadsticks (recipe 357; p.200)/Pitta Bread Chips (recipe 333, p.187)

Put the houmous and the yogurt dip into eggcups. Place in the center of a large plate and arrange the vegetables and breadsticks around them to serve. *Makes 1 serving*

136 toasted peanut butter and banana sandwiches

Peanut butter is an excellent high-protein food. The best brands contain only roasted peanuts, with nothing added.

PREPARATION
5 minutes

2 slices wholewheat bread
2 tbsp smooth peanut butter
½ small banana, sliced

STORAGE
Best made just
before serving

Toast the bread. While it is warm spread both slices with peanut butter. Place the banana slices on top of the peanut butter on one slice and sandwich toast together. Cut into triangle shapes or small fingers, or use cookie-cutters to make more interesting shapes. *Makes 1–2 servings*

137 toasted cream cheese and apple sandwiches

PREPARATION
5 minutes

2 slices raisin bread
2–3 tbsp cream cheese
3–4 slices eating apple

STORAGE
Best made just
before serving

Toast the bread. Spread both slices with the cream cheese. Place the apple slices on top of the cream cheese on one slice. Sandwich toast together, cut into quarters, and serve. *Makes 1–2 servings*

138 open salmon rolls

PREPARATION
5 minutes

3 tbsp canned salmon, drained and
  mashed
1 tbsp mayonnaise
1 tsp chopped fresh parsley
1 tsp chopped fresh chives

squeeze of lemon juice
1 mini wholewheat or granary
  bread roll
2 slices cucumber
1 black olive, pitted and cut in half

STORAGE
Best made just
before serving

Mix together the salmon, mayonnaise, parsley, chives, and lemon juice in a bowl. Split the roll in half and spread the salmon mixture on both sides. Top with twisted slices of cucumber and the olive halves. *Makes 1–2 servings*

139 smoked salmon pinwheel sandwiches

PREPARATION
5 minutes

2 slices smoked salmon, chopped
4 slices cucumber, finely chopped
2 tbsp cream cheese
1 small flour tortilla

STORAGE
Keeps for up
to 5 hours in
the fridge

Mix the salmon and the cucumber with the cream cheese in a small bowl. Spread over the tortilla, then roll up into a sausage shape. Cut into small slices. *Makes 1–2 servings*

140 wholewheat bacon and egg sandwiches

PREPARATION
5–10 minutes

1 hard-boiled egg
1 tsp mayonnaise
1 slice crispy bacon, crumbled
a little shredded iceberg lettuce
2 slices wholewheat bread

STORAGE
Best made just
before serving

Mash the egg in a small bowl. Add the mayonnaise and mix together. Add the crumbled bacon. Spread the mixture onto one slice of bread, top with lettuce, and cover with the second slice of bread. Cut into 4 triangles and serve with cucumber sticks and cherry tomatoes. *Makes 1–2 servings*

141 New York-style pastrami on rye

"Pastrami on rye" is a classic American sandwich from the delis of New York. If your child doesn't like rye bread, use white or wholewheat instead.

PREPARATION
5 minutes

¼ tsp mustard
1 tsp mayonnaise
2 slices rye bread

1 slice pastrami
1 tbsp grated cheese
½ tomato, sliced

STORAGE
Keeps for up
to 5 hours in
the fridge

Mix together the mustard and the mayonnaise in a bowl. Spread onto one side of both slices of bread. Place one slice of pastrami, then the tomato slices, onto one slice of bread and sprinkle on the grated cheese. Sandwich together with the other slice and cut into 4 squares or triangles, or other shapes. *Makes 1–2 servings*

142 tuna mayonnaise pitta pockets

PREPARATION
10 minutes

STORAGE
Keeps for up
to 5 hours in
the fridge

2 small pitta breads
3 tbsp canned tuna, well drained
¼ green/red bell pepper, deseeded
and diced

1 tbsp cooked corn
1 tbsp mayonnaise
1 tbsp grated Cheddar (optional)

Lightly toast the pitta breads. Meanwhile, mix together all the other ingredients in a bowl. Cut toasted pittas in half and open each half a little. Push equal amounts of the tuna mixture into each. *Makes 2 servings*

143 houmous and alfalfa pitta pockets

PREPARATION
5 minutes

STORAGE
Keep for up
to 5 hours in
the fridge

2 small pitta breads
4 tbsp houmous (recipe 125; p.98)
½ tomato, chopped

4 slices cucumber, chopped
4 tsp alfalfa sprouts

Lightly toast the pitta breads. Meanwhile, mix together the houmous, tomato, and cucumber in a bowl. Cut toasted pittas in half and open each half a little. Stuff with the houmous mixture and top with a few alfalfa sprouts. *Makes 2 servings*

144 easy lunch platter

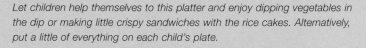

Let children help themselves to this platter and enjoy dipping vegetables in the dip or making little crispy sandwiches with the rice cakes. Alternatively, put a little of everything on each child's plate.

PREPARATION
5 minutes

STORAGE
Best made just
before serving

3 tbsp mayonnaise/Spicy Curry Dip
(recipe 336; p.189)
4 slices of ham, chicken, turkey,
salami, or pastrami, rolled and
secured with a toothpick
8 cubes of Cheddar or feta
a selection of rice cakes, breadsticks,
bagel chips, or toast triangles

4 slices of cucumber
4 slices of carrot
4 cherry tomatoes, cut in half
1 stick celery, cut into small sticks
4 slices each of green, red, and
yellow bell peppers
4 sugarsnap peas

Put the mayonnaise/Spicy Curry Dip into an eggcup or a small bowl. Place in the center of a large plate or platter and arrange the other ingredients around it to serve. *Makes 4 servings*

145 vegetable bruschettas

PREPARATION
15 minutes

4 thick slices ciabatta bread
1 clove garlic, crushed
3 tbsp olive oil

1 zucchini, thinly sliced
1 large tomato, sliced
4 tbsp Cheddar, grated

STORAGE
Best made just
before serving

Lightly toast the ciabatta. Pour the oil into a small cup and stir in the crushed garlic. Brush the bread slices on one side with the oil and place in a baking pan. Put a slice of tomato on each. Preheat the broiler. Using the remainder of the oil, stir-fry the zucchini for about 5 minutes until soft and golden. Place them on the bread on top of the tomato and sprinkle with the grated Cheddar. Broil for 1–2 minutes until the cheese has melted. Serve with salad. *Makes 2–4 servings*

146 tuna mayonnaise pinwheel sandwiches

PREPARATION
5–10 minutes

3 tbsp canned tuna, well drained
¼ small carrot, grated
¼ eating apple, cored and grated

1 tbsp mayonnaise
2 small flour tortillas

STORAGE
Keep for up to 5
hours in the fridge

Mix together all the ingredients for the filling in a bowl. Spread half the mixture onto each tortilla and roll them up into sausage shapes. Cut into small slices. *Makes 2 servings*

147 cream cheese and ham pinwheel sandwiches

PREPARATION
5 minutes

1 tsp chopped chives
1 tbsp cream cheese
1 small flour tortilla
1 slice ham

STORAGE
Keep for up to 5
hours in the fridge

Mix the chives with the cream cheese in a bowl. Spread the mixture onto the tortilla. Place the slice of ham on top of the cream cheese and then roll up into a sausage shape. Cut into small slices. *Makes 1–2 servings*

148 Greek salad

PREPARATION
15 minutes

STORAGE
Best made just
before serving

1lb 2oz tomatoes, sliced
1 small cucumber, peeled, halved
  lengthwise, and sliced
½ small red onion, peeled and finely
  sliced
4 scallions, finely sliced
1 green bell pepper, deseeded and

  thinly sliced
⅔ cup black olives, pitted
¾ cup feta, cubed
1 tbsp fresh parsley, chopped
3 tbsp olive oil
juice of 1 lemon

Arrange the tomatoes in a bowl. Scatter the cucumber, onion, scallions,
and bell pepper on top. Add the olives and cheese, and top with the
parsley. Combine the oil and lemon juice to make a dressing and drizzle
over just before serving. Serve with bread. *Makes 4–6 servings*

149 pink pasta and bean salad

PREPARATION
10 minutes

STORAGE
Keeps for up
to 12 hours
in the fridge

½ cup pasta spirals, cooked
14oz canned black-eye peas,
  well drained
1 medium cooked beet, peeled and
  diced
1 stick celery, sliced
1 carrot, grated

1 green bell pepper, deseeded and
  diced
juice of ½ lemon
½ tsp balsamic vinegar
½ tsp sesame seed oil
½ tbsp olive oil
pinch of black pepper

Mix the pasta, beans, and vegetables together in a bowl. Mix the remaining
ingredients together, pour over the salad, and toss. *Makes 6–8 servings*

150 Chinese noodle salad

PREPARATION
35 minutes

STORAGE
Best made just
before serving

1½ cups Chinese egg noodles
6oz sugarsnap peas, topped and
  tailed
6 scallions, sliced
10 small radishes, sliced
1½ cups cooked, peeled shrimps
2 tbsp chopped fresh coriander

2 tsp grated fresh ginger
1 clove garlic, crushed
grated rind of 1 lime
juice of 2 limes
1 tbsp runny honey
¼ cup walnut oil
pinch of black pepper

Half-fill a medium-size saucepan with water. Bring to the boil and add the
noodles. Cover the pan, remove from the heat, and leave to stand for
5 minutes until the noodles are just tender. Drain. When cool, transfer to a
salad bowl. Bring a small saucepan of water to the boil. Add the sugarsnap
peas and cook for 1 minute. Drain and leave to cool. Wash the shrimps and
drain. Add the shrimps, sugarsnap peas, scallions, and radishes to the
salad bowl. Sprinkle the coriander over and set aside. Mix the ginger and
garlic in a bowl. Add the lime rind and juice, honey, oil, and black pepper.
Combine, drizzle over the salad, and toss. *Makes 3–6 servings*

151 tuna pasta salad

PREPARATION
15–20 minutes

STORAGE
Keep for up
to 5 hours in
the fridge

2 cups pasta bow ties
1 tbsp olive oil
1 tbsp walnut oil
2 tsp lemon juice
1 tsp Dijon mustard
1 tsp chopped fresh parsley

½ cup frozen or canned corn
3 ripe tomatoes, chopped
½ red bell pepper, deseeded and
  finely chopped
5 scallions, sliced
7oz canned tuna, drained and flaked

Cook the pasta according to the instructions on the packet. Drain well and place in a salad bowl. Make the dressing by mixing the oils, lemon juice, and mustard together in a small bowl. Add the parsley. Pour onto the cooled pasta and add the corn, tomatoes, bell pepper, scallions, and tuna, mixing well. *Makes 4–6 servings*

152 coronation chicken salad

PREPARATION
45 minutes

STORAGE
Keeps for up
to 2 days in
the fridge

1 tbsp olive oil
½ small onion, peeled
1 clove garlic, peeled and crushed
1 tsp finely grated ginger
1 tsp ground cumin
1 tsp curry powder
½ cup chicken stock/water
⅓ cup mayonnaise

2 tbsp natural bio-yogurt
1 tbsp chopped fresh coriander
½ tbsp mango chutney
1 small iceberg lettuce, finely
  chopped
2 cooked chicken breasts, skinned
  and diced

Heat the oil in a skillet and cook the onion, garlic, and ginger until soft. Add the cumin and curry powder and cook for 2–3 minutes, stirring occasionally. Add the chicken stock/water, bring to the boil, and cook uncovered for 15 minutes until all the liquid has evaporated. Leave to cool. When cool, mix with the mayonnaise, yogurt, fresh coriander, and mango chutney. Add the lettuce and chicken pieces and toss to coat. *Makes 4–6 servings*

153 hot bacon salad

PREPARATION
20 minutes

STORAGE
Best made just
before serving

12 mixed lettuce leaves, such as
  oakleaf, Little Gem, and Romaine
few leaves of rocket/watercress
12 cherry tomatoes
½ small cucumber, peeled and diced

1 small avocado, peeled and diced
2 tbsp olive oil
6 slices lean back bacon, sliced
handful of croutons (recipe 260; p.158)
1 tbsp lemon juice/balsamic vinegar

Place the leaves, tomatoes, cucumber, and avocado in a salad bowl. Add half the oil and the lemon juice/vinegar and toss. Heat the rest of the oil in a skillet and add the bacon slices. Fry for about 5 minutes until cooked right through. Add the croutons and warm them through. Tip the bacon and croutons onto the salad. Toss and serve immediately. Serve with warm ciabatta bread. *Makes 4–6 servings*

154 spinach and feta triangles

PREPARATION
40 minutes

STORAGE
Suitable for freezing; keep for up to 2 days in the fridge

10½oz frozen spinach
⅔ cup feta
½ cup Cheddar
pinch of nutmeg

pinch of black pepper
8–10 sheets filo pastry
3 tbsp melted butter

Preheat the oven to 180°C/350°F/gas mark 4. Put the spinach in a small saucepan and thaw over a gentle heat, stirring occasionally until all the liquid has evaporated. Allow to cool. In a bowl, mix the spinach with the cheese, nutmeg, and black pepper. Lay out a sheet of filo pastry and brush with butter, then place another sheet on top and brush with butter again. Cut the pastry into strips about 3in wide and 8in long. Place a heaped teaspoonful of spinach mixture in the top corner of the strip and fold diagonally to form a triangle. Continue to fold over until you use up the whole strip. Place in a baking pan and brush with a little melted butter. Make triangles in this way until all the filling /strips are used up. Bake in the oven for 15–20 minutes until golden and crisp. *Makes 12–14 triangles*

155 minted beef samosas

These delicious pastry parcels are rich in protein, iron, zinc, and many vitamins. They are ideal picnic foods or as part of a packed lunch. You can also make them with very lean ground lamb.

PREPARATION
1 hour

STORAGE
Suitable for freezing; keep for up to 2 days in the fridge

2 tsp olive oil
1 small onion, chopped
2 cloves garlic, crushed
1 tsp ground cumin
1 tsp ground coriander
1¼ cups lean ground beef
3 tbsp fresh mint, chopped

½ stick celery, thinly sliced
2 medium potatoes, peeled and chopped
½ cup Cheddar, grated
10 sheets filo pastry
3oz butter, melted

Preheat the oven to 200°C/400°F/gas mark 6. Heat the oil in a skillet and add the onion, garlic, and spices, and sauté until the onion is soft. Add the ground beef, mint, and celery and stir until the beef is browned. Meanwhile, steam or boil the potatoes. When cooked, mash the potatoes with the cheese. Add the beef mixture to the potatoes and mix. Lay out a sheet of filo pastry and brush with butter, then place another sheet on top and brush with butter again. Cut the pastry into strips about 3in wide. Place a heaped tablespoonful of beef mixture at the top end of each strip and fold diagonally to form a triangle. Continue to fold over until you use up the whole strip. Place in a baking pan and brush the top with a little melted butter. Make triangles in this way until all the filling/strips are used up. Bake in a baking pan for about 10 minutes or until golden brown. Serve with Tomato and Basil Sauce (recipe 161; p.112), Mango Salsa (recipe 242; p.146) or Spicy Tomato Salsa (recipe 243; p.147). *Makes about 15 samosas*

156　vegetable samosas

To add variety you can vary the vegetables you use in these tasty samosas, which can be eaten hot or cold.

PREPARATION
1 hour 20 minutes

STORAGE
Suitable for freezing; keeps for up to 2 days in the fridge

1 potato, peeled and cut into small cubes
1 large carrot, peeled and cut into small cubes
1 sweet potato, peeled and cut into small cubes
6–8 string beans, trimmed and cut into small pieces
2 tbsp vegetable oil
½ tsp turmeric
½ tsp ground cumin

pinch of garam masala
1 clove garlic, crushed
1 tsp grated fresh ginger
2 tbsp cooked chickpeas, mashed slightly
¼ onion, peeled and chopped
1 tsp lemon juice
10–12 filo pastry sheets
1oz butter
2 tbsp olive oil

Preheat the oven to 180°C/350°F/gas mark 4. Place the potato in a saucepan, cover with water, and bring to the boil. Reduce heat and simmer for 4 minutes. Add the carrot, sweet potato, and beans and simmer for a further 4 minutes until the vegetables are beginning to soften. Drain. Put the vegetable oil in a skillet and sauté the onion, spices, garlic, and ginger for 3–4 minutes until the onion is soft. Remove from the heat and add the chickpeas, lemon juice, and the cooked vegetables, stirring well. In a small saucepan, melt the butter and mix with the olive oil. Lay out 1 sheet of filo pastry and brush the top with the butter and oil mixture; then lay another sheet on top and brush with the butter and oil mixture again. Cut the pastry into strips about 3in wide and 8in long. Place a heaped teaspoonful of the vegetable mixture in the top corner of the strip and fold diagonally to form a triangle. Continue to fold over until you use up the whole strip. Place in a baking pan and brush the top with a little melted butter and oil. Make triangles in this way until all the filling/strips are used up. Bake in the oven for 15–20 minutes until golden and crisp. Serve with Mint and Cucumber Yogurt Dip (recipe 245; p.147) or mango chutney. *Makes 16–18 samosas*

DINNERS

The mouthwatering recipes in this section form the basis of the main family meal, either as complete dishes or served with accompaniments from the next section. The taste, texture, and presentation of the recipes will instantly appeal to young children, while the use of more sophisticated ingredients, including many herbs and spices, ensures that the rest of the family will enjoy them too. The general emphasis is on lower-fat and healthy-fat choices with little or no added salt. Vegetables,

and sometimes fruit, have often been incorporated to help meet your child's "5-a-day" target. All of the recipes are quick and easy, and many can be made ahead of time and frozen. A selection of vegetarian dishes is also included, all of which contain good sources of vegetable protein.

157 quick tomato sauce

PREPARATION
15 minutes

STORAGE
Suitable for
freezing; keeps
for up to 2 days
in the fridge

2 tbsp olive oil
2 cloves garlic, finely chopped
1lb 12oz canned tomatoes

1 tbsp chopped fresh basil
1 tbsp chopped fresh parsley
salt and pepper to taste

Gently heat the oil in a saucepan and sauté the garlic until lightly browned.
Add the tomatoes and cook over a high heat for 5–10 mintues, stirring to
break them up. Turn down the heat, add the herbs, and cook for a minute
or two longer. Remove from heat, taste, and add salt and pepper if required.
Serve with pasta shapes, and grated cheese if desired. *Makes 4–6 servings*

158 spaghetti with cherry tomatoes

PREPARATION
10–15 minutes

STORAGE
Best made just
before serving

7oz ripe cherry tomatoes
1 clove garlic, peeled and crushed
2 tbsp chopped fresh basil
3 tbsp olive oil

2 tsp balsamic vinegar
a pinch of salt
7oz spaghetti
grated Parmesan (optional)

First, prepare the tomato sauce by quartering the tomatoes and putting them
in a large bowl with the garlic, basil, olive oil, and vinegar. Use your hands
to mix the ingredients together, squashing the tomatoes a little. Add a pinch
of salt to help bring out the flavor of the tomatoes. Leave to stand at room
temperature for at least 30 minutes to allow the flavors to blend and intensify.
Cook the spaghetti according to directions on the packet. Once cooked,
drain it and stir in the tomato mixture. Serve with Parmesan sprinkled on top
if desired. For a colorful variation, try using red and yellow cherry tomatoes.
This sauce can also be made using large tomatoes—just chop them up into
smaller pieces. *Makes 2–4 servings*

159 pasta shapes with asparagus and ham

PREPARATION
25 minutes

STORAGE
Best made just
before serving

1 onion, peeled and finely chopped
2 cloves garlic, peeled and crushed
2 tbsp olive oil
¼ tsp dried thyme
7oz asparagus, thinly sliced
  diagonally

3–4 slices cooked ham, chopped
2 cups pasta shapes (such
  as bow ties or small tubes)
1 tbsp water
juice of ½ lemon
grated Parmesan

In a large, heavy-bottomed saucepan, sauté the onion and garlic in the oil
until soft. Add the thyme, followed by the asparagus and ham. Cook over
a moderate heat for 2–3 minutes stirring occasionally until the asparagus
is slightly softened. Meanwhile, cook the pasta shapes according to the
instructions on the packet. Remove the sauce from the heat and add the
water and lemon juice, followed by the drained, cooked pasta. Mix well and
stir in the Parmesan. Serve immediately with a salad. For variation, try using
crispy cooked bacon instead of ham. *Makes 2–4 servings*

160 bolognaise bell pepper sauce with pasta

PREPARATION
30 minutes

STORAGE
Sauce suitable for freezing; keeps for up to 2 days in the fridge

1 large onion, peeled and sliced
1 red bell pepper, deseeded and sliced
1 green bell pepper, deseeded and sliced
1 tbsp olive oil
1lb lean ground beef
14oz canned, chopped

tomatoes
3 tbsp tomato paste
1 tsp dried basil
1 tsp dried oregano
½ tsp thyme
pinch of black pepper
12oz spaghetti
grated Parmesan

In a skillet, sauté the onion and bell peppers in the oil for 2–3 minutes. Add the ground beef and sauté until browned. Add the chopped tomatoes, tomato paste, herbs, and black pepper and stir to mix well. Cover with a lid and simmer for 10 minutes. Meanwhile, cook the spaghetti according to the instructions on the packet. Serve the pasta topped with the sauce and sprinkled with a little Parmesan. *Makes 4–6 servings*

161 tomato and basil sauce

PREPARATION
15–25 minutes

STORAGE
Suitable for freezing; keeps for up to 2 days in the fridge

1 onion, peeled and chopped
2 red bell peppers, deseeded and chopped
1 tbsp olive oil

2 cloves garlic, peeled and crushed
1lb 12oz canned, chopped tomatoes
2–3 tbsp chopped fresh basil

Place the onion, red bell pepper, and oil in a saucepan and sauté until soft. Add the garlic, tomatoes, and basil. Stir well. If using with the Mini Meatballs (recipe below), simmer for 3–4 minutes only. If using on its own as a pasta sauce, simmer for a further 5–10 minutes. *Makes enough sauce for the meatballs recipe (below), or 4 servings as a pasta sauce*

162 mini meatballs

PREPARATION
1 hour 15 minutes

STORAGE
Suitable for freezing; keep for up to 2 days in the fridge

1 portion Tomato and Basil Sauce
2 slices wholewheat bread
½ onion, peeled
½ red bell pepper, deseeded
1 small zucchini
1 small clove garlic, peeled
½ tbsp chopped fresh parsley

½ tsp dried oregano
2 tsp tomato paste
1 cup lean ground turkey
1 cup lean ground beef
½ beaten egg
flour for coating
olive oil for frying

Preheat the oven to 190°C/375°F/gas mark 5. First, make the Tomato and Basil sauce and set aside. Then crumb the bread in a food processor. Add the vegetables and garlic and mix until well chopped. Add the remaining ingredients and combine. Take small handfuls of mixture, dip in flour, and form into balls. Shallow fry until brown. Put in a casserole dish and pour over the sauce. Cover and bake for 40–50 minutes.
Makes 12–15 small meatballs

163 veggieburgers

PREPARATION
50 minutes

STORAGE
Suitable for
freezing; keep
for up to 2 days
in the fridge

12oz red kidney beans, precooked
   or canned
9oz sweet potato, peeled and
   chopped
1 medium carrot or parsnip, peeled
   and sliced
1 small onion, peeled and chopped
2 cloves garlic, peeled and chopped

1 stick celery, washed thoroughly
   and finely diced
2 tbsp olive oil
1 tbsp tomato paste
1 tsp ground cumin
1 tbsp chopped fresh coriander
flour to rub on hands

Drain the kidney beans and dry on kitchen towels. Steam the sweet potato
and carrot/parsnip for about 15–20 minutes until tender. Mash together. In
a large skillet, gently cook the onion, garlic, and celery in half the oil for
about 5 minutes, stirring occasionally. Add the mashed sweet potato mixture
and cook for another 5 minutes. Turn into a large bowl and mash everything
together well. Stir in the beans, tomato paste, cumin, and coriander. With
floured hands shape the mixture into 4–6 burgers. Place the burgers in a
baking pan and brush them with oil. Broil for 5- 6 minutes before turning,
brushing with oil and broiling for another 5–6 minutes on the other side.
Alternatively, fry the burgers in a little oil for 3–4 minutes on each side. Serve
in a bun topped with shredded lettuce and tomato. *Makes 4–6 servings*

164 beef burgers in buns *(below)*

PREPARATION
20 minutes

STORAGE
Suitable for
freezing; keep
for up to 2 days
in the fridge

1¼ cups lean ground beef
¼ small onion, peeled and finely
   chopped
1 carrot, peeled and finely grated

1 egg yolk
3 sesame seed burger buns
3 thin slices tomato
3 lettuce leaves

Put the beef, onion, carrot, and egg yolk in a bowl and mix together well.
Form into 3 burger patties. Broil for 3–4 minutes on each side until cooked
through. These burgers can also be cooked on a barbecue. Place on the
burger bun with a slice of tomato and lettuce. Serve with a dressed salad
or a salsa. *Makes 3 servings*

165 Asian-style turkey burgers

🍔➀⚙

PREPARATION
40 minutes

STORAGE
Suitable for
freezing; keep
for up to 2 days
in the fridge

2 slices wholewheat bread
1lb 9oz lean ground turkey
2 scallions
1 clove garlic, peeled and chopped
1 tsp finely grated ginger root

2 tbsp hoisin sauce
2 tsp toasted sesame oil
6–8 burger buns
cucumber slices, tomato slices, and
    shredded lettuce to garnish

Preheat the oven to 180°C/350°F/gas mark 4. Put the bread into a food
processor and whizz until crumbed. Add the turkey, garlic, scallions, grated
ginger, and hoisin sauce and process lightly. Take handfuls of the mixture
and form into 6–8 burger shapes. Place in an ovenproof pan and brush
both sides with a little of the oil. Cook in the oven for approximately
20 minutes until golden on the outside and cooked through. Alternatively,
cook under the broiler or on the barbeque. To serve, put each burger on
a warmed bun and top with the tomato, cucumber, and lettuce, and some
Sesame Mayonnaise (recipe 167; p.114). *Makes 6–8 burgers*

166 turkey patties

🍔➀⚙

PREPARATION
45–55 minutes

STORAGE
Suitable for
freezing; keep
for up to 2 days
in the fridge

½ medium onion, peeled
2 slices wholewheat bread
1lb 5oz lean ground turkey
1 egg

1 tsp dried oregano
2 tsp chopped fresh parsley
flour to rub on hands
3 tbsp olive oil

Preheat oven to 180°C/350°F/gas mark 4. Mix the onion and bread slices
in a food processor, then add the turkey, egg, and herbs. Whizz everything
together but be careful not to overprocess, or you will end up with a paste.
With floured hands, form the mixture into small patties. Pour enough oil into
a baking pan to cover the base. Put the patties in the pan. Bake for 30–40
minutes, turning them halfway through. Remove when golden and the meat
is thoroughly cooked. Alternatively, shallow fry in a little oil. Serve in mini
bread rolls with a salsa. *Makes 12 small patties*

167 sesame mayonnaise

Ⓐ✖✖➀

This low-fat sauce is a great accompaniment to the Asian-style Turkey Burgers.

PREPARATION
5 minutes

STORAGE
Keeps for up to 2
days in the fridge

2 tbsp reduced-fat mayonnaise
2 tbsp natural bio-yogurt
1 tsp soy sauce
½ tsp toasted sesame oil

Combine all the ingredients together in a bowl. Serve with turkey burgers or
use as a dip with vegetable crudités. *Makes 4–6 servings*

168 sesame chicken fingers

*These delicious chicken fingers have boosted nutritional value from the
sesame seeds, which are rich in iron and zinc, and contain some calcium.*

PREPARATION
15 minutes

4 boneless, skinless chicken breasts
2–3 tbsp sesame seeds
1–2 tbsp toasted sesame oil

STORAGE
Suitable for
freezing; keep
for up to 2 days
in the fridge

Cut each chicken breast into 5 or 6 fingers. Press the sesame seeds
into the chicken fingers to coat. Heat the oil over a medium heat in a
heavy-bottomed skillet, add the chicken pieces, and cook for 8–10
minutes, depending on the size of the chicken pieces, until golden brown
on all sides, and cooked through. This can be quite messy as the sesame
seeds tend to jump out of the skillet, so keep young children away! Once
cooked, serve immediately or keep warm in the oven. Serve with Honey
Mustard Dipping Sauce (recipe below). *Makes 6–8 servings*

169 honey mustard dipping sauce

PREPARATION
2 minutes

1 tbsp mild wholegrain mustard
4 tbsp runny honey

STORAGE
Keeps for up to a
week in the fridge

Mix the mustard and honey together in a small serving bowl. Serve with
Sesame Chicken Fingers (recipe above). *Makes 6–8 servings*

170 chicken nuggets

*This easy recipe produces tasty chicken nuggets that are far superior in
quality and nutrients to the pre-made varieties.*

PREPARATION
30 minutes

2 boneless, skinless chicken breasts
6 tbsp dried breadcrumbs
½ tsp paprika
1 tsp oregano

pinch of garlic powder (optional)
1 egg, beaten
2 tbsp olive oil

STORAGE
Suitable for
freezing; keep
for up to 2 days
in the fridge

Preheat the oven to 200°C/400°F/gas mark 6. Cut the chicken breasts
into nugget-size strips, trimming off any fat. Mix together the breadcrumbs,
paprika, oregano, and garlic powder (if using). Dip each strip of chicken in
the egg and then coat in the breadcrumb mixture. For a thick, crispy crust,
dip and coat again. Brush a baking pan with the oil and place the nuggets
in the pan. Bake for 10 minutes, then turn and bake for a further 5–10
minutes until cooked through and crispy. The cooking time will vary
according to the size of the chicken pieces. Serve with Traditional Oven
Fries (recipe 218; p.137) or Paprika Potato Wedges (recipe 219; p.138),
vegetables, and ketchup or salsa. *Makes 2–4 servings*

171 crispy coated turkey breasts

PREPARATION
15 minutes

3 wholewheat cereal cakes
2 tsp paprika
2 tsp mixed herbs

1 egg, beaten
4 thin turkey breast steaks
3–4 tbsp vegetable oil

STORAGE
Suitable for
freezing; keeps
for up to 2 days
in the fridge

Put the wholewheat cereal cakes in a plastic bag with the paprika and
mixed herbs. Crush, then tip out onto a plate. Pour the beaten egg into a
flat dish. Dip the turkey breasts in the egg and then in the crumbs until they
are fully coated. Heat the oil in a skillet. Put the turkey steaks in the pan
and fry on a medium heat for a couple of minutes on each side until golden
all over. Serve with vegetables or salad, and Paprika Potato Wedges (see
recipe 219; p.138). *Makes 4–6 servings*

172 chicken and vegetable noodles

*Experiment with the vegetables used in this recipe to get different colors
and textures. Thai fish sauce is available in most supermarkets.*

PREPARATION
30 minutes

5oz rice noodles
½ onion, peeled and chopped
2 tbsp toasted sesame oil
1 scallion, chopped
1 clove garlic, peeled and crushed
1 tsp chopped fresh ginger
2–3 tbsp Thai fish sauce
2 boneless, skinless chicken

breasts, cut into thin strips
¼ red bell pepper, deseeded and
sliced
⅛ cabbage, shredded
2 carrots, peeled and cut into
thin strips
1 cup bean sprouts

STORAGE
Keep for up to
2 days in the
fridge

Cook the rice noodles according to the instructions on the packet and set
aside. Heat the oil in a large skillet or wok and sauté the onions until just
soft. Add the scallions, garlic, ginger, and fish sauce, and continue to cook
for a few minutes. Turn up the heat a little and add the chicken and fry
until tender and slightly brown. Add the vegetables and continue to cook,
stirring until just tender. Stir in the cooked noodles and serve. Add more
fish sauce if needed. *Makes 3–4 servings*

173 mango-glazed chicken parcels

PREPARATION
40 minutes

4 boneless, skinless chicken breasts
4 tsp mild mango chutney
½ small onion, diced

STORAGE
Suitable for
freezing; keep
for up to 2 days
in the fridge

Preheat oven to 190°C/375°F/gas mark 5. Place each chicken breast on
a square of foil large enough to fold over and make into a parcel. Add a
teaspoonful of mango chutney and a little diced onion to each breast. Seal
the parcels and place in a baking pan. Cook for 30 minutes or until the
chicken is cooked through. *Makes 4 servings*

174 Mexican chicken parcels

PREPARATION
40 minutes

STORAGE
Keep for up to
2 days in the
fridge

4 boneless, skinless chicken breasts
8 tsp Spicy Tomato Salsa (recipe 243; p.147)
4 tsp walnut oil

Preheat oven to 190°C/375°F/gas mark 5. Place each chicken breast on a square of foil large enough to fold over and make into a parcel. Add 2 teaspoonfuls of salsa and a teaspoonful of walnut oil to each one. Seal the parcels and place on a baking tray. Cook for 30 minutes or until chicken is cooked through. *Makes 4 servings*

175 chicken and bacon parcels

PREPARATION
50 minutes

STORAGE
Keep for up to
2 days in the
fridge

4 slices streaky bacon, chopped
1 tsp olive oil
4 large field mushrooms, peeled and
    finely chopped

½ onion, finely chopped
pinch of nutmeg
½ tsp dried sage
4 boneless, skinless chicken thighs

Preheat oven to 190°C/375°F/gas mark 5. Chop the bacon into small pieces, cook in a skillet until crisp, then set to one side. Add oil and sauté the onion and mushrooms with nutmeg and sage until softened. Mix in the bacon pieces. Stuff the underside of each chicken thigh with a quarter of the mixture and place each one on a foil square. Seal into parcels and place in a baking pan. Cook for 30 minutes or until chicken is cooked through. *Makes 4 servings*

176 chicken and mushroom pot pie

PREPARATION
1 hour 15 minutes

STORAGE
Keeps for up to
2 days in the
fridge

⅔ cup chicken stock (recipe 251;
    p.151)
4 boneless, skinless chicken thighs,
    cut into small pieces
2oz butter
2 cups button mushrooms, sliced
¼ cup all-purpose flour

⅔ cup milk
2 tsp chopped fresh parsley
1 tbsp lemon juice
3 potatoes, peeled, cooked, and
    thinly sliced
8oz basic pie dough

Preheat the oven to 200°C/400°F/gas mark 6. Put the stock in a saucepan with the chicken pieces. Simmer for about 15 minutes. Remove the chicken pieces onto a plate, strain the stock through a sieve, and reserve. Melt half the butter in a saucepan, add the mushrooms, and cook gently for 3–4 minutes. Transfer to the plate. Add the remaining butter to the pan and melt. Mix in the flour, then add the stock and milk, stirring continuously. Add the parsley, lemon juice, chicken, and mushrooms. Transfer the contents of the saucepan to a pie dish. Cover with the potato slices. Roll out the pastry to cover the pie dish. Trim the sides and cut extra strips of pastry to lay around the edge of the dish to form a double edge. Stick these down with a little milk. Cut a small slit in the top of the pastry to allow steam to escape. Bake in the oven for 30–40 minutes until the pastry is golden and the filling is bubbling. Serve with a green vegetable. *Makes 4–5 servings*

177 chicken korma

PREPARATION
1 hour

STORAGE
Suitable for freezing; keeps for up to 2 days in the fridge

2 onions, peeled and chopped
1 garlic clove, peeled and crushed
4 tbsp olive oil
1in root ginger, grated
1 tsp mild chili powder
1 tsp turmeric
1 tsp ground coriander
½ tsp ground cardamom
½ tsp ground cinnamon

2 boneless, skinless chicken breasts, cut into chunks
2 boneless, skinless chicken thighs, cut into chunks
1 tbsp flour
1 cup water/chicken stock
⅔ cup natural bio-yogurt
3 tbsp light cream
chopped fresh coriander to garnish

In a large saucepan, gently sauté the onion and garlic in the oil for 2–3 minutes until the onion begins to soften. Add the ginger and the spices. Continue to cook for another minute or two, then add the chicken pieces, stir well, and sauté for 3–4 minutes to seal. In a cup, mix the flour with a little of the water, and add this to the pan, followed by the remaining liquid. Stir and bring to the boil before reducing the heat and allowing to simmer for 20–25 minutes. Once the chicken pieces are cooked through, add the yogurt and cream, stir, and simmer for a few minutes more. Garnish with the coriander leaves. Serve with rice or naan bread and slices of cucumber and tomato. *Makes 4–6 servings*

178 chicken tikka

PREPARATION
30 minutes plus 2 hours marinading

STORAGE
Keeps for up to 2 days in the fridge

2 cloves garlic
1 small piece root ginger
⅔ cup natural bio-yogurt
2 tsp garam masala/curry powder
½ tsp ground coriander
½ tsp ground cumin

1 tsp paprika
juice of ½ lemon
1 tsp chopped fresh coriander
4 skinless, boneless chicken breasts, cut into pieces

Peel and cut the garlic and ginger root into small pieces and crush in a pestle and mortar. (Alternatively, crush the garlic and grate the ginger.) In a large bowl, mix these together with the yogurt, spices, lemon juice, and coriander. Add the chicken pieces and stir until they are well covered with the mixture. Leave in the fridge to marinade for at least 2 hours. Thread the chicken onto metal or wooden kebab skewers. Place under a medium broiler or on a barbeque until cooked through and slightly blackened at the edges. Alternatively, put the kebabs on a rack above a baking pan and cook in a hot oven at 230°C/450°F/gas mark 8 for 15–20 minutes, turning once, until the chicken is cooked through. Serve with warm naan bread, salad, and Spicy Curry Dip (recipe 336; p.189). *Makes 4–6 servings*

179 chicken fajitas

PREPARATION
30 minutes

STORAGE
Keeps for up
to 2 days in
the fridge

¼ tsp paprika
¼ tsp ground cumin
½ tsp dried oregano
2 boneless, skinless chicken
  breasts, cut into thin strips
1 clove garlic, peeled and crushed
2 tbsp olive oil
1 onion, peeled, halved, and sliced

1 red bell pepper, cored and sliced
6 small flour tortillas
a small bowl of shredded lettuce
½ cup grated Cheddar and
  mozzarella, mixed
sour cream (optional)
Salsa (recipes 242–244; pp.146–147)
  or Guacamole (recipe 128; p.99)

Mix together the paprika, ground cumin, and oregano in a bowl. Add the
chicken pieces and coat with the spices. Heat half the oil in a large skillet
and sauté the chicken for 4–5 minutes until just cooked. Remove the
chicken to a plate. Now add the remaining oil to the skillet and sauté the
onions, bell pepper, and garlic over a medium heat for approximately
5 minutes until soft. Add the chicken and cook for a further minute or two,
making sure it is hot through. Warm the tortillas according to the
instructions on the packet. To serve, put the various fajita ingredients (the
chicken mixture, a bowl of lettuce, the grated cheese, the sour cream,
Salsa or Guacamole, and the warmed tortillas) on plates and let your
children make their own fajita by taking a tortilla, adding the fillings of
their choice, and rolling it up. *Makes 2–4 servings*

180 roast chicken

PREPARATION
1 hour 30 minutes–
2 hours 30 minutes

STORAGE
Keeps for up
to 2 days in
the fridge

1 chicken
1 onion, peeled and cut into quarters
1–2 tsp dried thyme

Preheat the oven to 190°C/375°F/gas mark 3. Rinse the chicken outside
and inside the cavity. Place in a roasting pan. Put the onion in the body
cavity (this gives the chicken some additional flavor) and sprinkle the skin
with a little thyme. Put in the oven. The cooking time will vary according
to the size of the chicken but allow 20 minutes for every 1lb, plus an
additional 20 minutes. Baste with the juices from the bottom of the pan
once or twice during cooking. Toward the end of the cooking time, turn
the oven temperature up to 220°C/425°F/gas mark 7 to crisp and brown
the skin. The chicken is cooked when all the juices run clear and the leg
can easily be tugged away from the body. When cooked, remove from oven
and allow to rest for 5–10 minutes before carving. Serve with gravy made
from the juices at the bottom of the pan, vegetables, and mashed potato.
Makes 4–8 servings depending on size of chicken

181 duck breast in orange sauce

PREPARATION
55 minutes

STORAGE
Suitable for freezing; keeps for up to 2 days in the fridge

2 duck breasts
juice of 1 orange
juice of ½ lemon

grated rind of 2 oranges
½ tsp dried tarragon

Preheat the oven to 180°C/350°F/gas mark 3. Place the duck breasts in a small ovenproof dish, skin uppermost. Pour over the orange and lemon juices and sprinkle on the orange rind and tarragon. Bake for 30–35 minutes uncovered. Allow to stand for 5 minutes and then lift out of the dish and put on a hot serving plate. Stand for another 5 minutes before cutting into slices. Serve with roasted vegetables. *Makes 4–6 servings*

182 apple-stuffed roast pork

PREPARATION
1 hour–1 hour
15 minutes

STORAGE
Suitable for freezing; keeps for up to 2 days in the fridge

1 tbsp butter
1 tbsp olive oil
1 small onion, peeled and chopped
1 large eating apple, grated (with the skin left on)

2 tbsp chopped fresh parsley
2 tbsp chopped fresh thyme
grated rind and juice of ½ lemon
1lb 5oz pork tenderloin
2 slices streaky bacon

Preheat the oven to 200°C/400°F/gas mark 6. To make the stuffing, melt the butter and olive oil in a skillet, add the chopped onion, and sauté until just beginning to soften. Add the grated apple and cook for about 10–15 minutes. Add the herbs, lemon rind, and juice. Remove from heat and allow to cool. Meanwhile, split the pork lengthwise and open out flat. Spoon on stuffing, wrap the meat around it, and tie with string. Put in a roasting pan, and lay the bacon slices on top. Cook for 40–50 minutes until pork is tender. Allow to stand for a couple of minutes before slicing. Serve with garlic roast potatoes and vegetables. *Makes 4–6 servings*

183 pork and apple stew

PREPARATION
1 hour 20 minutes

STORAGE
Suitable for freezing; keeps for up to 2 days in the fridge

1 onion, peeled and chopped
2 tbsp olive oil
2 eating apples, cored and chopped
1lb 5oz pork tenderloin, cut into chunks
2 tbsp all-purpose flour
⅓ cup cider vinegar

1½ cups unsweetened pure apple juice
⅔ cup water
1 tsp dried/1 tbsp fresh, chopped thyme
2 bay leaves
2–3 tbsp crème fraîche (optional)

Preheat oven 170°C/325°F/gas mark 3. In a large casserole dish sauté the onion in the oil until softened. Add the apples and cook for a minute or two before adding the pork. Seal the meat, then sprinkle the flour into the dish. Cook for a minute over a medium heat, then slowly add the vinegar, apple juice, and water, stirring continuously. Add the thyme and bay leaves, bring to simmering point, cover, and transfer to the oven. Cook for an hour, or until pork is tender, stirring occasionally. Remove from the oven. Stir in the crème fraîche, if using. Serve with rice and a green vegetable. *Makes 4–6 servings*

184   roast lamb with spiced yogurt crust

A Middle Eastern variation on the traditional roast dinner. Lamb is an excellent source of protein, iron, and zinc.

PREPARATION
2 hours 15 minutes
plus marinading
time

STORAGE
Suitable for
freezing; keeps
for up to 2 days
in the fridge

4lb 8oz leg of lamb
3 cloves garlic, peeled and quartered
1lb 2oz natural bio-yogurt
2 tsp paprika
2 tsp ground cumin
1 tsp ground turmeric

1 tsp ground coriander
½ tsp ground black pepper
½ tsp ground cardamom
pinch of saffron threads
grated rind of 1 lemon

Make cuts into the surface of the lamb and push in the garlic pieces. Combine the rest of the ingredients in a bowl and mix well. Put the lamb in a roasting dish and spread the yogurt mixture all over it. Cover and refrigerate for several hours or overnight to allow the flavors to penetrate the lamb. To roast, place the lamb on a wire rack in a baking pan and add enough water to cover the bottom of the pan. Cook uncovered for 1½ hours at 190°C/375°F/gas mark 4 or until the crust is brown and the lamb cooked to your preference. Remove from the oven and let the meat rest for 20–30 minutes before carving. Serve with roasted potatoes and roasted vegetables or, for the full Middle Eastern experience, with Warm Vegetable Couscous (recipe 246; p.148). *Makes 8–10 servings*

185   lamb hotpot

Another slow-cooking traditional dish with very tender meat. Prepare the potatoes just before using so that they do not discolor.

PREPARATION
2 hours 30 minutes

STORAGE
Keeps for up
to 2 days in
the fridge

1lb 10oz lean neck fillet of lamb,
   diced
2 medium onions, peeled and sliced
1 leek, sliced
2 large carrots, peeled and sliced

1lb 9oz potatoes, peeled and sliced
½ tbsp chopped fresh rosemary
pinch of black pepper
⅔ cup vegetable stock
1oz butter

Preheat the oven to 300°C/150°F/gas mark 1. Put one third of the potatoes in the bottom of a casserole dish. In a bowl, combine the lamb pieces with the leeks, carrots, and onion rings. Spread half of this mixture over the layer of potatoes. Season with half the rosemary and black pepper. Make another layer of half of the remaining potato slices. Add the rest of the meat, onion, leek, and carrot mixture, and pour in the stock. Arrange a final layer of potatoes on top, making sure that the slices are slightly overlapping. Dot with butter. Put in the oven uncovered for 15 minutes to allow the butter to melt. Cover with a tight-fitting lid and cook for 2 hours, removing the lid for the last 20 minutes so that the top layer of potatoes browns and crisps. Serve with steamed or stir-fried vegetables. *Makes 4–6 servings*

186 marinated lamb kebabs *(above)*

❌❌🚫🅿

Marinating meat gives it a soft and tender texture, which most children prefer. If you use a loin fillet you can broil these kebabs, but if you use a cheaper cut they are better fried as this will further tenderize the meat.

PREPARATION
25 minutes plus
marinading time

STORAGE
Suitable for
freezing; keep
for up to 2 days
in the fridge

1lb 2oz boneless lamb, cubed
1 large onion, peeled and cut into
    pieces
1 clove garlic, peeled and crushed
5 tbsp olive oil

juice of 2 lemons
½ tsp ground cumin
½ tsp ground ginger
½ tsp ground coriander

Put all of the ingredients except the lamb into a food processor and whizz until well mixed and the onion is finely chopped. Pour into a bowl, add the lamb cubes, and stir to coat them with the marinade. Cover and refrigerate for at least 4 hours, or overnight if possible. When ready to cook, thread the lamb onto skewers, brush with the marinade, and place under a preheated broiler for 5 minutes. Turn the kebabs and broil each side for about 5 minutes until they are brown all over and cooked through. Serve inside pitta breads with salad vegetables or over a bed of Warm Vegetable Couscous (recipe 246; p.148). *Makes 4–6 portions*

187   lamb koftas

PREPARATION
25 minutes

STORAGE
Suitable for
freezing; keep
for up to 2 days
in the fridge

1 cup lean ground lamb

1 small onion, peeled and finely
  chopped

1 clove garlic, peeled and crushed

1 tbsp chopped fresh mint

1 tbsp chopped fresh coriander

½ tsp ground cumin

½ small mild chilli, deseeded and
  chopped

1–2 tbsp vegetable oil

Put all the ingredients except the oil into a food processor and mix for a few
seconds to combine well and finely grind the lamb. Divide the mixture into
about 8 portions and roll into sausage shapes. Push a skewer lengthwise
into the middle of each sausage and mold the meat around the skewer.
Brush or rub with a little oil and place under a preheated broiler for 5–6
minutes. Turn as necessary to ensure they are brown all over. Serve with
Mint and Cucumber Yoghurt Dip (recipe 245; p.147) *Makes 4–6 servings*

188   pumpkin lamb stew

*This delicious autumn stew, packed full of vegetables and protein, is fun to
serve as a family meal for Halloween.*

PREPARATION
1½–2 hours

STORAGE
Keeps for up
to 2 days in
the fridge

1 medium pumpkin,
  approximately 8–10ins in diameter

2 tbsp water

2 tbsp olive oil

2 lb lean boneless lamb, cut into
  1in cubes

2 onions, peeled and chopped

2 cloves garlic, peeled and finely
  chopped

2 tbsp all-purpose flour

2 cups vegetable or chicken stock

1 cinnamon stick

¼ tsp ground cloves

¼ tsp ground ginger

dash of cayenne pepper

5 carrots, peeled and cut into strips

2 zucchini, cut into rounds

Preheat the oven to 180°C/350°F/gas mark 4. Prepare the pumpkin by
cutting a lid from the top, approximately 6ins in diameter. Scrape out the
seeds and fiber from the center of the pumpkin. Wrap the stem in foil and
replace lid. Place the pumpkin in a shallow baking pan and pour in the
water to ½inch deep. Bake in the oven for about an hour until the pumpkin
feels very slightly tender. Meanwhile, heat half of the oil in a large
heavy-bottomed skillet over a medium heat and brown the lamb. Remove
and set aside in a dish so that the meat juices are retained. Add the
remaining oil to the pan and sauté the onions and garlic until soft. Return the
meat and juices to the skillet. Sprinkle over the flour and stir. Slowly add the
stock, stirring all the time to prevent lumps forming. Add the spices. Bring
to the boil while stirring, then reduce the heat, and simmer until the meat is
tender (approximately 1 hour). Add the carrots and zucchini, and continue
to cook for a further 10 minutes until they begin to soften a little. Ladle the
stew into the cavity of the hot pumpkin and return to the oven for a further
30 minutes until the pumpkin is tender when pierced with a knife. Carefully
transfer the pumpkin to a deep serving dish and bring to the table. When
serving, make sure you scrape some of the pumpkin flesh into the stew.
Serve with brown rice or couscous. *Makes 6–8 servings*

189 pot roast beef

Slow pot roasting ensures the meat will be very soft and tender. Serve thin slices of Pot Roast Beef with hot vegetables or use it for a sandwich filling when cold. The red wine gives extra flavor and helps to tenderize the meat —the alcohol will evaporate during the slow cooking process.

PREPARATION
2 hours 50 minutes

STORAGE
Keeps for up
to 2 days in
the fridge

2 tbsp olive oil
3lb 5oz beef topside
  or silverside
1 large onion, peeled and chopped
14oz canned, chopped
  tomatoes
2 tsp dried basil

few pinches of black pepper
½ cup red wine
½ cup water
3 small potatoes, peeled
3 carrots, peeled and sliced
3 sticks celery, sliced
3 small zucchini, sliced

Preheat the oven to 190°C/375°F/gas mark 5. In an ovenproof casserole dish, brown the beef in the oil over a medium heat by cooking it for a minute on each side. Remove the beef and sauté the onion in the oil until soft. Add the tomatoes, basil, and pepper, and return the beef to the dish. Pour over the water and the wine. Cover and cook for 30 minutes, then turn the meat, reduce the heat to 160°C/325°F/gas mark 2, and cook for another 1½ hours, turning the beef every 25–30 minutes. Add the vegetables and cook covered for another 30 minutes until they are tender. *Makes 6–10 servings*

190 shepherd's pie

This family favorite, often made with ground beef, traditionally contains ground lamb—a good source of protein, iron, and zinc. Try making it in individual portions if you have a set of small ovenproof dishes.

PREPARATION
1 hour 15 minutes

STORAGE
Suitable for
freezing; keeps
for up to 2 days
in the fridge

1 tbsp olive oil
1 medium onion, peeled and finely
  chopped
1 small carrot, peeled and diced
1 clove garlic, peeled and crushed
1 tbsp chopped thyme
1 tbsp chopped rosemary
1lb lean ground lamb

1 tbsp all-purpose flour
1 tbsp tomato paste
dash of Worcester sauce
⅔ cup water
1lb potatoes, peeled and cut into
  chunks
1 tbsp butter
½ cup milk

Preheat the oven to 200°C/400°F/gas mark 6. Heat the olive oil in a saucepan and sauté the onion, carrot, garlic, and herbs over a gentle heat until soft. Add the lamb and continue cooking until brown right through. Add the flour, tomato paste, and Worcester sauce, and stir well. Cook for a minute, then gradually add the water, bring to the boil, cover, and simmer for 20 minutes. Meanwhile, steam the potatoes or boil in a small amount of water until soft. Mash them with the butter and milk. Put the lamb mixture into an ovenproof dish and cover with the mashed potatoes. Cook for 30 minutes or until lightly browned on top. Serve with some Roasted Vegetables (recipes 221; p.138 and 222; p.139) that can be cooked in the oven at the same time as the pie. *Makes 4–6 servings*

191 toad-in-the-hole (below)

PREPARATION
45 minutes

STORAGE
Best made just
before serving

3–4 tbsp vegetable oil
8 good-quality chipolata sausages
1 cup all-purpose flour

small pinch of salt
2 large eggs
1¼ cups semi-skimmed milk

Preheat the oven to 180°C/350°F/gas mark 4. Put the sausages in a baking pan and cook in the oven for about 15 minutes, turning once or twice, until just beginning to brown (don't overbrown them as they continue to cook with the batter later on). While the sausages are cooking make the batter. Put the flour and salt in a bowl, add the eggs and a little of the milk, and whisk using an electric or hand whisk. Gradually whisk in the remaining milk. Place a little oil in the bottom of 4 small loaf pans (or a large ovenproof dish), put in the oven, and turn the temperature up to 220°C/425°F/ gas mark 6. When the oil starts to smoke, take out the tins, place two cooked sausages in each one, and then add some of the batter mixture to fill the tin somewhere between quarter- and half-full. Quickly return to the oven and cook for at least 20 minutes before opening the oven door. The secret of well risen batter is to keep the oven door closed! If you have a glass oven door it is great fun to watch these rise. Once they are golden brown and crispy, remove from the oven and serve immediately. Serve with Onion Gravy (recipe 192; p.126) and green vegetables. *Makes 4–8 servings*

192 onion gravy

PREPARATION
25 minutes

STORAGE
Keeps for up
to 2 days in
the fridge

1 large red onion, peeled and
  chopped
1 tbsp olive oil

1 tbsp all-purpose flour
⅔ cup vegetable stock

Slowly sauté the onion in the oil until browned. Stir in the flour and cook
for a few minutes over a medium heat. Add the vegetable stock, stirring all
the time. Bring to the boil to thicken. Serve with Toad-in-the-Hole (recipe
191; p.125) or any roast meat. *Makes 4–5 servings*

193 vegetable chili

PREPARATION
1 hour 15 minutes

STORAGE
Suitable for
freezing; keeps
for up to 2 days
in the fridge

1 garlic clove, peeled and crushed
1 onion, peeled and sliced
1 tbsp olive oil
1 tsp chili powder
½ large eggplant, cut into chunks
1 zucchini, sliced diagonally
1 small cauliflower, cut into florets
14oz canned, chopped tomatoes

1 cup water
pinch of black pepper
1½ cups button mushrooms
½ fresh chili, deseeded and finely
  sliced (optional)
14oz canned red kidney
  beans, drained
3 tbsp chopped fresh parsley

In a saucepan, sauté the garlic and onion in the oil until soft. Add the chili
powder and eggplant and cook for 2–3 minutes. Stir in the zucchini,
cauliflower, tomatoes, water, and pepper. Bring to the boil and simmer for
15 minutes. Add the button mushrooms and chili (if using) and cook for a
further 15 minutes. Finally, add the kidney beans, and cook for 10 minutes.
Sprinkle with parsley. Serve with rice or noodles. *Makes 4–6 servings*

194 creamy vegetable curry

PREPARATION
1 hour

STORAGE
Suitable for
freezing; keeps
for up to 2 days
in the fridge

1 onion, peeled and chopped
1 clove garlic, peeled and crushed
2 tbsp vegetable oil
2 tsp grated fresh ginger
½ tsp mild chili powder
½ tsp turmeric
½ tsp ground cumin
½ tsp ground coriander
½ tsp garam masala
2 tomatoes, skinned and chopped

1 yellow bell pepper, deseeded and
  chopped
1 potato, peeled and chopped
4oz cauliflower florets
6oz cooked chickpeas
½ cup water or vegetable stock
⅔ cup natural bio-yogurt
2 tbsp light cream
chopped fresh coriander to garnish
salt to taste

In a large saucepan, sauté the onion and garlic in the oil for 2–3 minutes
until soft. Add the ginger and spices. Cook for another 1–2 minutes, stirring.
Add the vegetables, mix well, and sauté for 3–4 minutes. Pour in the water
or stock, stir, and bring to the boil. Reduce the heat and simmer for 20–25
minutes. Once the vegetables are tender, stir in the yogurt and cream, and
simmer for 1–2 minutes more. Garnish with the coriander. Serve with rice or
naan bread and slices of cucumber and tomato. *Makes 4–6 servings*

195 shrimp paella

PREPARATION
50 minutes

STORAGE
Suitable for
freezing; keeps
for up to 24 hours
in the fridge

2 tbsp olive oil
1 onion, peeled and diced
1 red bell pepper, deseeded
 and diced
1 clove garlic, peeled and crushed
few strands of saffron

1 cup paella or risotto rice
1 pt vegetable stock
4 tbsp frozen peas
4 tbsp frozen corn
1lb frozen peeled shrimps
black pepper to taste

Heat the oil in a paella pan or large heavy-bottomed skillet, add the onion,
bell pepper, and garlic, and sauté until softened. Sprinkle over a few
strands of saffron and then add the rice. Stir it in and cook over a medium
heat for a couple of minutes before adding the vegetable stock. Stir and
bring to the boil. Turn the heat down and simmer for about 10 minutes
before adding the frozen vegetables and shrimps. Bring back to a simmer
and continue to cook, stirring occasionally, until the rice is soft and all of the
water is absorbed. Season and serve immediately, on its own or with a
salad. *Makes 4–6 servings*

196 marinated tuna kebabs

PREPARATION
30 minutes plus
marinading time

STORAGE
Keep for up
to 2 days in
the fridge

2lb 4oz fresh tuna, cubed
6–8 tbsp chopped parsley
6–8 tbsp chopped coriander leaves
3 cloves garlic, peeled and crushed
1 tsp ground cinnamon
1 tsp ground cumin
1 tsp ground paprika

1 tsp ground coriander
juice of 3 limes or lemons
4 tbsp olive oil
grated rind of 1 lime or lemon
3 red or green bell peppers,
 deseeded and cut into squares
1 cup small button mushrooms

Combine all the ingredients except the tuna in a bowl. Add the tuna cubes
and cover. Marinate in fridge for 4–5 hours or overnight. Thread tuna onto
skewers, alternating pepper and mushroom between each cube. Broil or
barbeque, turning occasionally until cooked through. *Makes 4–6 kebabs*

197 fishy stir-fry

PREPARATION
35 minutes

STORAGE
Keeps for up
to 2 days in
the fridge

12oz fresh white fish fillets (such as
 haddock or cod), skinned and cut
 into chunks
2 tbsp cornstarch
3 tbsp olive oil
1 leek, sliced

4 scallions, sliced
1 red bell pepper, cored and sliced
½ zucchini, sliced
1 tbsp mild curry paste
⅓ cup orange juice
½ cup frozen peas

Coat the fish chunks in the cornstarch. Heat the oil in a skillet and add the
sliced fresh vegetables. Stir-fry for about 5 minutes until softened. Remove
from the skillet, add the fish chunks, and stir-fry for about 3 minutes until
cooked right through. Add the curry paste, orange juice, peas, and cooked
vegetables. Stir-fry until the peas have cooked and the dish is hot through.
Serve with rice or noodles. *Makes 3–5 servings*

198 salmon fish cakes *(above)*

As an alternative to fresh salmon, you could try canned salmon or other oily fish, such as mackerel or trout, to make these tasty cakes.

PREPARATION
1 hour 30 minutes
plus 30 minutes
chilling
STORAGE
Suitable for
freezing; keep
for up to 24 hours
in the fridge

1lb potatoes, peeled and cut into
   pieces
1lb skinless salmon fillet
2 tbsp butter
1 tbsp chopped chives

1 tbsp chopped parsley
1 tbsp chopped dill
2 tbsp mayonnaise
fresh white breadcrumbs
2 tbsp melted butter

Preheat the oven to 200°C/400°F/gas 6. Boil the potatoes until soft, drain well, and set aside. Cut the fish into small fillets and place on a sheet of foil. Dot with butter and wrap into a foil parcel. Bake in the oven for 12–15 minutes until the fish is opaque and flakes easily. Remove the fish parcel from the oven and mash the potatoes with the juices from the fish. Flake the fish into a bowl with the mashed potatoes, carefully checking for any remaining bones, add the herbs and mayonnaise, and mix everything together. Divide the mixture into 12 round fish cakes, roll each one in the breadcrumbs, place in a pan or on a plate, cover, and chill in the fridge for at least 30 minutes. Turn up the oven to 220°C/425°F/gas 7. Lightly grease a baking sheet and arrange the fish cakes on it. Brush with melted butter and bake for 20–25 minutes until golden, crisp, and hot through. Serve with lemon wedges and vegetables. *Makes 12 fish cakes*

199 salsa salmon

A quick and easy, tasty dish that is an excellent source of omega-3 fats.

PREPARATION
20 minutes

1 salmon fillet per person (or half for a small child)
2 tsp Peach and Mango Salsa (recipe 246; p.147) per fillet, or any mild,
  store-bought salsa

STORAGE
Keep for up
to 2 days in
the fridge

Preheat the oven to 180°C/350°F/gas mark 4. Put each salmon fillet on
a piece of foil approximately 6in square and top each one with a couple
of teaspoonfuls of salsa. Close up the foil to make a parcel and put the
parcels in a baking pan. Cook in oven for 15 minutes until the salmon flakes
easily. When ready, take the salmon out of the foil, put on a plate, and pour
a little of the juice over the top. Serve with extra salsa, a squeeze of lemon,
and Squashed Potato Roasties (recipe 217; p.137). For variation, cook the
salmon without salsa and then serve with Avocado and Tomato Salsa
(recipe 241; p.146). Salmon parcels can be made in advance and stored in
the fridge until needed. This will allow the salsa marinade to seep into the
salmon to give a more intense flavor.

200 teriyaki orange salmon parcels

PREPARATION
20 minutes

1 salmon fillet per person (or half for a small child)
2 tsp bottled teriyaki marinade per fillet
1 tsp fresh orange juice per fillet

STORAGE
Keep for up
to 2 days in
the fridge

Preheat the oven to 180°C/350°F/gas mark 4. Put each salmon fillet
on a piece of foil approximately 6in square and drizzle the teriyaki marinade
and orange juice over each one. Close up the foil to make a
parcel and put the parcels in a baking pan. Cook in the oven for 15
minutes until the salmon flakes easily. When ready, take the salmon out of
the foil, put on a plate, and pour a little of the juice over the top. Serve with
stir-fried vegetables and rice. For variation, try adding a slice of mango on
top of the salmon before cooking.

201 cod fish fingers

PREPARATION
25 minutes

4oz skinless cod fillet
1 egg, beaten
4 tbsp cornmeal
1 tbsp olive oil

STORAGE
Suitable for
freezing; best
made just before
serving

Cut the fish into 4 pieces, checking carefully for any remaining bones. Put the
egg in a bowl and the breadcrumbs on a flat plate and heat the oil in a skillet.
Dip the fish pieces in the egg, then coat them on all sides with the cornmeal,
and place in the hot skillet. Fry for 4–5 minutes, turning once, until the fish is
cooked right through, and the breadcrumbs are golden brown. Serve with
mashed potato and steamed vegetable sticks. *Makes 2–4 servings*

202 salmon fish fingers

OO

A delicious alternative to white fish fingers and packed full of LCPs.

PREPARATION
20 minutes

STORAGE
Suitable for
freezing; best
made just before
serving

12oz skinless salmon fillet
¼ cup dried breadcrumbs
1 egg, beaten

1 clove garlic, peeled and crushed
(optional)
2 tbsp butter

Preheat the oven to 200°C/400°F/gas mark 6. Cut the salmon into fingers, checking carefully for any remaining bones. Dip the salmon pieces in the beaten egg and then coat in the breadcrumbs. Place in a lightly greased baking pan. Mix together the crushed garlic (if using) and butter. Dot each breaded salmon finger with a little of the butter mixture. Bake in the oven for 5–6 minutes, turn the fingers over, and cook for a further 4–5 minutes until golden brown and cooked through. Serve with a salsa and Traditional Oven Fries (recipe 219; p.137) or Sweet Potato Fries (recipe 213; p.135). *Makes 4–5 servings*

203 fisherman's pie

O

This is a popular way to serve fish to children. By mixing white and oily fish you are providing plenty of omega 3 LCPs without too strong a flavor.

PREPARATION
1 hour 45 minutes

STORAGE
Keeps for up
to 24 hours
in the fridge

1lb mixed fish fillets, such as
haddock and salmon
2–3 tsp butter
12oz potatoes, peeled and diced
12oz butternut squash, peeled and
diced

2 cups milk
1oz butter for white sauce
½ cup all-purpose flour
1 tsp wholegrain mustard
½ cup breadcrumbs
2 tsp chopped parsley

Preheat the oven to 190°C/375°F/gas mark 5. Put the fish fillets on a piece of kitchen foil. Top each white fish fillet with a knob of butter and wrap the foil to make a parcel. Bake in the oven for 20 minutes. While the fish is cooking, steam the potatoes and butternut squash until soft. Mash together with about a quarter of the milk and set aside. When the fish is ready, pour the juices into the bottom of a greased ovenproof dish. Flake the fish, taking care to remove any remaining bones, and add to the dish. To make the white sauce, melt the butter in a saucepan, add the flour, and cook for a couple of minutes on a low heat, taking care that the flour does not turn brown. Slowly pour in the remaining milk while stirring with a wooden spoon or whisk. Keep stirring until you have a smooth sauce. Bring to the boil and simmer gently for 2–3 minutes to thicken. Stir in the wholegrain mustard and pour over the flaked fish. Spread the mashed vegetables on top and sprinkle over the breadcrumbs and parsley. Bake in the oven for 25 minutes until golden brown. Serve with peas or green beans. *Makes 8–10 servings*

204　rosti-topped fish pie

●

PREPARATION
2 hours

STORAGE
Keeps for up
to 24 hours
in the fridge

1lb 2oz mixed fish (such as salmon,
  white fish, or shrimps)
1¾ cups milk
1 cup fish stock
1 bay leaf
1oz butter

2 tbsp all-purpose flour
2 tbsp chopped parsley
1lb 2oz waxy potatoes, washed and
  scrubbed
2 tbsp olive oil
2 tbsp butter, melted

Preheat the oven to 200°C/400°F/gas mark 6. Put the fish in a large
saucepan with the milk, fish stock, and bay leaf, and simmer gently until the
fish is cooked and flakes easily. Strain the liquid from the pan into a jug and
set aside. To make the sauce, melt the butter in a small saucepan, add the
flour, and cook for a minute or two before gradually stirring in the milk and
stock mixture. Continue to cook over a low heat until the sauce thickens.
Stir until smooth. Add the fish and parsley to the sauce and spoon the
mixture into an ovenproof dish. Boil the potatoes in a pan with water for
12 minutes, remove from the heat, drain, cover with a clean cloth, and
leave to cool. When cool enough to handle, peel the potatoes and grate
into long shreds using a coarse grater. Put them in a bowl with the oil and
melted butter and mix to coat the potatoes. Spoon on top of the fish
mixture and bake for 20–30 minutes until the fish is bubbling and the
potato is crisp on top. *Makes 4–8 servings*

205　tofu stir-fry

Ⓥ Ⓧ Ⓧ Ⓧ ● ●

PREPARATION
25 minutes

STORAGE
Keeps for up
to 2 days in
the fridge

1 tbsp reduced-salt soy sauce/
  yellow bean sauce
1 tbsp smooth peanut butter
juice of ½ lemon
1 tbsp olive oil
1 tsp grated fresh ginger
½ tsp chopped fresh mild chili
  (optional)

1 clove garlic, peeled and crushed
⅔ cup firm tofu, drained and sliced
½ zucchini, diced
2 large mushrooms, diced
1 red bell pepper, deseeded and
  sliced
3oz fresh bean sprouts, sliced

In a bowl, mix together the soy/yellow bean sauce, peanut butter, and
lemon juice. Heat the oil in a skillet/wok and stir-fry the ginger, chili (if
using), and garlic for a minute. Add the tofu and stir-fry for a minute more.
Add the zucchini, mushrooms, bell pepper, and bean sprouts and continue
stir-frying for 2–3 minutes. Pour in the sauce mixture and stir-fry for a
further 1–2 minutes until all of the ingredients are well combined. Serve with
noodles or rice. *Makes 2–4 servings*

206 butternut squash and chickpea risotto

PREPARATION
1 hour 10 minutes

STORAGE
Suitable for
freezing; keeps
for up to 2 days
in the fridge

3½ pts vegetable stock
2 cloves garlic, peeled
large pinch of saffron strands
2 tbsp tomato paste
1 small butternut squash, peeled,
    deseeded, and diced
1 tbsp olive oil

2 tbsp butter
1 small onion, peeled and chopped
1lb risotto rice
4oz canned chickpeas, drained
2oz grated Parmesan
3 tbsp chopped parsley

In a large saucepan, place the stock, garlic, saffron, tomato paste, and squash. Simmer for 10–15 minutes until the squash is soft. Using a slotted spoon transfer the squash to a plate and set aside. Discard the garlic. Melt the oil and butter in a heavy-based pan, add the onion, and sauté for a few minutes until soft. Add the rice, stir well, and cook gently for 1–2 minutes. Now add the stock a ladle at a time. Stir constantly, gradually adding more liquid as the rice absorbs it. When the rice is almost cooked, add the squash and chickpeas. Keep adding the stock and stirring until rice has absorbed all the liquid. When cooked, stir in the Parmesan and sprinkle with chopped parsley. Serve with a salad or green vegetable. *Makes 4–6 servings*

207 lentil moussaka

PREPARATION
2 hours 20 minutes

STORAGE
Suitable for
freezing; keeps
for up to 2 days
in the fridge

1 cup Puy lentils
1 large eggplant, trimmed
1 tbsp olive oil
1 small onion, peeled and finely sliced
2 small red bell peppers, deseeded,
    and finely sliced
2 cloves garlic, peeled and crushed

2 tsp dried mixed herbs
½ cup sun-dried tomatoes,
    finely chopped
1½ cups passata
½ cup grated Cheddar
¼ cup breadcrumbs

Preheat the oven to 180°C/350°F/Gas mark 3. Rinse the lentils thoroughly, place in a saucepan, cover with cold water, and bring to the boil. Keep boiling rapidly for 10 minutes, then simmer for 30–40 minutes or until they are soft. Drain. Slice the eggplant, brush with a little of the oil, and broil under a medium heat, turning once, until golden brown on both sides. In a skillet, gently sauté the onion and bell pepper in the oil until soft. Stir in the garlic and herbs, cook for 1 minute, and turn off heat. Put half the lentils in the bottom of an ovenproof dish, layer on half the eggplants, half the onion and bell pepper mixture, and half the sun-dried tomatoes and passata. Repeat with a second layer in the same order. Mix together the cheese and breadcrumbs and sprinkle over the top. Bake for 30 minutes until golden and bubbling. Serve with pasta or rice. *Makes 4–6 servings*

208 chickpeas with cumin and potatoes

PREPARATION
50 minutes

STORAGE
Suitable for freezing; keeps for up to 2 days in the fridge

1 small onion, peeled and chopped
2 tsp olive oil
1 tsp cumin seeds
¼ tsp turmeric
1 garlic clove, peeled and crushed
1lb potatoes, peeled and diced
7oz broccoli florets

1 dried red chili, deseeded and finely diced
5 tbsp water
14oz canned chickpeas, drained and rinsed
1 tbsp chopped fresh coriander

In a skillet, sauté the onion in the oil for 4–5 minutes until soft. Add the cumin seeds, turmeric, and garlic and cook for a further 2–3 minutes. Add the potatoes, broccoli, chili, and water. Stir well, cover, and cook until the potatoes are soft, adding more water if needed. Stir in the chickpeas and cook gently for another 2 minutes. Sprinkle with coriander and serve with naan bread and Mango Salsa (see recipe 242; p.146). *Makes 3–5 servings*

209 rice and "peas"

This is a very popular dish with children in the Caribbean. The "peas" are actually beans, but this is the traditional name.

PREPARATION
1 hour 20 minutes

STORAGE
Keeps for up to 2 days in the fridge

2 tbsp olive oil
1 medium onion, peeled and chopped
1 red bell pepper, cored and sliced
1 tsp dried thyme
pinch of black pepper

2 cups long grain brown rice
1¼ cups cold water
14oz can coconut milk
14oz can kidney beans, drained

Heat the oil in a large skillet and sauté the onions until soft. Add the red bell pepper, thyme, black pepper, rice, water, and coconut milk, and bring to the boil. Reduce heat and simmer gently for about 45 minutes until all the liquid is absorbed and the rice is tender. Stir in the kidney beans and cook for a further 5 minutes. Serve with salad or roasted vegetables. *Makes 4–6 servings*

COMPLETING MEALS WITH SIDE DISHES

In order to be nutritionally balanced, a meal should include some portions of starchy foods, vegetables, and fruit. In this next section you will find ideas for tasty side dishes to help you to "complete" main meals. These are dishes intended to be served as an accompaniment to any meat, fish, or vegetarian main meal. Preparing and cooking vegetables in interesting ways and taking the time to present them attractively will help to encourage your child to eat them. Children do tend to prefer the stronger flavor of vegetables that have been cooked in a little fat to the taste of boiled or steamed vegetables, so we have included some oven-roasted and stir-fried dishes. Salads are also a good way of offering vegetables, and adding oil-based dressings will provide small amounts of polyunsaturated and omega-3 fats.

210 basic sweet potato mash

PREPARATION
20 minutes

STORAGE
Best served
immediately

6 orange sweet potatoes, peeled and quartered
1–2 tbsp walnut oil

Put 2in of water in a saucepan and bring to the boil. Add the sweet potatoes and bring back to the boil. Reduce heat, cover and cook for about 15–20 minutes until soft. Drain the potatoes, return them to the warm saucepan, add the oil, and mash until smooth. *Makes 4–6 servings*

211 buttery sweet potato mash with maple syrup

A delicious enriched sweet potato mash with a velvety texture.

PREPARATION
20 minutes

STORAGE
Best served
immediately

6 orange sweet potatoes, peeled and quartered
1 tbsp butter
2 tbsp milk
2 tsp maple syrup

Cook the potatoes following the instructions given in the recipe above. Return the drained potatoes to the warm saucepan, add the butter, milk, and syrup, and mash until smooth. *Makes 4–6 servings*

212 sweet potato fries

Although these fries are relatively high in fat, the sweet potatoes are full of carotenes and using rapeseed oil provides essential omega-3s. Children love to eat them with a little dish of ketchup for dipping.

PREPARATION
25 minutes

STORAGE
Best served
immediately

6 orange sweet potatoes, scrubbed and ends trimmed
vegetable oil (for deep frying)

Half fill a deep-sided saucepan with vegetable oil. Slice the sweet potatoes and cut them into chunky fries. Heat the oil over a fairly high heat. When hot, carefully add the sweet potato pieces and fry until golden and crispy. Depending on the size of the potato pieces, this will take between 15 and 20 minutes. Remove them from the pan using a slatted spoon and place on paper towels to drain off excess oil. *Makes 4–6 servings*

213 layered potato and onion bake

PREPARATION
1½–2 hours

STORAGE
Best served
immediately

4 medium red-skinned potatoes
4 orange sweet potatoes
1 large white onion, peeled
2–3 tbsp walnut oil
pinch of black pepper

Preheat the oven to 180°C/350°F/gas mark 4. Wash the red-skinned potatoes and remove any black spots with a sharp knife. Cut into thin slices. Peel the sweet potatoes and cut them into thin slices. Halve and thinly slice the onion. Rub a little oil around the base and sides of an oven-proof dish. Arrange a layer of red potato slices on the bottom of the dish and follow this with a layer of onion slices and then a layer of sweet potato slices. Repeat these layers until all the slices are in the dish. Drizzle the remaining oil over the top and season. Cover with kitchen foil. Place in the preheated oven and bake for 1–1½ hours, removing the foil for the last 15 minutes to allow the top layer to crisp. *Makes 5–7 servings*

214 potato and parsnip mash

PREPARATION
20 minutes

STORAGE
Best served
immediately

4 large potatoes, peeled
  and diced
1 large parsnip, peeled

and diced
3 tbsp milk
1 tbsp butter/margarine

Put 2in of water in a pan and bring to the boil. Add the potatoes and parsnip, and bring back to the boil. Reduce heat, cover and cook for about 15 minutes until soft. Drain, return to the warm saucepan, add the milk and butter, and mash until smooth. *Makes 4–6 servings*

215 cheese and tomato mash

PREPARATION
10 minutes

STORAGE
Best served
immediately

4 large potatoes, peeled and cut into
  large chunks
3 tbsp milk
1 tbsp butter/margarine
1 scallion, finely chopped

2 tbsp chopped fresh parsley
4 medium tomatoes, skinned
  and chopped
½ cup grated Cheddar

Put 2in of water in a pan and bring to the boil. Add the potatoes and bring back to the boil. Reduce heat, cover, and cook. Drain, return to the warm saucepan, add the milk and butter, and mash well. Add all the remaining ingredients and stir gently to combine. *Makes 4–6 servings*

216 garlicky roast potatoes

A tasty and popular lower-fat version of traditional roast potatoes

PREPARATION
1 hour 10 minutes

STORAGE
Best served
immediately

2–3 tbsp olive oil
1 tsp dried oregano/mixed herbs
1 clove garlic, peeled and finely chopped
6 medium potatoes, peeled and diced

Preheat the oven to 200°C/400°F/gas mark 6. Place the oil, oregano, and garlic in a large bowl. Add the diced potatoes and toss until they are well coated with the oil and herb mixture. Place in a single layer in a roasting pan. Roast in the oven for approximately 1 hour, turning occasionally, until the potatoes are crisp and golden. *Makes 5–6 servings*

217 squashed potato roasties

These little squashed potatoes are a delicious and fun idea, plus they require a shorter roasting time as they are parboiled before they go in the oven.

PREPARATION
40 minutes

STORAGE
Best served
immediately

12 small new potatoes, unpeeled
4 tbsp olive oil
1 tsp dried thyme/mixed herbs
pinch of salt

Preheat the oven to 220°C/425°F/gas mark 7. Place the potatoes in a saucepan and add sufficient water to cover. Bring to the boil, reduce heat, and cook for about 15 minutes until just turning soft. Drain. Arrange on a lightly oiled baking pan. Using a potato masher, gently squash each one before brushing it with oil and sprinkling with thyme and a little salt. Cook for 25 minutes until crisp and brown. *Makes 4–6 servings*

218 traditional oven fries

These are much tastier, lower in fat, and almost as quick to prepare as the ready-made frozen variety.

PREPARATION
35 minutes

STORAGE
Best served
immediately

2 tbsp olive oil
2 large potatoes, peeled and cut into chunky fries

Preheat the oven to 220°C/435°F/gas mark 7. Toss the potatoes in the oil until well coated. Place in a lightly oiled baking pan. Cook for 20–30 minutes, turning once, until golden and crisp. *Makes 2–3 servings*

219 paprika potato wedges

V ⊗ ⊗ ⊛

PREPARATION
45 minutes

STORAGE
Best served
immediately

4 tbsp olive oil
1 tsp paprika
1½ tsp dried oregano
2 cloves garlic, peeled and crushed
4 large potatoes, peeled and cut into wedges

Preheat the oven to 220°C/425°F/gas mark 7. Place the oil in a large bowl and add the paprika, oregano, and garlic. Toss the potato wedges in the oil mixture until well coated. Tip the wedges into a hot baking pan. Cook for 35–40 minutes, turning once, until crisp and brown. *Makes 4–6 servings*

220 warm potato salad

V ⊗ ⊗ **O**

This light and nutritious potato salad is a big improvement on the simple boiled potato and is a hit with grown-ups, too!

PREPARATION
20 minutes

STORAGE
Keeps for up to 2
days in the fridge

10½oz small new potatoes, unpeeled
1 tbsp natural bio-yogurt
1 tbsp mayonnaise

1 tsp wholegrain mustard
2 tbsp chopped
fresh chives

Put 2in of water in a saucepan and bring to the boil. Add the new potatoes and bring back to the boil. Reduce heat, cover, and cook until tender. Mix the remaining ingredients together in a serving dish. Drain the potatoes and toss until well coated with the yogurt mixture. *Makes 3–6 servings*

221 roasted autumn vegetables

V ⊗ ⊗ ⊛

Roasted vegetables can be served either hot or cold and leftovers make an excellent filling for sandwiches.

PREPARATION
45 minutes

STORAGE
Keep for up to 24
hours in the fridge

2 red bell peppers, cored and sliced
1 red onion, halved and sliced thinly
½ marrow squash, peeled and diced
2 carrots, peeled and sliced

2 tbsp olive oil
1 tsp dried oregano
2–3 tsp chopped fresh
parsley (optional)

Preheat the oven to 200°C/400°F/gas mark 6. Place the vegetables in a large bowl. Add the oil, herbs, and toss until well coated. Spread the vegetables out on a large oven tray. Cover with foil. Cook covered for 10–15 minutes to just soften the vegetables then remove the foil and roast for a further 30–35 minutes. *Makes 4–5 servings*

222 roasted winter vegetables with potatoes *(below)*

This dish is good with Toad-in-the-Hole (recipe 191; p.124).

PREPARATION
40–50 minutes

STORAGE
Best served
immediately

2 red bell peppers, cored and sliced
1 red onion, halved and sliced thinly
2 leeks, sliced thinly
3 large red-skinned potatoes, peeled
  and diced

4 carrots, peeled and sliced
  lengthwise
2 tbsp olive oil
½ tsp dried rosemary
½ tsp dried thyme

Preheat the oven to 200°C/400°F/gas mark 6. Place the vegetables in a large bowl. Add the oil and herbs and toss until well coated. Spread the vegetables out in a large oven pan. Cover with kitchen foil. Cook for 10–15 minutes to just soften the vegetables, then remove the foil and roast for a further 30–35 minutes until they are beginning to turn crisp at the edges.
Makes 4–6 servings

223 oven-roasted tomatoes

A tasty way to enjoy tomatoes and ideal served with any egg dish.

PREPARATION
15 minutes

STORAGE
Best served
immediately

1 tbsp olive oil
2 cloves garlic, peeled and crushed
1 tsp dried oregano
6 medium tomatoes, quartered

Preheat the oven to 200°C/400°F/gas mark 6. Put the oil, garlic, and oregano in a large bowl and add the tomatoes. Toss until they are well coated with the oil mixture. Tip into a shallow roasting pan. Roast in the oven for 5–10 minutes, until the tomatoes are just beginning to collapse. Allow to cool slightly before serving. *Makes 4–8 servings*

224 roasted pumpkin

You can cook most varieties of squash in this way.

PREPARATION
40 minutes

STORAGE
Best served
immediately

1 medium pumpkin/squash,
    approximately 2lb in weight
1 clove garlic, peeled and crushed

2 tsp dried oregano
2 tsp ground coriander
2 tbsp olive oil

Preheat the oven to 200°C/400°F/gas mark 6. Prepare the pumpkin by cutting it in half, scooping out the seeds and then slicing it into wedges. Place the garlic, oregano, coriander, and oil in a large bowl and add the pumpkin wedges. Toss well and make sure that the pumpkin is coated with the oil mixture. Lay the wedges out in a large baking pan and cook for 30–35 minutes, until the flesh is tender and the skin is beginning to crisp. You can eat the entire wedge, including the skin, but if you prefer not to eat the skin, the flesh can easily be scraped away from the skin before serving. *Makes 4–6 servings*

225 carrot and celeriac mash

This unusual and nutritious vegetable mash has a great flavor and is a surprise hit with children.

PREPARATION
25 minutes

STORAGE
Best served
immediately

5 large carrots, peeled and sliced
1 celeriac, peeled and diced
1 tbsp butter/margarine

Add the carrot and celeriac to a pan of boiling water, reduce the heat and simmer for about 20 minutes until tender. Drain the vegetables and return them to the warm saucepan. Add the butter or margarine and mash with a potato masher until smooth, adding a little water if necessary. *Makes 4–6 servings*

226 vegetable rosti cakes

PREPARATION
10–15 minutes

STORAGE
Best served
immediately

4 carrots, peeled and grated
1 zucchini, grated
1 small onion, peeled and grated
4 large floury potatoes, peeled

and grated
1 tbsp all-purpose flour
½ egg, beaten
vegetable oil (for shallow frying)

Mix the vegetables together in a large bowl. Tip the mixture out onto a clean tea towel, pull up the sides, and squeeze it tightly to remove excess water. Put the mixture back in the bowl, add the flour and egg, and mix well. Take a small amount of mixture and shape it into a flat cake. Repeat until all the mixture has been used. Heat the oil in a large skillet and add the cakes using a fish slice. Gently fry until golden on both sides. Drain on paper towels to remove excess oil. *Makes 8–10 servings*

227 multicolored corn

PREPARATION
15 minutes

STORAGE
Best served
immediately

1 tbsp olive oil for sautéing
½ green and ½ red bell pepper,
  finely chopped

½ onion, peeled and chopped
7oz corn (canned
  or frozen)

Heat the oil in a saucepan and add the bell peppers and onion. Sauté until soft. Add the corn and stir. Cover with a lid and cook over a low heat for 5–10 minutes, until the corn is tender. *Makes 3–4 servings*

228 spaghetti squash in soy ginger sauce

PREPARATION
1 hour 45 minutes

STORAGE
Best served
immediately

1 spaghetti squash, washed
4 tbsp soy sauce
4 tbsp apple juice

1 tbsp maple syrup
pinch of ground ginger
2 scallions, finely sliced

To oven cook, preheat the oven to 200°C/400°F/gas mark 6, pierce the skin in several places, and put in a baking pan. Bake uncovered for about 1½ hours, turning once during cooking. The squash is ready when the shell gives to pressure. Once cooked, allow to cool slightly, split in half, and remove the seeds. Alternatively microwave by splitting the squash in half, removing the seeds, and placing it cut-side up in a microwavable dish. Cover with microwave wrap and cook on "high" for 10–12 minutes. Meanwhile, put the soy sauce, apple juice, maple syrup, ginger, and scallions in a bowl and mix them together. Cover and leave to stand until the squash is cooked. Once the squash is ready, gently fork out the flesh to form strands that resemble spaghetti. Place these in a serving dish and pour over the sauce. *Makes 6–8 servings*

229 sesame green beans

PREPARATION
5 minutes

STORAGE
Best served
immediately

1 tbsp sesame oil
9oz green beans, trimmed and halved
1 scallion, finely chopped
1 tbsp sesame seeds, toasted

Heat the sesame oil in a large skillet or wok. Add the beans and scallion and stir-fry over a high heat for 2–3 minutes. Toss regularly during cooking to avoid burning. Add the toasted sesame seeds and cook for a further minute. *Makes 2–3 servings*

230 stir-fried mixed vegetables

Stir-frying is a versatile and quick way of cooking vegetables. You can prepare most vegetables this way—simply cut them into bite-size pieces.

PREPARATION
15 minutes

STORAGE
Best served
immediately

2 tbsp olive oil
1 small onion/1 small leek/
   3 scallions, chopped
1 stick celery, sliced/1 celeriac,
   sliced
⅛ cup green beans/mangetout

6 broccoli/cauliflower florets
1 red/green bell pepper, cored
   and sliced
1 zucchini, diced
6 mushrooms, sliced

Heat the olive oil in a large skillet or wok. Add the vegetables in the order shown in the ingredients list above (allowing approximately 2 minutes between each new addition) and cook over a high heat, stirring constantly to avoid burning. Once all of the ingredients are in the skillet or wok, cook for a further 5 minutes. *Makes 6–8 servings*

231 stir-fried mangetout and carrot

Both mangetout and carrots are a good source of beta-carotene and children enjoy their sweet flavor.

PREPARATION
10 minutes

STORAGE
Best served
immediately

1 tbsp sesame oil
1 stick celery, chopped
2 carrots, peeled and cut into
   matchsticks
4oz mangetout/sugarsnap peas,

trimmed
3 scallions, chopped
juice of 1 lemon
1 tbsp sesame seeds, toasted
black pepper to taste

Heat the oil in a large skillet or wok, add the celery and carrots, and stir-fry over a high heat for 2 minutes. Add the mangetout/sugarsnap peas and scallions, and stir-fry for a further 2–3 minutes until cooked through but still crisp. Add the lemon juice and toasted sesame seeds, season to taste with pepper, and toss to distribute the seasoning evenly through the vegetables. Remove from the heat and serve. *Makes 4–6 servings*

232 stir-fried fresh spinach

Always wash fresh spinach leaves very thoroughly and keep rinsing them until no grit or sand is visible in the water.

PREPARATION
10 minutes

STORAGE
Best served
immediately

1 tbsp olive oil
1 onion, peeled and finely chopped
7oz canned tomatoes, chopped

8oz fresh spinach, washed, stalks
    removed, and chopped

Heat the oil in a large skillet or wok, and add the onion. Fry over a low heat until soft. Add the tomatoes and simmer for 2 minutes. Add the prepared spinach, stir, and simmer for 1–2 minutes, until the spinach leaves have just wilted. *Makes 2–4 servings*

233 mixed leaf and herb salad

PREPARATION
15 minutes

STORAGE
Best served
immediately

12 lettuce leaves (any variety)
1 small bunch watercress
12 leaves rocket
3 tbsp chopped fresh parsley
3 tbsp chopped fresh coriander
1 tbsp balsamic vinegar

juice of 1 lemon
1 clove garlic, peeled and crushed
1 tsp mustard powder
1 tbsp walnut oil
1 tbsp olive oil
black pepper to taste

Combine all the salad leaves and chopped herbs in a large salad bowl. Put the balsamic vinegar, lemon juice, garlic, mustard powder, walnut oil, and olive oil in a bowl and whisk vigorously with a fork. Season to taste with pepper before pouring over the leaves. Toss well before serving. *Makes 4–6 servings*

234 baby spinach and radish salad

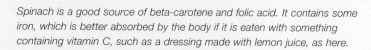

Spinach is a good source of beta-carotene and folic acid. It contains some iron, which is better absorbed by the body if it is eaten with something containing vitamin C, such as a dressing made with lemon juice, as here.

PREPARATION
10 minutes

STORAGE
Best served
immediately

12 leaves baby spinach, washed and drained
12 radishes, thinly sliced
salad dressing from recipe above

Place the spinach leaves and radishes in a salad bowl and mix together. Pour over the dressing and toss well to distribute evenly through the salad before serving. *Makes 2–4 servings*

235 fresh beet salad

Kids are often not keen on beet pickled in vinegar as the taste is too sharp for them, but when it's freshly prepared it's a different story!

PREPARATION
35 minutes

STORAGE
Keeps for up to 2
days in the fridge

3 medium beets, unpeeled
3 tbsp chopped fresh parsley

juice of ½ lemon
1 tbsp olive oil

Put the beets in a saucepan and add sufficient water to cover. Bring to the boil, cover, reduce heat, and simmer for 20–25 minutes until the beets are tender right through. Drain and allow to cool. The skin should peel off very easily when you rub it with your fingers. Chop the cooked beets into small dice and sprinkle with the fresh parsley, lemon juice and oil before serving. *Makes 3–6 servings*

236 nutty celery and carrot salad

PREPARATION
5–10 minutes

STORAGE
Keeps for up to 6
hours in the fridge

3 tbsp mayonnaise
1 tbsp lemon/lime juice
3 carrots, peeled and grated
3 sticks celery, finely chopped

1 eating apple, cored and chopped
4 tbsp raisins
3 tbsp chopped walnuts

Put the mayonnaise and lemon/lime juice in a bowl and mix together. Add the carrots, celery, apple, raisins and walnuts and stir so that the dressing is distributed evenly. This is particularly good when served in half an avocado. *Makes 3–5 servings*

237 tomato and avocado salad

The key to this salad is to choose full-flavored tomatoes.

PREPARATION
10 minutes

STORAGE
Best served
immediately

4 tomatoes, sliced
1 ripe avocado, stoned, peeled,
    and sliced
2 tbsp olive oil

1 tbsp balsamic vinegar
½ tsp Dijon mustard
1 tbsp chopped fresh basil

Arrange the tomatoes and avocado on a large plate. Place the oil, vinegar, and mustard in a small bowl and whisk vigorously with a fork. Pour over the salad, sprinkle with the basil, and serve. *Makes 2–3 servings*

238 homemade coleslaw

PREPARATION
15 minutes

STORAGE
Keeps for up to 24
hours in the fridge

¼ white cabbage, finely shredded
2 carrots, peeled and finely grated
1 red bell pepper, cored and diced
1 green bell pepper, cored and diced

1 tbsp olive oil
1 tbsp mayonnaise
1 tbsp natural bio-yogurt
black pepper to taste

Place the vegetables in a large bowl. Combine the oil, mayonnaise, and yogurt in a small bowl and whisk with a fork. Pour over the vegetables and toss well. Season to taste with pepper. *Makes 2–4 servings*

239 crunchy salad with honey mustard dressing *(below)*

PREPARATION
15 minutes

STORAGE
Best served
immediately

20 sugarsnap peas, trimmed, strings
  removed, and halved
1 red and 1 green bell pepper, cored
  and chopped
2 sticks celery, sliced
1 Little Gem lettuce, chopped
½ cucumber, chopped

1 clove garlic, peeled and crushed
1 tsp Dijon mustard
1 tbsp runny honey
2 tbsp cider vinegar
3 tbsp olive oil
1 tbsp walnut oil

Place the vegetables in a large salad bowl. Combine the garlic, mustard, honey, vinegar, olive oil, and walnut oil in small bowl and whisk vigorously with a fork before pouring over the vegetables. Toss well to distribute the dressing evenly before serving. *Makes 3–4 servings*

240 fruity coleslaw
V ⊗ ⊗ O

PREPARATION
15 minutes

STORAGE
Best served immediately

¼ green cabbage, shredded
¼ red cabbage, shredded
1 red onion, finely sliced
2 sticks celery, finely sliced
4 radishes, sliced
½ fresh pineapple, peeled and diced or 14oz canned pineapple

5 tbsp mayonnaise
3oz natural bio-yogurt
1 tbsp olive oil
1 tbsp lemon juice
2 tbsp chopped fresh parsley
black pepper to taste

Combine all the vegetables and the pineapple in a salad bowl. Place the mayonnaise, yogurt, oil, lemon juice, parsley, and pepper in a bowl and whisk with a fork. Pour over the salad and mix well. *Makes 4–6 servings*

241 tomato and avocado salsa
V ⊗ ⊗ ⊠

PREPARATION
10 minutes

STORAGE
Best served immediately

1 ripe avocado, halved and diced
2 large tomatoes, skinned and finely chopped
¼ small red onion, finely chopped (optional)

1 tsp balsamic vinegar
2 tsp chopped fresh coriander
juice of ½ lemon or lime
pinch of salt and pepper

Place the avocado, tomato, onion, vinegar, coriander, and lemon/lime juice in a bowl and mix together well. Season to taste with salt and pepper. *Makes 3–4 servings*

242 mango salsa
V ⊗ ⊗ ⊠

Mangoes are a great source of vitamin C, beta-carotene, and potassium.

PREPARATION
10 minutes

STORAGE
Keeps for up to 4 hours in the fridge

1 ripe mango, peeled and diced
½ small cucumber, peeled, deseeded, and diced
½ tbsp chopped fresh coriander

juice of ½ lime
hot pepper sauce to taste (optional)
pinch of salt and pepper

Mix all the ingredients together in a bowl. Allow to stand for at least 10 minutes before serving. *Makes 4–6 servings*

243   spicy tomato salsa

PREPARATION
20 minutes

STORAGE
Keeps for up to 24
hours in the fridge

1 tbsp olive oil
½ small white onion, finely chopped
½ green bell pepper, cored and finely
  chopped
1 clove garlic, peeled and
  crushed

½ tsp balsamic vinegar
7oz canned tomatoes, chopped
½ tbsp chopped fresh coriander
½ tbsp chopped fresh parsley
hot chili sauce to taste (optional)

Heat the oil in a saucepan. Add the onion and bell pepper and gently
sauté until softened. Add the garlic and vinegar and cook for a few more
seconds. Add the tomatoes, coriander, parsley, and chili sauce (if using).
Simmer uncovered for a further 15 minutes. Serve warm or cover and chill
in the fridge. *Makes 4–6 servings*

244   peach and mango salsa

PREPARATION
15 minutes

STORAGE
Keeps for up to 4
hours in the fridge

1 ripe mango, peeled
1 ripe (but firm) peach, skinned and
  diced
½ small red onion, finely chopped

4 tbsp white wine/cider vinegar
2 tbsp chopped fresh coriander
½ tsp sugar to taste

Using a sharp knife, remove the mango flesh from the stone. Chop half of it
into small dice and put to one side. Place the remaining flesh in a bowl and
use a fork to mash it to a pulp. Add all the remaining ingredients to this
bowl (including the diced mango) and mix well. Cover and chill in the fridge
before serving. *Makes 4–5 servings*

245   mint and cucumber yogurt dip

PREPARATION
5 minutes

STORAGE
Keeps for up
to 24 hours in
the fridge

⅔ cup natural bio-yogurt
2 tbsp mayonnaise
juice of ½ lime
½ cucumber, chopped

1 clove garlic, peeled and crushed
2 tsps chopped fresh mint
pinch of salt

Place the yogurt, mayonnaise, and lime juice in a bowl and whisk with a
fork. Add the cucumber, garlic, and mint, mix well, adding a pinch of salt if
necessary. Cover and leave in the fridge for at least 1 hour before serving
to allow the flavors to intensify. *Makes 4–6 servings*

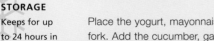

246 warm vegetable couscous

PREPARATION
20 minutes

STORAGE
Best served
immediately

½ cup couscous
¾ cup boiling water/Basic Vegetable
   Stock (recipe 252; p.151)
1 tbsp olive oil
3 scallions, sliced

1 small leek, sliced
1 green bell pepper, cored and diced
1 red bell pepper, cored and diced
½ zucchini, diced
2 sticks celery, sliced

Place the couscous in a large bowl, pour on the boiling water or stock,
and set aside to stand for 10–15 minutes, until all the liquid is absorbed.
Meanwhile, heat the oil in a skillet and add the vegetables. Stir-fry them for
10 minutes until softened. Add the couscous to the skillet and gently stir as
it warms through. Serve warm. *Makes 4–6 servings*

247 fruity couscous salad *(below)*

PREPARATION
10 minutes

STORAGE
Keeps for up to 6
hours in the fridge

½ cup couscous
¾ cup boiling water/Basic Vegetable
   Stock (recipe 252; p.151)
2 tbsp raisins
6 dried apricots, chopped

½ red bell pepper, cored and diced
2 tbsp frozen peas, defrosted
1 tsp ground allspice
2 tsp olive oil

Put the couscous in a bowl, pour on the boiling water or stock, and set
aside to stand for 5 minutes until all the liquid is absorbed. Add the raisins,
apricots, red pepper, peas, allspice and oil and mix well with a fork until
fluffy. *Makes 4–6 servings*

248 brown rice risotto

Brown rice makes a risotto with a slightly nutty flavor. It contains more fiber and B-vitamins than white rice so it is a healthier choice.

PREPARATION
30 minutes

STORAGE
Keeps for up to 6
hours in the fridge

2oz butter
1 onion, chopped
1 red bell pepper and 1 green bell
pepper, cored and chopped
2 sticks celery, sliced
1¼ cups brown rice

2 cups Basic Chicken Stock or
Basic Vegetable Stock (recipe 251;
p.151/252; p.151)
2 cups hot water
3 tbsp grated Parmesan
2 tbsp fresh chopped parsley

Melt the butter in a saucepan and add the onion. Gently sauté over a
low heat until soft and transparent. Add the red and green bell peppers,
celery, and brown rice. Stir in half the hot stock, bring to the boil, reduce
heat, and allow to simmer, gradually adding the remaining stock until all
the liquid has been absorbed by the rice and vegetables. Pour in the hot
water in the same way, a little at a time and stirring often during cooking.
This will take about 45 minutes and the risotto should be moist, soft,
and creamy. Stir in the Parmesan and fresh parsley just before serving.
Makes 6–8 servings

249 rice salad

PREPARATION
25 minutes

STORAGE
Keeps for up to 6
hours in the fridge

1 cup basmati/long
grain rice
½ red bell pepper, cored and finely
chopped
⅓ cup frozen peas, cooked
½ cup canned corn,
well drained

¼ cup currants
2 tbsp olive oil
2 tsp balsamic vinegar
1 tbsp unsweetened orange juice
½ clove garlic, crushed
3 tbsp fresh chopped chives

Cook the rice according to the instructions on the packet. Drain and
allow to cool slightly. Stir in the bell pepper, peas, corn and currants.
Mix the oil, vinegar, orange juice, and garlic in a small jug and whisk
with a fork. Pour the dressing over the rice and vegetable mixture and
stir well to combine. Sprinkle on the chives and stir through.
Makes 6–10 servings

250 tabbouleh

PREPARATION
10 minutes

STORAGE
Keep in the fridge
for up to 6 hours

½ cup couscous
⅔ cup boiling water
4 scallions, finely chopped
5 tomatoes, skinned and finely
chopped

4 tbsp chopped fresh parsley
4 tbsp chopped fresh mint
juice of 1 lemon
4 tbsp olive oil
black pepper to taste

Mix all the ingredients together in a salad bowl. Cover and stand for 1 hour
until couscous absorbs the liquids and softens. Stir well. *Makes 4–6 servings*

SOUPS

Soup is a healthy, fast-to-make, and economical food that can be made from virtually anything in any season. It is often popular with children and can be a very useful way of disguising vegetables and ensuring that more are eaten. A warm bowl of soup makes an ideal light lunch or evening meal which, with the addition of some bread and cheese, a simple sandwich, or eggy bread and a piece of fruit, will become nutritionally complete. Making your own stock is surprisingly simple and has the added advantage of letting you control salt and sugar levels as you can use less than you would find present in canned soup or even the increasingly popular fresh soups now sold in supermarkets. Most of the recipes here will freeze well so they are ideal if you want to cook soup in large batches and store for use at a later date.

251 basic chicken stock

PREPARATION
1 hour 45 minutes

1 chicken carcass from a roast chicken
4½ cups cold water
1 white onion, peeled and quartered (optional)

STORAGE
Suitable for
freezing

Place the chicken carcass in a large saucepan or flameproof casserole. Add the water, and the onion, if using (it will add a little extra flavor but the stock works equally well without it). Bring to the boil, reduce the heat and cover the saucepan/casserole with a tight-fitting lid. Allow to simmer gently for at least 1½ hours. Remove from the heat and when cool pour through a sieve to strain. Pour the stock into containers ready to store. *Makes 4½ cups*

252 basic vegetable stock

PREPARATION
45 minutes

3 sticks celery, chopped
2 large carrots, peeled and chopped
2 small onions, peeled and chopped

1 bay leaf
2–3 tbsp chopped fresh parsley
4½ cups cold water

STORAGE
Suitable for
freezing

Place the prepared vegetables in a large saucepan, add the herbs and the water. Bring to the boil, reduce the heat and cover with a tight-fitting lid. Allow to simmer gently for 20–25 minutes. Remove from the heat, allow to cool and then strain through a sieve, discarding the vegetables. Pour the stock into containers ready to store. *Makes 4½ cups*

253 butternut squash soup

This warming and nutritious soup is packed with antioxidants, as well as providing some protein, iron, and calcium.

PREPARATION
55 minutes

1 white onion, peeled and chopped
2 tbsp olive oil
½ tsp garam masala
4 large carrots, peeled and sliced
1 potato, peeled and chopped
1 sweet potato, peeled and chopped
1 butternut squash, peeled,

deseeded, and chopped
4½ cups vegetable stock
   (see Basic Vegetable Stock, above)
4 tbsp red lentils
1 tbsp tahini
pinch of salt and pepper

STORAGE
Suitable for
freezing

In a large saucepan sauté the onion in the oil until softened, add the garam masala and cook for a few seconds then add all the remaining vegetables followed by the stock. Stir well and then add the lentils. Bring to the boil stirring continuously to prevent sticking, then reduce the heat and allow to simmer gently for 30 minutes until all the vegetables are soft. Remove from the heat and blend in a liquidizer until smooth, adding a little water if too thick. Stir in the tahini and season to taste with salt and pepper. Serve with fresh crusty bread. *Makes 6–8 servings*

254 mushroom soup

PREPARATION
50 minutes

STORAGE
Suitable for
freezing

1 white onion, peeled and chopped
2 tbsp olive oil
1 medium potato, peeled and
  chopped
2¼ cups mushrooms, washed and
  sliced

1¼ cups Basic Vegetable Stock
  (recipe 252; p.151)
1¼ cups milk
pinch of nutmeg
⅛ cup white rice
1–2 tbsp chopped fresh parsley

In a large saucepan sauté the onion in the oil until soft. Add the potato and
the mushrooms followed by the stock, milk, nutmeg, and rice. Bring to the
boil and then reduce the heat and allow to simmer for about 20 minutes
until the vegetables and rice are soft. Remove from the heat and blend in
a liquidizer until smooth, adding a little extra milk if too thick. Pour into
serving bowls and sprinkle with chopped parsley. *Makes 4–6 servings*

255 creamy leek and potato soup

PREPARATION
40–50 minutes

STORAGE
Suitable for
freezing; keeps
for up to 24 hours
in the fridge

1oz butter
1 tbsp olive oil
4 large leeks, washed and sliced
2 medium potatoes, peeled and
  chopped

1 white onion, peeled and chopped
2¼ cups Basic Vegetable Stock
  (recipe 252; p.151)
2 cups milk
salt and pepper to taste

In a large saucepan melt the butter with the oil. Add the leeks, potato and
onion, stir well to coat in the butter and oil mixture. Cover with a lid and
allow to sweat over a low heat until all the vegetables are softened. Add the
stock and milk and bring to the boil. Reduce the heat, recover and allow to
simmer for 20–25 minutes until the vegetables are fully cooked and soft.
Blend in a liquidizer, season to taste and serve with croutons or fresh
bread. *Makes 6–8 servings*

256 speedy lentil soup

PREPARATION
40 minutes

STORAGE
Suitable for
freezing

1 white onion, finely chopped
1 tbsp olive oil
1 cup red lentils
3½ cups Basic Vegetable Stock
  (recipe 252; p.151)
1 carrot, peeled and chopped finely

1 stick celery, chopped finely
juice of a lemon
black pepper to taste
½ tsp ground ginger
4 tbsp natural bio-yogurt (optional)

In a large saucepan, gently sauté the onion with the olive oil. Add the
lentils, vegetable stock, carrot, and celery and bring to the boil. Reduce the
heat and allow to simmer for 20 minutes or until the lentils and vegetables
are tender. Add the lemon juice, pepper, and ginger and simmer for a
further 5 minutes. Either leave as is or blend in a liquidizer until smooth.
Pour into serving bowls, add a spoonful of natural bio-yogurt, if desired,
and serve with crusty bread. *Makes 4–6 servings*

257 spicy carrot, lentil, and coriander soup

V 🍤 🌾 🥚

This thick soup is a good source of antioxidants, protein, and iron and an excellent choice for vegetarian children.

PREPARATION
50 minutes

STORAGE
Suitable for freezing

1 medium onion, sliced
1 clove garlic, peeled and crushed
1 tbsp olive oil
1 medium carrot, peeled and sliced
5 tbsp red lentils
2 cups Basic Vegetable Stock

(recipe 252; p.151)
1 tsp ground cumin
1 tsp ground coriander
black pepper to taste
1 tbsp chopped fresh coriander
4 tbsp natural bio-yogurt (optional)

In a large saucepan sauté the onion and garlic in the olive oil until the onion is transparent and soft. Add the carrots and red lentils and stir for a few minutes. Pour in the vegetable stock and add the cumin, coriander, and a little black pepper to taste. Bring to the boil then reduce the heat and allow to simmer for 20 minutes or until the vegetables are cooked through and soft. Blend until smooth in a liquidizer. Add the fresh coriander, stir, and pour into serving bowls. Garnish with a spoonful of natural bio-yogurt, if desired. *Makes 2–4 servings*

258 minestrone

V

This hearty Italian bean and pasta soup is a meal in itself. Involve your children by letting them choose the pasta shapes.

PREPARATION
55 minutes

STORAGE
Suitable for freezing

3 tbsp olive oil
1 white onion, finely chopped
1 stick celery, chopped
1 large carrot, peeled and chopped
14oz passata or canned chopped
   tomatoes
9 cups Basic Vegetable Stock
   (recipe 252; p.151)

1 bay leaf
6oz any small pasta shapes
14oz navy beans, precooked
black pepper to taste
8oz fresh spinach, chopped
⅓ cup Parmesan cheese, finely
   grated

In a large pan heat the olive oil. Add the onion, celery, and carrot and gently sauté for about 10 minutes until the vegetables have softened. Add the passata/chopped tomatoes, stock, and bay leaf and bring to the boil. Reduce the heat and allow to simmer for 15 minutes. Add the pasta shapes and navy beans and continue to simmer, stirring occasionally until the pasta is cooked. Add a little black pepper and the prepared spinach and cook for a few minutes, just until the spinach is tender. Pour into serving bowls and sprinkle with the Parmesan cheese. *Makes 4–6 servings*

259 gazpacho *(above)*

Ⓥ 🔥 ❌ 🚫 O

This traditional chilled Spanish soup is packed full of antioxidants.

PREPARATION
1 hour 30 minutes

STORAGE
Suitable for
freezing but add
garnish before
serving

6 medium tomatoes, skinned,
   quartered and deseeded
1 small red onion, peeled and
   quartered
1 clove garlic, peeled and chopped
1 red bell pepper, deseeded and
   chopped
1 small cucumber, ½ roughly
   chopped, ½ diced
1 tbsp cider vinegar

14oz passata or canned chopped
   tomatoes
salt and pepper to taste
dash of Tabasco sauce (optional)
1 egg, hardboiled, shelled, and
   chopped
1 tbsp chopped fresh flat-leaf
   parsley
croutons (recipe 260; p.155)

Place the tomatoes, onion, garlic, red bell pepper, chopped cucumber (put
the diced to one side), cider vinegar, and passata/canned tomatoes in a
liquidizer and blend until smooth. Pour into a large jug or bowl and add
the reserved cucumber. Season to taste with salt and pepper and Tabasco
sauce (if using) and stir. Cover and place in the fridge for at least 1 hour
before serving (to allow the flavors to develop fully). Place a little crushed
ice in serving bowls before pouring or ladling in the soup. Sprinkle with the
chopped hardboiled egg, a little parsley, and some homemade croutons.
Makes 6–8 servings

260 croutons

PREPARATION
15–20 minutes

2 tbsp olive oil
2 thick slices stale white bread, diced

STORAGE
Will keep in an
airtight container
for several days

Preheat the oven to 180°C/350°F/gas mark 4. Pour the olive oil into a bowl and add the diced bread, tossing it in the oil until each piece is well coated. Next tip the bread pieces onto a baking pan and spread them out evenly. Bake in the preheated oven for about 10–15 minutes, until crisp and golden. Remove from the oven and allow to cool before serving.
Makes 4–6 servings

261 cheesy ciabatta croutons

PREPARATION
15–20 minutes

2 tbsp olive oil
4 thick slices ciabatta bread, diced
1 tbsp finely grated Parmesan

STORAGE
Will keep in an
airtight container
for several days

Preheat the oven to 180°C/350°F/gas mark 4. Pour the olive oil into a bowl and add the diced bread, tossing it in the oil until each piece is well coated. Add the grated Parmesan and mix well to ensure all the croutons are covered with a thin layer of cheese. Tip the bread pieces onto a baking pan and spread them out evenly. Bake in the oven for about 10–15 minutes, until crisp and golden. Remove from the oven and allow to cool before serving. *Makes 4–6 servings*

262 tomato and bacon soup

This is so easy to make and a delicious alternative to traditional tomato soup. Leave out the bacon for vegetarians.

PREPARATION
45 minutes

STORAGE
Suitable for
freezing

4 slices lean back bacon, chopped in
  small pieces
1 tbsp olive oil
1 white onion, peeled and chopped
2 large carrots, peeled and chopped
1 medium potato, peeled and chopped

1 stick celery, chopped
14oz canned chopped tomatoes
⅔ cup water
1 bay leaf
⅔ cup milk

In a large pan gently sauté the bacon bits until the fat is rendered. Add the oil followed by the onions and sauté until softened. Add all the remaining vegetables, tomatoes, water, and bay leaf. Bring to the boil, reduce the heat and allow to simmer gently for 20–30 minutes, until all the vegetables are softened. Blend the soup in a liquidizer and then add the milk. Reheat if necessary before pouring into serving bowls. *Makes 4–6 servings*

263 turkey noodle soup with lemon grass and ginger

If you don't have tamari, you can use soy sauce.

PREPARATION
35 minutes

STORAGE
Suitable for freezing

4½ cups Basic Chicken Stock/Basic Vegetable Stock (recipes 251 and 252; p.151)
1 piece of lemon grass, about 1in in length
1 piece ginger root, about 1in in size, cut into 2 pieces
½ cup turkey breast, cut into small

strips
10 chestnut mushrooms, thinly sliced
3 tsp tamari/soy sauce
¾ cup rice noodles, broken into small pieces
2 scallions, thinly sliced
2 tbsp chopped fresh coriander

Place the stock, lemon grass, ginger, and turkey pieces in a large saucepan and bring to the boil. Reduce the heat and allow to simmer for 15 minutes. Add the mushrooms and tamari/soy sauce and simmer for a few minutes before adding the broken noodles. Continue to cook the soup for about 3–4 minutes, until the noodles are soft. Use a slatted spoon to lift out the lemon grass and ginger and then stir in the scallions and fresh coriander before serving. Pour into serving bowls and offer rice crackers as an accompaniment. *Makes 4–6 servings*

264 creamy chicken soup

This creamy soup is more delicious than the store-bought variety and has a much lower salt content. The chicken and milk provide protein.

PREPARATION
45 minutes

STORAGE
Suitable for freezing

1 small onion, peeled and finely chopped
3 sticks of celery, finely chopped
1 tbsp olive oil
½ tbsp butter
2 tbsp all-purpose flour
2½ cups Basic Chicken Stock (recipe 251; p.151)

½ tsp nutmeg
½ cup cooked chicken, diced
½ tsp lemon juice
½ cup milk
salt and pepper to taste
croutons (recipe 260; p.155)

In a large saucepan gently sauté the onion and celery in the olive oil and butter until softened. Stir in the flour, cook for a few minutes, then remove from the heat. Stir in the stock. Return the saucepan to the heat and bring to the boil while stirring continuously. Reduce the heat, add the nutmeg and allow to simmer gently for 10–15 minutes until the vegetables are soft. Remove from the heat and blend. Return to the saucepan, add the chicken, lemon juice, and milk, and gently reheat. Season to taste and sprinkle with croutons before serving. *Makes 4–6 servings*

265 corn chowder

This soup is a mixture of bright colors with a sweet taste that children love.

PREPARATION
55 minutes

STORAGE
Suitable for freezing

4 slices lean back bacon, cut into small strips
2 tbsp olive oil
1 small onion, peeled and chopped
1 tbsp all-purpose flour
2 cups Basic Vegetable Stock (recipe 252; p.151)

1 large potato, peeled and chopped
1 red bell pepper, deseeded and chopped
1lb corn, canned/ frozen
½ cup milk
2 scallions, sliced
1 tbsp chopped fresh coriander

In a large saucepan gently sauté the bacon bits until the fat is rendered. Add the oil followed by the onions and cook for about 5 minutes until softened. Add the flour and cook for a few minutes more, stirring continuously. Add the stock and potato and continue to cook over a low heat for 12–15 minutes. Once the potatoes are beginning to soften, add the pepper, corn, and milk. Cook for a further 5–7 minutes then add the scallions. Cook for a little longer until the onions begin to soften but do not lose their bright green colour. Pour into serving bowls and sprinkle with the coriander before serving with crusty bread. *Makes 4–6 servings*

DESSERTS

It's important not to give a dessert to your child as a reward. Instead, view including one as a further opportunity to provide valuable nutrients. Always offer a dessert as part of a meal, even if it is just a simple piece of fruit with a yogurt, or a cookie. If you know that what you are offering is healthy, you can be happy for your child to eat it. The recipes in this section are made using nutritious ingredients and all feature fruit or a fruit sauce to provide immune-boosting flavonoids. Cocoa and good-quality chocolate are also used in certain recipes, as these also contain them. A child who eats a balanced meal including a dessert is less likely to want to snack on candy later on in the day.

266 speedy frozen strawberry yogurt

Ⓥ ⓧ ⓧ ⊙

We've used strawberry here as it is a family favorite, but you can use any other soft fruit along with the same flavor of yogurt, such as raspberries.

PREPARATION
5 minutes

2 cups frozen strawberries
2 x 3½oz pots full-fat strawberry-
    flavored yogurt, chilled
1 cup natural bio-yogurt, chilled

STORAGE
Suitable for
freezing

Place the frozen strawberries in a liquidizer and add the yogurt (cold from the fridge). Blend until smooth. Spoon into dishes and serve immediately. *Makes 6–8 servings*

267 iced mango yogurt

Ⓥ ⓧ ⓧ ⊙

PREPARATION
15 minutes plus
overnight freezing

½ cup golden superfine sugar
⅓ cup water
2 large ripe mangoes
juice of 1 lemon
2 cups natural bio-yogurt

STORAGE
Suitable for
freezing

Gently heat the sugar and water in a saucepan until the sugar dissolves and forms a syrup. Leave to cool. Peel the mangoes and cut the flesh off the stone. Place the mango in a liquidizer, add the lemon juice and blend until smooth. Add the cooled syrup and yogurt and mix well. Pour the mixture into a plastic container and place in the freezer for approximately 2 hours. When it is just starting to set around the edges, remove from the freezer and whisk vigorously to thicken. Return to the freezer for a minimum of 2 hours, preferably overnight, before serving. *Makes 6–8 servings*

268 elderflower apples with yogurt

Ⓥ ⓧ ⓧ

PREPARATION
10–15 minutes

1lb eating apples, peeled, cored, and chopped
¼ cup water
2 tbsp elderflower cordial
⅔ cup natural bio-yogurt
2 tsp light brown sugar

STORAGE
Keeps for up to 2
days in the fridge

Place the apples and water in a pan and simmer gently until the apples are soft, adding a little extra water if necessary. Put the cooked apple in a bowl and mash or blend to form a purée. Add the elderflower cordial. Allow the mixture to cool. Stir in the yogurt and spoon into small individual serving dishes. Chill in the fridge for at least 30 minutes and sprinkle the top of each dish with a little light brown sugar before serving. *Makes 3–4 servings*

269   winter dried fruit salad

*A delicious blend of dried fruit lightly spiced to make a warm fruity dessert
to serve with yogurt, custard, or ice cream.*

PREPARATION
15 minutes

STORAGE
Keeps for up to 2
days in the fridge

¼ cup dried apricots
¼ cup dried prunes, pitted
½ cup dried peaches/pears
¾ cup dried apple rings
¼ cup dried banana chips
¼ cup golden raisins

1¼ cups orange juice
1 cup water
3 cloves
1in cinnamon stick
1 tsp grated orange rind

Place all the ingredients in a saucepan and bring to the boil. Reduce the
heat, cover, and allow to simmer until the fruit is tender. Remove the cloves
and cinnamon and allow to cool slightly before serving. *Makes 4–8 servings*

270   exotic fruit salad

PREPARATION
20 minutes

STORAGE
Best served
immediately

2 star anise
¼ cup superfine sugar
¼ cup unsweetened
  pineapple/orange juice
¼ cup water
½ pineapple, peeled, cored, and cut

into chunks
1 canteloupe melon, peeled, pips
  removed, and diced
1 banana, peeled and sliced
1 mango, peeled, pitted, and diced
2 kiwis, peeled and diced

Place the star anise, sugar, juice, and water in a saucepan. Bring to the boil,
reduce the heat and allow to simmer until the sugar dissolves and forms a
syrup. Remove from the heat and set aside to cool. Put the prepared fruit
into a serving bowl. Remove the star anise from the syrup and pour it over
the fruit. Serve with vanilla ice cream or yogurt. *Makes 4–6 servings*

271   apple, lychee, and clementine fruit salad

PREPARATION
5–10 minutes

STORAGE
Best served
immediately

2 sweet eating apples (preferably russett)
2 clementines
15oz lychees in syrup

Core and dice the apples and place them in a large bowl. Peel the
clementines, cut them into slices, and then quarter each slice to make
small triangles. Add to the bowl. Drain the lychees (reserve a little of the
syrup and discard the rest). Cut the lychees in half and add them to
the bowl. Mix all the fruit together, add the reserved syrup, and serve.
Makes 4–6 servings

272 Caribbean bananas (below)

This quick and easy dessert is deliciously sweet.

PREPARATION
5 minutes

STORAGE
Best served
immediately

1 tbsp sweet butter
2 ripe bananas, peeled and sliced
½ cup orange juice
1 tsp soft dark brown sugar

Gently melt the butter in a frying pan. Once it is sizzling add the banana slices and cook them for 1 minute, until slightly softened. Add the orange juice followed by the sugar. Use a wooden spoon or spatula to stir and allow them to cook for a few seconds, just until the sauce is thickened and bubbling. Serve hot with a little whipped cream or natural bio-yogurt.
Makes 2–3 servings

273 chocolate fondue with fruit

PREPARATION
10 minutes

STORAGE
Best served
immediately

3 ripe bananas, thickly sliced
30 strawberries, hulled
2 eating apples, cut into chunks
6oz good quality dark
   chocolate, broken into pieces

3oz good quality milk
   chocolate, broken into pieces
⅔ cup heavy cream
6–8 fondue forks or wooden skewers

Arrange the prepared fruit on a large platter or individual plates. Place the chocolate pieces in a glass bowl and set this over a saucepan of hot water. Gently heat the water and stir the chocolate until melted. Add the cream and stir until mixed in. Pour the chocolate sauce into a warmed dish and serve immediately as a fondue-style dip for the fruit. *Makes 6–8 servings*

274 elderflower and berry jello

PREPARATION
10 minutes plus
2–3 hours to set

STORAGE
Keeps for up to 2
days in the fridge

2½ cups water
juice of 1 lemon
1¼ cups superfine sugar
1oz leaf gelatine
⅛ cup elderflower cordial
1¼ cup mixed berries, such as

raspberries, strawberries,
   blueberries and loganberries

(Note: don't use pineapple, kiwi
or papaya as enzymes they
contain break down the gelatine)

Place the water and lemon juice in a saucepan and bring to the boil. Remove from the heat, add the sugar, and stir until dissolved. Soak the gelatine leaves in cold water until soft. Squeeze out the water, add the leaves to the sugar syrup and stir until dissolved. Next add the elderflower cordial, stir, and leave the jello mixture to cool but not set. Meanwhile wash and hull the berries and cut any large fruits into bite-size pieces. Arrange the berries in the bottom of individual jello molds (or one large one) and then pour in the jello mixture. Refrigerate until set. *Makes 3–6 servings*

275 baked strawberry soufflé

PREPARATION
5–10 minutes

STORAGE
Best served
immediately

3oz unsalted butter
4 tbsp all-purpose flour
½ cup milk
¼ cup superfine sugar

2 cups strawberries, washed
   and hulled
4 eggs, separated

Preheat the oven to 350°C/180°F/gas mark 4 and grease a large soufflé dish. Melt the butter in a saucepan and stir in the flour. Cook over a gentle heat for 2 minutes. Add the milk and stir continuously until the mixture thickens. Remove from the heat and stir in the sugar and strawberries. Beat the egg yolks until fluffy and add to the strawberry mixture. In a separate clean bowl beat the egg whites until stiff peaks form. Gently fold the egg whites into the strawberry mixture. Pour the soufflé mixture into the prepared dish and bake for 25–30 minutes. *Makes 6–8 servings*

276 apple and pear crêpes

PREPARATION
30 minutes

STORAGE
Suitable for
freezing but
best served
immediately

1¼ cups all-purpose flour
1 egg, beaten
1¼ cups milk
1 tbsp sweet butter, melted
1 eating apple, cored, and diced
1 pear, peeled, cored, and diced

12–15 dried apricots, chopped
1 tbsp soft brown sugar
4 tbsp unsweetened orange/apple juice
6 scoops vanilla ice cream
confectioner's sugar (for dusting)

Place the flour in a large bowl and make a well in the center. Add the egg and mix. Pour in the milk slowly, beating continuously. Next add the melted butter. Beat the mixture well. Allow the batter to stand for 20–30 minutes. Meanwhile, put the fruit, sugar, and juice in a small saucepan and simmer for 5 minutes until soft. To make the crêpes, pour a little batter at a time into a hot skillet. Roll the mixture around the skillet and fry, turning once, until golden brown. To serve, put some fruit compote and a scoop of ice cream on one side of the crêpe, fold and dust with confectioner's sugar. *Makes 6 servings*

277 crêpes with tropical salsa

PREPARATION
20 minutes

STORAGE
Suitable for
freezing but
best served
immediately

1¼ cups all-purpose flour
1 egg, beaten
1¼ cups milk
1 tbsp sweet butter, melted
1 ripe mango, peeled, pitted,
    and halved

½ ripe papaya, peeled, seeds
    removed, and diced
1 kiwi, peeled and diced
2 tbsp elderflower cordial
6 scoops fruit sorbet (any flavor)
confectioner's sugar for dusting

Prepare the crêpe batter following the instructions given in recipe 276. While the batter is standing, prepare the tropical salsa. Begin by mashing half the mango flesh with a fork. Dice the remaining mango and mix it with the prepared papaya and kiwi. Add the elderflower cordial and stir. Make the crêpes following the instructions given in recipe 276. To serve, put some tropical fruit salsa and a scoop of sorbet on one side of the crêpe, fold, and dust with confectioner's sugar. *Makes 6 servings*

278 rhubarb muesli crumble

PREPARATION
40–55 minutes

STORAGE
Suitable for
freezing; keeps
for up to 2 days
in the fridge

1 cup all-purpose flour
3oz sweet butter, diced
1 cup unsweetened muesli
⅓ cup soft dark brown sugar

2lb rhubarb, chopped into chunks
4 tbsp water
⅓ cup light brown sugar

Preheat the oven to 180°C/350°F/gas mark 4. Place the flour in a large bowl and rub in the butter until the mixture resembles coarse breadcrumbs. Stir in the muesli and soft dark brown sugar. Place the rhubarb in a large saucepan and add the water and light brown sugar. Heat gently until the rhubarb begins to soften. Drain off excess water and tip the rhubarb into an ovenproof dish. Sprinkle the crumble mixture on top. Bake for 30–40 minutes until the top is golden brown. Serve with custard. *Makes 4–6 servings*

279 strawberry and apple crumble

Eating apples are used in this recipe, which reduces the amount of sugar you need to add. The crumble topping can be frozen, so why not make double the amount you need and freeze the remainder for use on another day.

PREPARATION
40–55 minutes

STORAGE
Suitable for freezing; keeps for up to 2 days in the fridge

1½ cups all-purpose flour
⅔ cup rolled oats
3oz butter, cut into small cubes
⅓ cup soft dark brown sugar

3 eating apples, peeled and sliced
4 tbsp water
3 cups strawberries, hulled and halved

Preheat the oven to 180°C/350°F/gas mark 4. Put the flour and oats in a large bowl and rub in the butter until the mixture resembles coarse crumbs. Stir in the sugar. Place the apple slices in an ovenproof dish and add 4 tablespoons of water. Cover and cook in the oven for approximately 10 minutes or until the apple is just beginning to soften. Remove from the oven and allow to cool slightly before adding the prepared strawberries. Sprinkle the crumble mixture over the top. Bake for 30–40 minutes until the top is golden brown. Serve with strawberry ice cream or custard.
Makes 4–6 servings

280 plum and almond crumble

PREPARATION
40–55 minutes

STORAGE
Suitable for freezing; keeps for up to 2 days in the fridge

16–18 plums, halved and pitted
1 cup self-rising flour
3oz sweet butter, diced
⅓ cup soft dark brown sugar
½ cup ground almonds

Preheat the oven to 190°C/375°F/gas mark 5. Place the prepared plums in an ovenproof dish. Add just enough water to cover the bottom of the dish. Cover and cook in the oven for 10–15 minutes until the plums are just beginning to soften. Meanwhile, make the crumble. Place the flour in a large bowl and rub in the butter until the mixture resembles coarse crumbs. Stir in the sugar and ground almonds. When the plums are ready, remove them from the oven and allow to cool slightly. Sprinkle the almond crumble mixture over the top of the plums. Bake for 30–40 minutes until the top is golden brown. Serve with vanilla ice cream or custard. *Makes 4–6 servings*

281 steamed fruit dessert
V O

This is a lovely light fruit dessert that is a good alternative to Christmas pudding, which young children often find too rich. You may use chopped dried apricots and dates instread of golden raisins and currants.

PREPARATION
2 hours 15 minutes

STORAGE
Suitable for freezing; keeps for up to 2 days in the fridge; steam for 30–40 minutes to reheat

3 cups fresh breadcrumbs
½ cup soft brown sugar
1 tsp baking powder
½ cup golden raisins
½ cup currants
2 eating apples, peeled and grated
grated rind of ½ lemon

4oz vegetable suet/hard margarine, diced
2 tbsp light corn syrup
1 egg, beaten
4 tbsp milk
1 tsp mixed spice

Grease a 2¼ pint dessert bowl with a little butter. In a large bowl mix together the breadcrumbs, sugar, and baking powder and then stir in the golden raisins, currants, apple, lemon rind, vegetable suet/margarine, and syrup. Combine the egg and milk, pour into the bowl, and mix everything together well. Spoon the mixture into the prepared bowl and cover with foil or waxed paper and secure tightly with string. Steam the dessert for 2 hours before serving hot with cream or custard. *Makes 6–8 servings*

282 lemon self-saucing dessert
V O

This clever baked dessert forms its own deliciously lemony sauce underneath a light sponge while it is cooking. The fresh lemon juice in the dessert also provides a good source of vitamin C.

PREPARATION
1 hour 10 minutes

STORAGE
Keeps for up to 2 days in the fridge

3 eggs, separated
1 cup white sugar
2 tbsp flour

1¼ cups milk
grated rind and juice of 2 lemons
1 tbsp shredded coconut (optional)

Preheat the oven to 180°C/350°C/gas mark 4. Place the egg yolks and ⅔ cup sugar in a large bowl and beat until light and fluffy. Add the flour, milk, lemon rind, and juice and beat vigorously. In a separate, clean bowl whisk the egg whites until they form stiff peaks. Add the remaining sugar and coconut (if using) while whisking. Gently fold the egg whites into the lemon mixture. Pour into an oven-proof dish and bake for 1 hour. Serve warm with cream or natural bio-yogurt. *Makes 6–8 servings*

283 orange almond dessert

V ✗ ✗ O 🥄

The almonds and eggs make this a high-protein dessert and a good source of iron for vegetarians.

PREPARATION
1 hour 20 minutes

STORAGE
Suitable for freezing; keeps for up to 2 days in the fridge or an airtight container

3 medium oranges, washed
8oz sweet butter, softened
6 medium eggs, separated
1 cup superfine sugar

2½ cups ground almonds
1 tbsp baking powder
confectioner's sugar to dust

Preheat the oven to 200°C/400°F/gas mark 6. Place whole oranges in a saucepan and cover with water. Bring to the boil and simmer for one hour. Drain and cool. Meanwhile grease a 9in cake pan and line the base with foil. Cut the cooled oranges into quarters and remove all the pips. Place them in a food processor and add the butter and egg yolks, and purée until smooth. Pour into a large bowl and mix in the sugar, ground almonds, and baking powder. Whisk the egg whites until soft peaks form and then fold into the mixture. Pour into the cake pan and place in the preheated oven to bake for 10 minutes. Then reduce the oven temperature to 160°C/325°F/gas mark 3 and continue baking for a further 50 minutes, or until the cake pulls away from the sides of the pan. Take out of the oven and leave to stand for 10 minutes. Tip out of the pan and cool on a wire rack. Sprinkle with confectioner's sugar before serving. *Makes 10–12 servings*

284 apple sponge dessert

V O

You can use almost any fruit in this dessert. For speed use diced, canned fruit, well drained, and just make the sponge topping.

PREPARATION
55 minutes

STORAGE
Suitable for freezing; keeps for up to 2 days in the fridge

3 medium cooking apples, peeled,
  cored, and chopped
2 tbsp white sugar
2 tbsp water
5oz butter

½ cup sugar
2 eggs
6oz self-rising flour
1 tsp baking powder
2 tsp vanilla essence

Preheat the oven to 180°C/350°F/gas mark 3. Place the apples, and the 2 tablespoonfuls of sugar and water in a saucepan. Bring to the boil and simmer gently for about 5–7 minutes until soft. Put into an ovenproof soufflé dish and allow to cool while mixing the sponge topping. Mix the butter and sugar until light and fluffy. Add the eggs and beat well. Next add the flour, baking powder, vanilla essence, and 2 tablespoons water and mix. Spoon the mixture over the fruit, making sure it is all covered. Bake for about 45 minutes. Serve with custard, yogurt or cream. *Makes 8–10 servings*

285 rice and golden raisin pudding

This pudding requires long, slow cooking to be at its best. It is rich in both calcium and protein.

PREPARATION
2 hours 5 minutes

⅛ cup short grain white rice
¼ cup light soft brown sugar
4 tbsp golden raisins

2½ cups milk
2 tsp butter
½ tsp ground nutmeg

STORAGE
Keeps for up to 2 days in the fridge

Preheat the oven to 150°C/300°F/gas mark 2. Put the rice, sugar and golden raisins in an ovenproof dish. Stir in the milk and float the butter on top. Sprinkle with the nutmeg and cook for 2 hours until the rice is tender and the top golden. *Makes 4–6 servings*

286 brioche pudding

PREPARATION
1 hour 10 minutes

½ cup golden raisins
2 tbsp unsweetened orange juice
12 thin slices of brioche
3 eggs

2 tbsp superfine sugar
2 cups milk
1 tsp vanilla extract

STORAGE
Keeps for up to 2 days in the fridge

Preheat the oven to 170°C/325°F/gas mark 3. Place the golden raisins and orange juice in a small bowl and leave to soak for at least half an hour. Layer the brioche slices in an ovenproof dish, sprinkling the golden raisins in between the layers. Beat the eggs and sugar together and then stir in the milk and vanilla extract. Pour this mixture over the brioche slices and bake for 1 hour until the top is crisp and golden. *Makes 6–8 servings*

287 upside down ginger and pear cake

PREPARATION
15 minutes

1 tbsp butter
1 tbsp soft brown sugar
1 tsp ground ginger
2 pears, peeled and sliced thickly
1½ cups self-rising flour

¾ cup superfine sugar
1 tsp ground ginger
2 tbsp milk
3oz soft butter/margarine
3 eggs

STORAGE
Keeps for up to 2 days in the fridge

Preheat the oven to 190°C/375°C/gas mark 5. Melt a tablespoonful of butter in the bottom of a 8in cake pan by putting the cake pan in the oven while it warms up. Mix together the brown sugar and the teaspoonful of ground ginger and sprinkle into the melted butter. Now place the pear slices in the butter mixture so that they cover the bottom of the pan. Mix the remainder of the ingredients in a food processor and process until they are well mixed. Pour over the pears and bake for about 30 minutes until golden brown and the cake springs back when touched. Allow to cool a few minutes in the pan and then put a plate over the pan and invert. Serve with natural bio-yogurt, cream, ice cream, or custard. *Makes 8–12 servings*

288 baked cheesecake *(below)*

V O

The eggs and cream cheese make this a high protein dessert. It is delicious served with a fruit coulis or fresh berries.

PREPARATION
45 minutes

STORAGE
Suitable for
freezing; keeps
for up to 2 days
in the fridge

1½ cups butter, melted
1½ cups sweet wheat cookies, crumbed
1lb cream cheese
2 eggs
1 cup superfine sugar
1 tsp vanilla extract

Preheat the oven to 180°C/350°F/gas mark 4. Put the butter in a bowl and melt it in the microwave. Add in the crumbed cookies and mix well. Press into the base of a 9in ovenproof flan dish. Now beat together the cream cheese, eggs, sugar, and vanilla extract and pour the mixture into the prepared cookie base. Bake for 30 minutes or until the top just begins to crack open. Serve with Red Berry Coulis (opposite page).
Makes 8–10 servings

289 moist chocolate cake

PREPARATION
50 minutes

STORAGE
Cake without topping suitable for freezing; keeps for up to 2 days in an airtight container

5oz plain chocolate
3oz butter
1¼ cups milk
1¼ cups all-purpose flour
⅓ cup superfine sugar
2 tsp baking powder
1 tsp baking soda
1 egg
1 tsp vanilla extract

Topping: (optional)
1oz sweet butter
3 tbsp superfine sugar
5 tbsp confectioner's sugar
½ cup cocoa
2 tbsp milk

Preheat the oven to 180°C/350°F/gas mark 4 and grease a 9in cake pan. Melt the chocolate and butter together in a large bowl (either in a bowl over a pan of hot water or in the microwave) and add the milk. Stir and put aside to cool slightly. Place the flour, sugar, baking powder and baking soda in a large bowl. Add the melted butter, chocolate, and milk mixture and beat well. Next, add the egg and vanilla extract and again beat well. Pour the cake mixture into the greased pan and bake for 35 minutes. Cool on a wire rack. Blend together all the ingredients for the topping and spread over the cake when cool. Serve with fresh strawberries. *Makes 10–12 servings*

290 red berry coulis

PREPARATION
10 minutes

STORAGE
Suitable for freezing; keeps for up to 2 days in the fridge

2 cups fresh strawberries
2 cups fresh raspberries
1 tbsp confectioner's sugar

Wash, hull and slice the strawberries and wash the raspberries. Put the prepared fruit into a liquidizer jug or food processor bowl with the confectioner's sugar and blend until smooth. If you would like a very fine coulis, push through a sieve to remove any seeds. *Makes 6–8 servings*

291 mini apple and pear strudels

PREPARATION
40–45 minutes

STORAGE
Suitable for freezing; keeps for up to 2 days in the fridge

1 sweet eating apple, grated
1 pear, peeled and sliced
½ tsp ground cinnamon
1 tsp light brown sugar

6 sheets filo pastry
2 tbsp fresh breadcrumbs
1oz butter, melted
confectioner's sugar (for dusting)

Preheat the oven to 190°C/375°F/gas mark 5. Mix the apple, pear, sugar, and cinnamon in a bowl. Place a sheet of filo on a board. Brush with melted butter and lay another sheet on top. Brush this with melted butter. Add a third sheet and brush with butter. Sprinkle half the breadcrumbs onto this and spoon half the fruit mixture onto the bottom third of the square of filo. Fold in the sides and roll it up into a sausage, and brush with melted butter. Repeat this process to create a second strudel. Place them on a lightly greased cookie sheet and bake in oven for 30–35 minutes until golden and crisp. Allow to cool slightly before dusting with confectioner's sugar, slicing and serving with vanilla ice cream. *Makes 4–6 servings*

292 apple and raisin strudel

PREPARATION
50 minutes

STORAGE
Suitable for
freezing; keeps
for up to 2 days
in the fridge

1 large cooking apple, peeled and
diced
2 tbsp light brown sugar
½ tsp mixed spice
1 tsp cinnamon
juice of ½ lemon

2 tbsp raisins
9 sheets filo pastry
2oz melted butter
3 tbsp wholewheat breadcrumbs
confectioner's sugar (for dusting)

Preheat the oven to 190°C/375°F/gas mark 5. Mix the apple, sugar, mixed
spice, cinnamon, lemon juice, and raisins together in a bowl. Place 3 sheets
of filo, long sides together and overlapping, on a board. Brush with melted
butter and then lay another 3 sheets of filo on top and brush with more
butter. Repeat this process for the final layer. Sprinkle the breadcrumbs on
top. Spoon the fruit onto the bottom third of the rectangle of filo. Fold in
the sides and roll up into a sausage. Place on a lightly greased cookie
sheet. Brush with melted butter. Bake in the oven for 30–35 minutes until
the pastry is golden and crisp. Leave to cool slightly before dusting with
confectioner's sugar and serving with vanilla ice cream. *Makes 6–8 servings*

293 sweet couscous with raisins and yogurt

PREPARATION
10 minutes

STORAGE
Best served
immediately

¾ cup couscous
4 tbsp raisins, soaked in hot water
for 20 minutes and then drained
1¼ cup milk

½ tsp cinnamon
¼ cup superfine sugar
4 tbsp natural bio-yogurt

Put the couscous and raisins in a bowl. Put the milk, cinnamon, and sugar
in a saucepan and bring to the boil. Stir to dissolve the sugar. Pour over the
couscous and raisins. Mix well, cover with plastic wrap and leave for about
10 minutes. Mix in the yogurt just before serving. *Makes 4–6 servings*

294 crispy fruit fritters

PREPARATION
15 minutes

STORAGE
Suitable for
freezing but
best served
immediately

½ cup all-purpose flour
½ tbsp oil
3 tbsp milk
2 tbsp water
1 egg

vegetable oil (for deep frying)
1 apple, cored, and sliced
1 small banana, sliced lengthways
confectioner's sugar (for dusting)

Put the flour, oil, milk, and water in a bowl and mix well together. Add the
egg and beat. Heat the oil for deep frying until it begins to smoke. Dip the
apple or banana slices in the batter, allow the excess to drip off then lower
into the oil. Fry until brown and crisp, removing with a slotted spoon. Drain
on paper towels. Dust with confectioner's sugar and serve when cool
enough to hold. The fruit inside will remain hotter than the batter so be
careful with young children. *Makes about 12 fritters*

295 quick strawberry mousse *(below)*

PREPARATION
10–15 minutes plus
1–2 hours to set

STORAGE
Keeps for up to 2
days in the fridge

1 strawberry jello
⅔ cup natural bio-yogurt
1½ cups frozen strawberries, defrosted
4–6 fresh strawberries, to decorate

Make up the jello according to the instructions on the packet but using only half the amount of water. Allow to partially but not fully set. Using an electric whisk beat until it forms a foamy mixture approximately double in size with lots of bubbles. Add the yogurt and strawberries (reserving a few for decoration). Continue to whisk until everything is well blended. Pour into glasses and return the mixture to the fridge and allow to set. Decorate with a little whipped cream and strawberries. *Makes 4–6 servings*

DRINKS

Children need 6–8 drinks per day, and more in hot weather. The best drinks to have in between meals are water and milk. Avoid fizzy drinks and squashes, which are loaded with sugar and low in nutrients. Dilute fruit juices with water to reduce their acidity to prevent damaging your child's tooth enamel.

The juice drinks included here are a great way of introducing fruit- and vegetable-based drinks to those who are unfamiliar with the taste. All of the drinks boast immune-boosting flavonoids, and the fruit smoothies retain all of their fruit's fiber. The flavored milk shakes and smoothies are an excellent way of giving milk to reluctant milk drinkers. They make delicious substitutes for desserts, and are ideal for giving your children energy in hot weather when they are not very hungry.

296 raspberry mango smoothie

PREPARATION
10 minutes

½ cup fresh raspberries, plus a few for decoration
½ ripe mango, peeled and cut into pieces
1 scoop vanilla ice cream
2–3 tbsp milk

STORAGE
Serve immediately

Put the ingredients into a food processor or blender and process until smooth. Pour into glasses, place a raspberry on top of each one for decoration, and serve. *Makes 2–3 servings*

297 peach smoothie

PREPARATION
10 minutes

3 fresh peaches, halved and pitted
2 small bananas, peeled and sliced
½ cup apple juice

STORAGE
Serve immediately

Put the prepared fruit and apple juice into a food processor or blender and process until smooth. Pour into glasses and serve with ice if desired. *Makes 2–3 servings*

298 frozen strawberry fruit shake

PREPARATION
5 minutes

¼ cup fresh strawberries, hulled
1 ripe banana, peeled and sliced
¾ cup pineapple juice
1 tsp runny honey

STORAGE
Serve immediately

3 ice cubes

Put the prepared fruit, pineapple juice, honey, and ice cubes into a food processor or blender and process until smooth. Pour into glasses and serve. *Makes 2–3 servings*

299 tropical fruit smoothie

PREPARATION
10 minutes

2 ripe mangoes, peeled and cut into pieces
¼ fresh pineapple, peeled and roughly chopped
2 passion fruit, peeled
½ cup pineapple juice

STORAGE
Serve immediately

Put the prepared fruit and pineapple juice into a food processor or blender and process until smooth. Pour into glasses and serve with ice if desired. *Makes 2–3 servings*

300 frozen blueberry smoothie

V ⊗ ⊗ ⊗

Blueberries are a popular choice with children as they have no pips and are naturally sweet when eaten raw (as in this recipe). They are also a good source of vitamin C.

PREPARATION
5 minutes

STORAGE
Serve immediately

1 cup fresh blueberries, plus a few for decoration
1 small banana, peeled and sliced
½ cup apple juice
4 tbsp crushed ice

Put the blueberries, banana, apple juice, and ice into a food processor or blender and process until smooth and foaming. Pour into small tumblers, place a couple of whole blueberries on top of each one for decoration, and serve. *Makes 2–3 servings*

301 very berry shake

Ⓥ ⓧ ⓧ ⓪

This recipe can be made using any combination of soft fruits.

PREPARATION
5 minutes

STORAGE
Serve immediately

8 fresh strawberries, hulled
4 tbsp fresh raspberries
4 tbsp fresh blueberries
⅔ cup strawberry fromage frais
1 scoop vanilla ice cream
½ cup semi-skimmed milk

Put the ingredients into a food processor or blender and process until smooth and foaming. Add more milk if a thinner shake is required. Pour into tall glasses, add drinking straws, and serve. *Makes 2–3 servings*

302 banana and honey milk shake

Ⓥ ⓧ ⓧ ⓪

PREPARATION
5 minutes

STORAGE
Serve immediately

1 medium banana, peeled and
  sliced
⅔ cup natural bio-yogurt
1 tbsp honey

½ cup milk
drinking chocolate for dusting
  (optional)

Put the banana, yogurt, honey, and milk into a food processor or blender and process until smooth. Pour into 2 tall glasses, sprinkle with a little drinking chocolate if desired, and serve. *Makes 2 servings*

303 tropical fruit yogurt drink

Ⓥ ⓧ ⓧ

Almost any blend of fruit and yogurt makes a delicious, nutritional snack.

PREPARATION
10 minutes

STORAGE
Serve immediately

1 ripe mango, peeled and cut into pieces
1 banana, peeled and sliced
5 tbsp natural bio-yogurt
⅔ cup orange juice

Put the mango, banana, yogurt, and orange juice into a food processor or blender and process until smooth. Pour into glasses, add drinking straws, and serve. *Makes 2–3 servings*

304   melon and grape juice drink

V 🏃 🏃 🍽

Melon and grapes are both high in antioxidants.

PREPARATION
5 minutes

½ ripe canteloupe/honeydew melon
½ cup pure unsweetened grape juice
4 ice cubes

STORAGE
Serve immediately

Remove the seeds and scoop the flesh out of the melon. Put the melon flesh into a food processer or blender with the grape juice and ice, and process until smooth. Pour into glasses and serve. *Makes 2–3 servings*

305   carrot and apple juice

V 🏃 🏃 🍽

If you have a juicer, try juicing blends of fruit and vegetables to create fresh tasting drinks that are packed with vitamins, minerals, and flavonoids. Most children enjoy straight carrot or apple juice so they will probably love this sweet combination of the two.

PREPARATION
10 minutes

3 medium carrots, peeled and topped
2 eating apples, peeled and cored

STORAGE
Serve immediately

Cut the carrots and apples into chunks. Put the chunks into a juicer and extract the juice. Pour into glasses and serve with ice if desired. *Makes 2–4 servings*

306   celery and grape juice

V 🏃 🏃 🍽

PREPARATION
10 minutes

2 sticks celery, washed
small bunch of white/red seedless
    grapes, washed and destalked

STORAGE
Serve immediately

Cut the celery into chunks. Put the grapes and celery in a juicer and extract the juice. Pour into glasses and serve. *Makes 2–3 servings*

307 carrot and bell pepper juice
V 🔪 ✂ 🍶

PREPARATION
10 minutes

3 carrots, peeled and topped
1 red bell pepper, washed
1 orange/yellow bell pepper, washed

STORAGE
Serve immediately

Cut the carrots and bell peppers into chunks. Put the chunks into a juicer and extract the juice. Pour into glasses and serve. *Makes 2–4 servings*

308 cucumber and pear juice
V 🔪 ✂ 🍶

PREPARATION
10 minutes

1 cucumber, washed
2 pears, peeled and cored
4 sprigs fresh mint, washed (optional)

STORAGE
Serve immediately

Chop the cucumber and pears into chunks and put them in a juicer with the mint. Extract the juice. Pour into glasses and serve. *Makes 2–4 servings*

309 tropical pear juice
V 🔪 ✂ 🍶

PREPARATION
10 minutes

3 pears, peeled, cored
¼ pineapple, peeled
juice of ½ a lime

STORAGE
Serve immediately

Chop up the pears and pineapple and put the pieces in a juicer with the lime juice. Extract the juice. Pour into glasses and serve. *Makes 2–4 servings*

310 mulled apple juice
V 🔪 ✂ 🍶

This is a great drink to serve on cold afternoons, particularly around Christmas time.

PREPARATION
15 minutes

2 cups unsweetened apple juice
½ cup water
1 cinnamon stick
1 clove
rind from ½ orange, cut into large strips

STORAGE
Serve immediately

Put the ingredients into a saucepan. Bring to the boil, then reduce the heat and allow to simmer for 10 minutes. Strain the liquid through a sieve. Allow to cool slightly, then pour into cups and serve. *Makes 4–5 servings*

SNACKS

Snacks provide children with important boosts of energy and are another good opportunity to give them more nutrients. Many children need to eat three small meals each day, supplemented by one or two small snacks rather than just three large meals. Most children are ready for a snack at the end of the school day, which bridges the hunger gap until dinner.

The snacks in this section all provide essential immune-boosting nutrients as well as energy. The fruit kebabs and vegetable platter are fun ways to encourage children to eat more of these foods; the recipes containing dried fruit provide iron; and our pitta bread and tortilla chips are lower in salt and much lower in fat than their commercial equivalents.

311 fruit and cereal snack bag

For convenience, why not make up several bags of these in advance?

PREPARATION
5 minutes

10 frosted wheat cereal mini-squares
10 rounds of dried banana chips
1 tbsp raisins

STORAGE
Keeps for 4 days in
an airtight container

Mix all the ingredients together in a small bag. Seal to retain freshness.
Makes 1–2 servings

312 tropical fruit snack bag

PREPARATION
5–10 minutes

4 strips (about 2in long) dried mango
1 tbsp dried raw coconut chips
2 tbsp dried pineapple pieces
10 rounds dried banana chips

STORAGE
Keeps for up to 4
days in an airtight
container

Cut each mango strip into 4–6 smaller pieces. Mix all the ingredients
together in a small bag. Seal to retain freshness. *Makes 1–2 servings*

313 apple, apricot, and raisin snack bag

PREPARATION
5 minutes

2 dried apple rings
3 small dried apricots
1 tbsp large raisins

STORAGE
Keeps for up to 4
days in an airtight
container

Cut the apple rings into quarters and the apricots into 6 small pieces.
Mix all ingredients together in a bag. Seal to retain freshness.
Makes 1–2 servings

314 bugs on a log

This nutritious snack is a great way to help your child get their "5-a-day".

PREPARATION
5–10 minutes

2 sticks of celery
1–2 tbsp cream cheese
1 tbsp dried cranberries

STORAGE
Best made just
before serving

Peel off any stringy bits from the back of the celery. Fill the hollows with
the cream cheese. Cut into pieces about 2in long. Dot the cream cheese
with the dried cranberries to resemble little creatures sitting on top of the
celery "log". *Makes 2–4 servings*

315 ants on a log

PREPARATION
5–10 minutes

2 sticks of celery
1–2 tbsp smooth pure peanut butter
1 tbsp raisins/currants

STORAGE
Best made just
before serving

Peel off any stringy bits from the back of the celery. Fill the hollows with the peanut butter. Cut into pieces about 2in long. Dot the peanut butter with the raisins/currants to resemble little creatures sitting on top of the celery "log". *Makes 2–4 servings*

316 peanut butter and apple rings

PREPARATION
5 minutes

1 red eating apple
2 tbsp smooth pure peanut butter

STORAGE
Best made just
before serving

Core the apple and cut into 4 rings. Spread the peanut butter on one side of the apple rings and serve immediately. *Makes 2 servings*

317 fruit kebabs

PREPARATION
10 minutes

2 thin plastic straws
8 small cubes of melon

4 medium strawberries, hulled
4 cherries, pitted

STORAGE
Best made just
before serving

Cut the bendy end off the straws and then cut them in half. Thread the fruit onto the straws, starting with melon and alternating with the red fruits. Serve on their own or with a fruit yogurt dip. *Makes 2 servings*

318 fruit and yogurt bars

PREPARATION
45 minutes

3oz butter
2 heaped tbsp runny honey
½ tsp baking soda
2 cups oats
½ cup sunflower seeds, finely

chopped
1 cup dried apricots, chopped
1 cup dates, finely chopped
4 tbsp natural bio-yogurt

STORAGE
Keeps for up
to 4 days in the
fridge or in an
airtight container

Preheat the oven to 170°C/325°F/gas mark 3. Lightly grease a square baking pan. In a small saucepan melt the butter and honey together. Transfer into a bowl and mix in the baking soda. Add the rest of the ingredients and stir well to mix. Spoon into the pan and level out. Bake for 15–20 minutes until light golden. Mark into bars, then leave to cool. Cut through when cool and lift out. Wrap the bars in plastic wrap to store. *Makes 20 bars*

319 baklava bars

Using ground as well as finely-chopped nuts in these mouth-watering high-protein snacks makes them easier for younger children to eat.

PREPARATION
1 hour 15 minutes–
1 hour 45 minutes

STORAGE
Keep for up to
1 week in an
airtight container

6oz butter, melted
12 sheets filo pastry
1 cup ground hazelnuts
1 cup finely chopped walnuts

1¼ cups superfine sugar
2 tsp ground cinnamon
⅔ cup water
1 tsp grated orange rind

Preheat the oven to 180°C/350°F/gas mark 4. Brush a medium-size baking dish with melted butter. Place 1 sheet of filo pastry in the dish, folding the sheet to fit, if necessary. Brush the top with melted butter. Repeat with 2 more filo sheets, brushing each with melted butter. In a bowl, mix the nuts, ¼ cup of superfine sugar and 1½ teaspoonfuls of cinnamon together. Spread a third of this mixture over the filo pastry in the dish. Cover with 3 more sheets of filo, each brushed with melted butter. Continue layering in the same way until you have 4 layers of pastry sheets with 3 layers of nut mixture in between them. Brush the top with melted butter. Cut 5 strips lengthwise and then cut them across to make small bars. Bake for 30 minutes before reducing the heat to 150°C/300°F/gas mark 2 and baking for a further 10 minutes, or until browned. While the bars are baking, make a syrup by putting the remaining sugar, the water, and the orange rind into a small saucepan. Stir over a low heat until the sugar dissolves. Simmer uncovered for a further 5 minutes until syrupy. Pour the syrup over the baklava when you take it out of the oven. Allow to cool in the dish. *Makes about 25 small bars*

320 almond and date spirals

Ⓥ

All the sweetness in these tasty treats comes from the dates which are a good source of vitamins and minerals. For younger children use ground rather than slivered almonds.

PREPARATION
1 hour 30 minutes

STORAGE
Keeps for up
to 4 days in
the fridge

1¼ cups dried seedless dates,
    chopped
½ tsp ground cinnamon
½ tsp ground nutmeg
½ tsp ground ginger
⅔ cup light cream

¼ cup ground almonds/
    toasted slivered almonds
2 tsp grated lemon rind
5 sheets filo pastry
1oz butter, melted

Preheat the oven to 180°C/350°F/Gas mark 4. Place the dates, spices, cream, nuts, and rind in a small saucepan over a gentle heat, stirring to combine until all the cream is absorbed. Remove from the heat and while mixture is cooling prepare the pastry sheets. Layer the sheets of filo pastry together, brushing each layer with melted butter. Now spread the cooled date paste over the pastry leaving a 2in border on one long side. Roll pastry up from the other long side toward the border. Cover with plastic wrap or a moist tea towel and refrigerate for 30 minutes. Cut the roll into ½in slices and place on a greased cookie sheet. Bake for about 20 minutes until the pastry is crisp. *Makes about 20 slices*

321 oatmeal chocolate chip cookies *(above)*

V O

These all-American cookies are delicious served with a glass of milk.

PREPARATION
40 minutes

STORAGE
Keeps for up
to 4 days in an
airtight container

4½oz butter, softened
½ cup sugar
¼ cup soft brown sugar
1 tsp vanilla extract
1 egg
1¼ cup all-purpose flour

1 tsp cinnamon
½ tsp baking powder
½ tsp baking soda
1 cup oats
1 cup chocolate chips

Preheat the oven to 190°C/375°F/gas mark 5. Lightly grease 2 large cookie sheets. Put the butter, sugars, vanilla, and egg in a bowl and beat with an electric whisk until the mixture is smooth. Add the flour, cinnamon, baking powder and baking soda and mix until well combined. Stir in the oats and chocolate chips. Put two tablespoonfuls of the sugar in a small bowl. Take a tablespoon of the cookie mixture and form it into a ball, dip one side in the sugar, and place sugar-side up on the cookie sheet. Press down the cookie using the bottom of a glass to make a flat circle. Repeat until all the dough is used. Bake in the oven for 5–10 minutes until golden. Remove from the oven and leave to cool. Serve with milk or a smoothie (see recipes 296–303; pp.173–175). *Makes 18–20 small cookies*

322   flapjacks

PREPARATION
50 minutes

4oz butter
¼ cup soft light brown sugar
3 tbsp runny honey
2 cups rolled oats

STORAGE
Keeps for up
to 4 days in an
airtight container

Preheat the oven to 190°C/375°F/gas mark 5. Grease a medium-size
baking pan. Melt the butter in a bowl in the microwave or in a saucepan
and transfer to a bowl. Add the sugar and honey, and stir until dissolved.
Mix in the oats. Press into the baking pan and bake for 20–30 minutes until
firm and golden brown. Allow to cool in the pan for 5 minutes and mark into
squares or fingers with a sharp knife. Leave until cold and you will be
able to break it into squares or fingers easily. *Makes 12–16 servings*

323   brownies

*The eggs and nuts make these delicious snacks full of protein and the
cocoa powder is a good source of flavonoids.*

PREPARATION
10 minutes

6oz plain chocolate
6oz butter
3 large eggs
1¼ cups superfine sugar

1 tsp vanilla extract
1 cup all-purpose flour
1 cup chopped hazelnuts

STORAGE
Suitable for
freezing; keep for
up to 2 days in an
airtight container

Preheat the oven to 180°C/350°F/gas mark 4 and line a square cake pan
with baking parchment. Melt the chocolate and butter in a bowl in the
microwave. In another bowl beat together the eggs, sugar, and vanilla.
Then beat into the chocolate mixture. Mix in the flour and hazelnuts and
transfer to the cake pan. Bake for about 20 minutes. Remove from the
oven and stand for 10 minutes. Cut into squares. Allow the brownies to
cool completely before removing from the pan. *Makes 25–30 brownies*

324   chocolate almond cakes

PREPARATION
50–55 minutes

3½oz good quality dark chocolate
2oz butter
¼ cup superfine sugar
½ cup ground almonds

2-3 drops vanilla extract
2 eggs, separated
confectioner's sugar (for dusting)

STORAGE
Suitable for
freezing; keep for
up to 2 days in an
airtight container

Preheat the oven to 180°C/350°F/gas mark 4. Line a muffin pan with
double-paper cases. Break the chocolate into a bowl, add the butter and
sugar, and melt over hot water, stirring continuously. Once melted, remove
from the heat and leave to cool for 3–5 minutes. Stir in the almonds and
the vanilla extract. Stir the egg yolk into the chocolate mixture. In a clean
bowl whisk the egg whites until stiff. Using a metal spoon fold them into the
chocolate mixture. Spoon the mixture into the muffin cases. Bake for
20–25 minutes. Allow to cool slightly before removing from the pans.
Dust the tops with confectioner's sugar before serving. *Makes 6 cakes*

325 chocolate muffins

These moist chocolate muffins contain bananas, eggs, milk, and flour to boost the nutrients of a chocolate snack.

PREPARATION
30 minutes

STORAGE
Suitable for freezing; keep for 1 day in an airtight container

1¼ cups self-rising flour
2 tbsp cocoa powder
⅓ cup chocolate chips
½ tsp baking powder

2 eggs, beaten
⅓ cup olive oil
½ cup milk
2 ripe bananas

Preheat the oven to 200°C/400°F/gas mark 6. Line a muffin pan with paper cases. Place the flour, cocoa powder, chocolate chips, and baking powder in a bowl and mix. In a separate bowl beat the eggs, oil, and milk together. Mash the bananas on a plate and then mix into the egg mixture. Combine the dry and wet mixtures, but do not over-blend. Spoon the mixture into the paper cases and bake for 15 minutes until the muffins are well risen and the tops spring back when slightly pressed. *Makes 12 muffins*

326 classic Victoria sponge

Children love home-baked cake and this is so easy to make. For variation try filling with different jellies, chocolate nut spread, or fresh fruit.

PREPARATION
50 minutes

STORAGE
Suitable for freezing; keeps for up to 3 days in an airtight container

8oz sweet butter, softened
1 cup superfine sugar
1 tsp vanilla extract
4 large eggs
1¾ self-rising flour

1 tsp baking powder
3–4 tbsp milk
4 tbsp strawberry jelly
6–8 strawberries, sliced
confectioner's sugar (for dusting)

Preheat oven to 180°C/350°F/gas mark 4. Lightly grease 2 layer cake pans and line the bases with waxed paper. To mix in the traditional way, cream the butter and sugar together in a large bowl. Add the vanilla extract, then the eggs, one at a time. Fold in the flour and baking powder. Add enough milk to achieve a soft, dropping consistency. To make in a food processor, put all ingredients except the milk in the bowl and whizz until smooth. Add the milk through the funnel top and pulse until the mixture reaches a soft, dropping consistency. Divide the mixture between the two cake pans. Bake for approximately 25 minutes until the cakes are beginning to come away from the edges of the pans, feel springy to touch and are golden. Remove from oven and allow to cool a little before turning out onto a wire rack. Leave to cool completely. When ready to serve, place one cake on a plate and spread it with jelly and sliced strawberries. Put the other cake on top. Dust with confectioner's sugar. *Makes 8 servings*

327 carrot cakes *(below)*
V O

These delicious cakes are quick and easy to make. Carrots are rich in beta-carotene, and olive oil contains some omega-3 fats.

PREPARATION
1 hour

STORAGE
Suitable for freezing; keep for up to 5 days in an airtight container

1 extra-large or 2 small eggs
½ cup soft brown sugar
½ cup dark muscovado sugar
1 cup wholewheat flour
½ tsp baking soda
½ tsp ground nutmeg
1 tsp ground cinnamon
3 tbsp olive oil

2 tbsp natural bio-yogurt
1 tsp vanilla extract
2 medium carrots, grated
⅓ cup shredded coconut
⅓ cup cream cheese (optional)
3 tbsp confectioner's sugar (optional)
juice of ½ lemon (optional)

Preheat the oven to 150°C/350°F/gas mark 4. Line a muffin pan with paper cases. Beat together the eggs and sugar in a food processor. Place flour, baking soda, nutmeg, and cinnamon in a bowl, pour in the egg and sugar mixture, and stir well. In a separate bowl mix together the oil, yogurt, and vanilla extract. Pour into the flour mixture and stir again. Add the grated carrot and coconut, and stir again. Spoon the mixture into the paper cases. Bake for about 25–30 minutes until well risen and golden brown. Cool on a wire rack. To make the icing (if required), place the cream cheese, confectioner's sugar, and lemon juice in a small bowl and beat until smooth. Spread a teaspoonful of icing on the top of each cake. *Makes 12 cakes*

328 banana bread

PREPARATION
1 hour 30 minutes

STORAGE
Suitable for freezing; keeps for up to 4 days in an airtight container

1¼ cups all-purpose flour
2 tsp baking powder
½ tsp baking soda
4½oz butter, melted
¾ cup brown sugar

2 eggs
1 tsp vanilla extract
4 large ripe bananas, mashed
½ cup raisins (optional)

Preheat the oven to 170°C/325°F/gas mark 3. Grease a loaf pan and line with baking parchment. In a large bowl mix together the flour, baking powder and baking soda. In another large bowl mix together the melted butter and sugar until well-blended. Add the eggs and vanilla extract, then the mashed bananas. Mix well. Stir in the raisins. Gradually add the flour mixture, stirring well. Scrape the mixture into a loaf tin. Bake for 1–1¼ hours until golden and springy to the touch. Leave in the pan to cool. Slice to serve. This is particularly delicious eaten warm, but can be wrapped in plastic wrap to store. *Makes 8–10 slices*

329 date and walnut loaf

The fruit and nuts make this sweet, moist loaf a nutritious snack. Walnuts are high in omega-3 fats.

PREPARATION
1 hour 20 minutes

STORAGE
Suitable for freezing; keeps for up to 4 days in an airtight container

2oz soft butter or margarine
¾ cup soft brown sugar
2 eggs
1 cup wholewheat flour
1 cup all-purpose white flour
1½ tsp baking powder

1 small cooking apple, peeled, cored, and chopped
1 cup walnuts, chopped
½ cup pitted dates, chopped
3–4 tbsp water

Preheat the oven to 180°C/350°F/gas mark 4. Grease a loaf pan and line with baking parchment. Put the butter, sugar, eggs, flour, and baking powder in a food processor. Process for a few seconds until mixed. Add the apple, walnuts, dates, and water. Mix for another few seconds, but do not over-process. Turn the mixture into the loaf pan, spreading it evenly. Bake for 1 hour until the loaf feels springy. Allow to cool in the pan for a few minutes before turning out. Serve warm or cold. *Makes 8–10 slices*

330 cheesey garlic bread

PREPARATION
15–20 minutes

STORAGE
Best made just before serving

2oz softened butter
1 tsp chopped parsley
2 cloves garlic, very finely chopped

pinch of black pepper
1 tbsp grated Cheddar
1 small baguette

Preheat the oven to 200°C/400°F/gas mark 6. Mix the butter, parsley, garlic, pepper, and grated cheese together in a bowl. Make a diagonal cut (but don't cut right through) roughly every 1in along the baguette. Spread the garlic butter into the cuts. Wrap the baguette in foil and heat in the oven for 10–15 minutes. Serve with fruit juice. *Makes 4–6 servings*

331   spicy cheese straws

This crunchy snack contains protein, calcium, and lots of B-vitamins, making it a more nutritious alternative to chips and other commercial snacks.

PREPARATION
30 minutes

STORAGE
Suitable for freezing; keep for up to 2 days in an airtight container

1 cup all-purpose/wholewheat flour
1tsp ground cumin (optional)
2oz butter, diced
¾ cup Cheddar
1 egg, beaten

Preheat the oven to 200°C/400°F/gas mark 6. Mix the flour, cumin (if using), and butter together in a food processor, until the mixture resembles breadcrumbs. Stir in the cheese and egg until you form a soft dough. Roll out the dough on a floured board, to a thickness of about ½in and cut into fingers, or shape into thin rolls. Place on a greased cookie sheet and bake for 10 minutes. Cool on a wire rack. *Makes 12 straws*

332   cheese and onion straws

PREPARATION
30 minutes

STORAGE
Suitable for freezing; keep for up to 2 days in an airtight container

1 small onion, finely diced
2oz butter, diced
1 cup all-purpose/wholewheat flour
¾ cup Cheddar
1 egg, beaten

Preheat the oven to 200°C/400°F/gas mark 6. Fry the onion in a little butter in a frying pan until it is soft and transparent. Allow to cool. Whizz the flour and the rest of the butter together in a food processor until the mixture resembles breadcrumbs. Add the onion and cheese and process again to ensure the onion is very finely diced. Stir in the egg until a soft dough forms. Roll out the dough on a floured board to a thickness of about ½in and cut into fingers, or shape into thin rolls. Place on a greased cookie sheet and bake for 10 minutes. Cool on a wire rack. *Makes 12 straws*

333   pitta bread chips

PREPARATION
10–15 minutes

STORAGE
Suitable for freezing; keep for up to 2 days in an airtight container

2 mini pitta breads
1 tbsp olive oil
½ tsp mixed herbs (optional)

Preheat the oven to 180°C/350°F/gas mark 3. Split the pitta breads in half and then cut each piece into 6 wedges. Brush with a little olive oil and sprinkle on a few mixed herbs. Place the pieces on a cookie sheet in a single layer. Bake in the oven for about 10 minutes until golden and crisp, checking frequently as they over-cook easily. Serve as a snack on their own or with a dip. *Makes 2–4 servings*

334 tortilla chips *(above)*

PREPARATION
10–15 minutes

STORAGE
Keep for up to 2 days in an airtight container

1 large flour tortilla

Preheat the oven to 180°C/350°F/gas mark 3. Cut the tortilla into 8 wedges. Place the pieces on a cookie sheet in a single layer. Bake in the oven for about 10 minutes until golden and crisp, checking frequently as they over-cook easily. Serve on their own or with a dip. *Makes 2–4 servings*

335 bagel chips

PREPARATION
10–15 minutes

STORAGE
Keep for up to 2 days in an airtight container

1 bagel
1 tbsp olive oil

Preheat the oven to 180°C/350°F/gas mark 3. Slice the bagel across the hole into 4 thin slices. Brush the pieces with a little olive oil, and place them on a cookie sheet in a single layer. Bake in the oven for about 10 minutes until golden and crisp, checking frequently as they over-cook easily. Serve on their own or with a dip. *Makes 2–4 servings*

336 vegetable snack platter with spicy curry dip

V O

The spicy dip perfectly complements the healthy raw vegetables.

PREPARATION
15–20 minutes

STORAGE
Best made just
before serving

1 stick celery
1 small carrot
1 small red/green bell pepper
1 piece cucumber, 2in long, peeled
2 broccoli florets
2 cauliflower florets

Tortilla Chips (recipe 334; opposite)
6 tbsp natural bio-yogurt
2 tbsp low-fat mayonnaise
2 tbsp freshly squeezed lemon juice
1 clove garlic, crushed
1 tsp curry powder

Chop the vegetables into small sticks. Arrange vegetables and Tortilla Chips attractively on a plate, leaving a gap in the center for the dip. Place all the ingredients for the curry dip in a bowl and mix together well. Put dip in a small cup or bowl and place in the center of the plate.
Makes 2–4 servings

337 plum fruit spread

V

This low-sugar spread is packed full of fruit. It makes an ideal accompaniment for English Breakfast Scones (recipe 098; p.85), toast, or crumpets.

PREPARATION
1 hour 15 minutes

STORAGE
Keeps in the fridge
for several weeks

1lb 5oz plums, pitted and sliced
1 medium eating apple, quartered,
  but not cored
1 tbsp apple/grape juice

2 tsp lemon juice
⅓ cup sugar
pinch of ginger, optional

Prepare 2 jelly jars and lids or covers, wash, and dry well. Put a small plate in the freezer for testing when the spread is set. Place the plums, apple, apple/grape juice, and lemon juice in a large saucepan. Bring to the boil, stirring occasionally. Reduce heat, and simmer for about 30 minutes until the fruit is very soft. Press the fruit through a sieve to remove the skins, stones, and pips. Return to the saucepan, add the sugar and ginger (if using). Bring to the boil and cook for a further 15–20 minutes. Test to see if spread is ready by dropping a little onto the cold plate. Run your finger through the center—if the jelly remains parted and does not flow to fill the hole, it is ready. Allow the spread to cool slightly before pouring into the jelly jars. Cover and store in the fridge. Serve with toast or crumpets.
Makes 2 small jars

PARTY FOOD

Glimpse the words "party food" and you probably think of foods that are full of sugar, fat, coloring, and additives. However, this needn't be the case. While it is true that parties are special occasions when children expect treats, there is no reason why the foods you serve can't also be nutritionally sound.

The secret of healthy party foods is to balance the high-fat and high-sugar food and drinks you offer with some healthier fruit and vegetables presented in fun and interesting ways. The recipes here include both sweet and savory foods, as well as drinks. You'll find everything you need for a great party, from new ideas, such as Humpty Dumpty Wall, to firm favorites, such as Honey Popcorn. Enjoy!

338 Humpty Dumpty wall

PREPARATION
25 minutes

STORAGE
Keeps for up to
3 hours covered
with plastic wrap

4 eggs
8 slices white bread
8 slices wholewheat bread
4 tsp butter

4 tbsp yeast extract
slivers of carrot and green bell
  pepper (for decoration)

Place the eggs in a small saucepan and cover with water. Bring to the boil and simmer for at least 6 minutes. When cool, peel off the shells and cut off about ¼ of the bottom, so they will sit. Make a face on each egg by cutting a slit for the mouth and two for the eyes. Push a sliver of carrot in for the mouth and two rounds of green bell pepper for the eyes. Butter the bread and spread with yeast extract, then make 8 sandwiches, using one white slice and one wholewheat slice for each one. Cut off the crusts and cut each one into 8 fingers. Stack the fingers on top of each other to build 4 separate brick walls. Sit a decorated egg on top of each wall. *Makes 4 servings*

339 fairy bread

PREPARATION
5 minutes

STORAGE
Keeps for up to
3 hours covered
with plastic wrap

2 slices white bread
1 tsp butter/cream cheese
2 tsp multicolored sugar strands

Spread the butter/cream cheese thinly on the bread. Sprinkle half the sugar strands on each slice of bread. Cut each slice into 4 triangles, or into angel or fairy shapes using a cookie-cutter. Place on a serving plate. *Makes 4–8 servings*

340 sausage hedgehog with homemade tomato ketchup

PREPARATION
35 minutes

STORAGE
Keeps for up
to 12 hours in
the fridge

14oz canned tomatoes, chopped
1 tsp balsamic vinegar
1 tbsp tomato paste
2 tsp superfine sugar
½ grapefruit

shredded lettuce
30 cocktail sausages, cooked
30 cocktail sticks or toothpicks
1 stuffed olive, cut in half
1 gherkin

Purée the tomatoes in a blender or food processor. Place them in a large saucepan and bring to the boil. Reduce heat, add the vinegar, tomato paste, and sugar, and simmer for about 15 minutes until the mixture is reduced by half. Cool and pass through a sieve. Place the grapefruit-half in the center of a large plate and cover the rest of the plate with shredded lettuce to look like grass. Put the sausages on the cocktail sticks and stick into the grapefruit for the hedgehog's "spines". Leave a small section clear for the hedgehog's face—use the olive-halves for the eyes and the gherkin for the nose, and fix them in place with cocktail sticks. Serve the ketchup in a bowl and let the children dip their sausages-on-sticks into the ketchup. *Makes 10–15 servings*

341 celery sailing boats

These crunchy "boats" provide a little calcium and protein.

PREPARATION
15 minutes

⅔ cup cream cheese
1 tbsp chopped chives
6 sticks celery

rice paper (for sails)
20 toothpicks
shredded lettuce (as garnish)

STORAGE
Keep for up
to 12 hours in
the fridge

Place the cream cheese and chives together in a bowl and mix. Cut the celery sticks into 2½in lengths. Fill the hollows with the cheese mixture. To make the sails cut the rice paper into triangular pieces, spear with toothpicks, and stick in the center of each celery stick. Arrange the lettuce on a plate and place the celery boats on top. *Makes about 20 boats*

342 honey popcorn in paper cones

Popcorn is a healthy alternative to chips. It can be made in a microwave, but this traditional way is more fun because you can hear the corn popping. And children love the way in which the almost-empty pan magically fills!

PREPARATION
35 minutes

4 tbsp vegetable oil
1 cup popcorn kernels
4 tbsp runny honey

wrapping paper (for the cones)
sticky tape (for the cones)

STORAGE
Best served
immediately

Heat 1 tablespoonful of oil in a large heavy-bottomed saucepan over a high heat. Add a quarter of the corn, cover, and cook, shaking the pan constantly until the kernels pop. Remove from the heat, transfer to a large bowl, and mix in 1 tablespoonful of the honey. Repeat the process three more times. Serve in paper cones. To make the cones, cut wrapping paper into 12in squares. Fold in half diagonally and make a firm crease along the fold line. Fold the points into each other to make a cone and secure along the join using sticky tape. *Makes about 10 cones*

343 chocolate-coated mini kebabs

PREPARATION
1 hour 50 minutes

1 small pineapple, peeled, cored, and cut into small chunks
½ melon, rind removed, deseeded, and diced
1 mango, peeled, pitted, and diced

2 kiwis, peeled and diced
1 punnet of strawberries, washed, and hulled
8oz milk/dark chocolate
toothpicks (to make the kebabs)

STORAGE
Keeps for up
to 12 hours in
the fridge

Thread 2 or 3 pieces of fruit onto each toothpick. Place them on a tray and put in the fridge for 1 hour. Melt the chocolate in a bowl over heat, or use a microwave. Take the kebabs out of the fridge and dip each one in the melted chocolate. Place on a serving plate and refrigerate for about 30 minutes before serving. *Makes 15–20 servings*

344 marshmallow cereal bars *(above)*

You can vary these by using different cereals and by making some with pink and others with white marshmallows.

PREPARATION
20 minutes plus
20 minutes to set

STORAGE
Keeps for up
to 2 days in an
airtight container

2oz sweet butter
5 cups pink and white marshmallows
1½ cups breakfast cereal such as cornflakes, hoops, crisped rice

Lightly oil a small baking pan. Melt the butter in a large saucepan over a low heat, add the marshmallows, and melt, stirring continuously. Remove from the heat and stir in the cereal. Tip into the baking pan. Press down using the back of a spoon (this works best if you lightly oil the spoon to stop it sticking). Leave to set. Cut into squares and serve. *Makes 10–12 bars*

345 frozen yogurt clown faces

Yogurt is a healthier choice than ice cream in this recipe, as it contains more protein and calcium.

PREPARATION
2hours 30 minutes

STORAGE
Suitable for
freezing but
best served
immediately

3½ pts frozen vanilla yogurt
60 colored, sugar-coated chocolate
  buttons
12 red jelly beans (for the mouths)
12 other-color jelly beans (for the
  noses)

2 tbsp chocolate sugar strands
2 tbsp buttercream icing
12 ice cream cones
12 chocolate-covered sweet
  wholewheat cookies

Chill a baking pan in the freezer. Scoop out 12 balls of frozen yogurt and put them in the pan. Freeze for 1 hour. Remove and quickly make the faces on each ball by pressing on chocolate buttons for the eyes and jelly beans for the mouths and noses. Freeze for another hour. Meanwhile, spread icing around the top of each cone and dip in the chocolate strands. Put 3 dots of icing in a line down the outside of the cones and stick on chocolate buttons to look like pom-poms on a clown's hat. Put a cookie on each plate. Place the frozen yogurt faces on the cookies and top with the cone "hats". Serve immediately. *Makes 12 clowns*

346 star-shaped cookies

There is endless scope for variety with these cookies—try using different shapes, icing them, sprinkling them with colored sugar or pressing chopped dried fruits into them.

PREPARATION
1 hour

STORAGE
Keep for up
to 3 days in an
airtight container

4½oz butter, softened
¾ cup superfine sugar
a few drops of vanilla extract

2 egg yolks
1¾ cups all-purpose flour
a little extra sugar (to decorate)

Preheat the oven to 180°C/350°F/gas mark 4. Grease 2 large baking pans. Beat together the butter, sugar, and vanilla extract until creamy. Add the egg yolks and beat well. Stir in the flour and mix to a firm dough using your hands. Turn onto a lightly floured surface, knead into a ball, and then roll out to a thickness of about ¼in. Cut into star shapes using a cookie-cutter. Place on the baking pans, sprinkle the tops with a little sugar (use multi-colored sugar if you can get it). Bake for 10–15 minutes until firm and golden brown. *Makes about 20 cookies*

347 party cupcakes

V O

You can easily decorate these cakes using candy to make faces. Alternatively, try out more elaborate designs or write names using ready-made tubes of writing icing, obtainable from larger supermarkets.

PREPARATION
45 minutes

1 tbsp milk
3 eggs
¾ cup superfine sugar
1 cup self-rising flour

3oz butter, melted
¼ cup low-fat cream cheese
½ cup confectioner's sugar

STORAGE
Suitable for freezing; keep for up to 3 days in an airtight container

Preheat the oven to 180°C/350°F/gas mark 4. Line 2 muffin pans with 15 paper cases. Whisk the milk, eggs, and sugar in a bowl until light and fluffy. Fold in the flour and then the butter. Fill the cases with the mixture (just over half full). Bake for 10–15 minutes until risen and golden. Cool on a wire rack. Beat the cream cheese and confectioner's sugar until smooth and spread on the cakes. Decorate with candy or icing. *Makes 15 cupcakes*

348 gingerbread men (and women!)

V O

Gingerbread men are traditional cookies that seem popular from generation to generation. You can find the cutters in kitchen-equipment stores.

PREPARATION
30–45 minutes

2½ cups all-purpose flour
2 tsp ground ginger
1 tsp baking soda
4oz butter

¾ cup soft brown sugar
4 tbsp light corn syrup
1 egg
currants (to decorate)

STORAGE
Keep for up to 2 days in an airtight container

Preheat the oven to 190°C/375°F/gas mark 5. Cover 2 baking pans with baking parchment. Mix the flour, ginger, and baking soda together in a food processor. Add the butter and whizz until the mixture resembles fine breadcrumbs. Add the sugar, syrup, and egg and process again until it forms a pliable dough. Roll out the dough thinly and cut into figure shapes with cookie-cutters. Transfer the figures carefully onto the baking parchment and put in currants for the eyes and mouths, and a line of 3 currants down the "bodies" as buttons. Bake for 15 minutes until golden brown. Be careful not to overcook. Leave in the pans until firm, then transfer onto a wire rack. *Makes about 12 figures*

349 hot chocolate with marshmallows *(below)*

PREPARATION
10 minutes

STORAGE
Best served
immediately

1¼ cups milk
8 tsp drinking chocolate/cocoa with
   a little sugar to sweeten
4 heaped tbsp whipped cream

16 small marshmallows
grated chocolate or cinnamon
   powder (to garnish)

Heat the milk either in a saucepan or in the microwave. Pour into a jug, add the chocolate powder/cocoa and sugar, and stir well until completely dissolved and well mixed with the milk. Pour into cups. Float the cream on top of the chocolate in each cup. Let the children add the marshmallows and grated chocolate/cinnamon powder to garnish. *Makes 4 servings*

350   elderflower ice cream floats

V ⊗ ⊗

PREPARATION
5 minutes

4 tsp elderflower cordial
1¼ cups sparkling water
4 small scoops vanilla ice cream

STORAGE
Best served
immediately

Put the elderflower cordial in a wide glass or plastic cup. Add the sparkling water and stir. Gently drop in the ice cream. Serve immediately with a straw and a spoon. *Makes 4 servings*

351   melon and orange slush

V ⊗ ⊗ ⊜

This bright orange frosted drink is packed full of beta-carotene and vitamin C.

PREPARATION
10 minutes

1 ripe canteloupe melon
1¾ cups orange juice
8 ice cubes

STORAGE
Best served
immedately

Remove the seeds and skin from the melon and cut it into cubes. Blend all the ingredients together in a food processor or liquidizer. Serve in chilled glasses, these will give a frosted effect as they warm up. *Makes 3–4 servings*

352   homemade lemonade

V ⊗ ⊗ ⊜

This old-fashioned lemonade is rich in vitamin C and contains no colorings or preservatives. It also works well as a still lemonade with non-fizzy water.

PREPARATION
15 minutes

juice of 3 lemons
2 tbsp superfine sugar
2 cups sparkling water

STORAGE
Best served
immediately

Put the lemon juice and sugar in a saucepan. Bring to the boil on a gentle heat, remove from the heat and leave to cool. Once cold, add the sparkling water and serve immediately. *Makes 3–4 servings*

COOKING WITH YOUR CHILD

Children love to help in the kitchen and are often more willing to eat food they have helped to prepare. Counting or weighing ingredients and stirring and mixing foods develop physical coordination and improve their math as well as teaching them how to cook. But the most important benefit is that your child is developing a very positive attitude to food. The key to success is to make the tasks simple and age-appropriate, but to involve him as much as possible. We have indicated in each recipe which jobs we feel should be done by the adult and which by the child. Always take the utmost care when your child uses knives and other potentially dangerous equipment. Above all, let him taste, enjoy, and be proud of his creations!

353 do-it-yourself pizza

Letting children choose their own pizza topping is a great way to entertain a small group. With imagination they can make faces or simple pictures.

PREPARATION
40 minutes

STORAGE
Best served
immediately

2 pizza bases
6 tbsp passata/canned tomatoes,
   chopped
1 tsp dried oregano
selection of washed and prepared
   vegetables, such as red and green
   bell peppers, zucchini, and
   mushrooms in separate bowls
   (for topping)

sliced cherry tomatoes (for topping)
canned corn, drained (for topping)
¼ cup diced ham or cooked chicken
4 tbsp grated mixed Cheddar and
   Parmesan
6–8 thin slices mozzarella, cut into
   strips

ADULT: Preheat oven to 200°C/400°F/gas mark 6.
CHILD: Spread the passata/chopped tomatoes over the pizza bases.
Sprinkle with oregano. Top with his choice of vegetables and meat (if using).
Sprinkle over the grated cheese and add strips of mozzarella.
ADULT: Place the pizzas in the oven and bake for about 10 minutes until
the cheese is bubbling. Serve with salad. *Makes 2–4 servings*

354 herby pasta salad

*If you do all the chopping, cooking, and blanching involved in this recipe,
your child can add and mix the ingredients. You can turn this dish into
a nutritionally complete lunch by adding flaked salmon or chopped ham.*

PREPARATION
40 minutes

STORAGE
Keeps for up
to 24 hours
in the fridge

2½ cups pasta spirals or similar small
   pasta
5 tbsp olive oil
6oz assorted vegetables,
   such as broccoli, celery, carrots,
   zucchini, cucumber, sugarsnap
   peas, red and green bell peppers,
   scallions, string beans

12 cherry tomatoes
juice of 1 lemon/lime
1 tbsp balsamic vinegar
1 tbsp chopped fresh parsley
1 tbsp chopped fresh basil
⅓ cup grated Parmesan
1 tbsp mild mustard
pinch of black pepper

ADULT: Bring a large saucepan of water to the boil. Add 1 tablespoonful
of oil and the pasta shapes. Reduce heat, cover, and simmer for 10–12
minutes until the pasta is just tender. Drain, rinse with hot water, and allow
to cool. Prepare the vegetables by cutting the celery, carrots, zucchini, and
cucumber into matchsticks. Top and tail the sugarsnap peas.
CHILD: Break the broccoli into small florets.
ADULT: Thinly slice the bell peppers, scallions, and string beans. Place all
the vegetables except the cucumber into a pan of boiling water and simmer
for about 3 minutes to blanch them. Drain. Allow to cool.
CHILD: Put the pasta into the salad bowl and then mix in the blanched
vegetables. Add the cucumber and the cherry tomatoes. In a separate bowl
mix together the lemon/lime juice, vinegar, herbs, Parmesan, mustard, and
pepper. Stir well, pour over the salad, and toss. *Makes 4–6 servings*

355 cottage cheese dip with vegetable sticks and baked chips

PREPARATION
15 minutes

STORAGE
Dip keeps for up to 2 days in the fridge; chips and vegetables best served immediately

1 cup cottage cheese
2 scallions, chopped
½ red bell pepper, finely chopped
½ tsp Dijon mustard

½ tsp mixed dried herbs
selection of vegetables, such as celery, carrots, broccoli florets, cut into sticks or small pieces

ADULT: Prepare all the vegetables. (An older child may be able to help do this with supervision.)
CHILD: Put all the ingredients in a bowl, measure out the herbs and the mustard, and mix everything together.
Serve with vegetable sticks and Tortilla Chips (recipe 334; p.188) or Bagel Chips (recipe 335; p.188). *Makes 6–8 servings*

356 apple smiles

PREPARATION
10 minutes

STORAGE
Best served immediately

1 red eating apple
3–4 tbsp smooth peanut butter
puffed rice cereal (for the teeth)

ADULT: Core and slice the apple into ¼in slices.
CHILD: Pat the apple slices with a paper towel to dry them. This will help the peanut butter to stick. Spread one side of each apple slice with peanut butter. Sandwich 2 slices together and squash them a little so that the peanut butter begins to ooze out onto the apple's skin—the "lips". Place 5–6 pieces of puffed rice in the peanut butter to form the "teeth", as if in a smiling mouth. *Makes 5–6 smiles*

357 breadsticks

PREPARATION
45 minutes

STORAGE
Keeps for up to 1 week in an airtight container

1¾ cups strong white/wholewheat flour
½ sachet of fast-action yeast
1 tbsp olive oil

½ cup water, at room temperature
1oz butter
sesame seeds (optional)

ADULT: Preheat the oven to 220°C/400°F/gas mark 6.
CHILD: Mix the flour and yeast in a bowl. Pour in the oil and water.
ADULT: Melt the butter and pour into the flour mixture.
CHILD: Mix (with help) to form a firm dough. Divide the dough into 15 pieces and roll into pencil shapes, about 6in long.
ADULT: You could shape these into letters and spell out your child's name.
CHILD: Brush the sticks and roll them in the sesame seeds (if using). Place in a greased baking pan.
ADULT: Bake for about 20 minutes until golden. *Makes 15 sticks*

358 kids' club sandwich

Even young children will find it easy to assemble this nutritious sandwich.
Let them serve their creation with pride and carry it to the table. For a
vegetarian option, use 1–2 tablespoons of houmous instead of the meat.

PREPARATION
5–10 minutes

STORAGE
Best served
immediately

3 thin slices white/wholewheat
   bread
2 tsp mayonnaise/softened butter
1 thin slice ham, cooked
   chicken/other cold meat

2 lettuce leaves
2 radishes, thinly sliced
1 thin square slice Cheddar (big
   enough to cover a slice of bread)
1 medium tomato, sliced

CHILD: Put the slices of bread on a plate and spread them with
the mayonnaise or the softened butter, using a pastry brush/knife.
ADULT: If your child is using a knife, make sure that it is not sharp.
CHILD: Take one slice of the bread, buttered-side up, and cover with the
slice of ham/cooked chicken/other cold meat (if using). Place a lettuce leaf
on top and then add the sliced radishes. Place the second slice of bread
on top, again buttered-side up. This time layer with the cheese, tomato
slices, and the other lettuce leaf. Top with the third bread slice,
buttered-side down.
ADULT: Press the sandwich down, cut off the crusts, and cut into
4 triangles.
Serve with carrot sticks or cucumber slices. *Makes 1–2 servings*

359 rice cake faces

PREPARATION
5–10 minutes

STORAGE
Best served
immediately

2 large plain rice cakes
4 tbsp cream cheese/houmous (recipe 125; p.98)
6 raisins
2 thin slices red apple, mouth-shaped
1 carrot, peeled and finely grated

ADULT: Cut the apples into quarters, remove the cores, and cut off 2 thin
slices. Grate the carrot.
CHILD: Spread the cream cheese/houmous onto the rice cakes. Make the
faces using the raisins for the eyes and the noses, and the apple slices for
the mouths. Sprinkle grated carrot around the tops to make hair, or below
the mouths to make beards. Serve with extra slices of apple or with
vegetable sticks. *Makes 2 faces*

360 crispy chocolate rice cakes
V ⊗ ⊗ ⊘

Most commercially produced rice cereals are fortified with iron and many vitamins, making them a very nutritious snack. You might like to try adding a few raisins for variety. Your child will be proud to take a couple of his creations to school in his lunch box or to share them with friends.

PREPARATION
15 minutes

STORAGE
Keep for up
to 2 days in an
airtight container

8oz good-quality dark/milk chocolate
1 cup crisped rice cereal

CHILD: Weigh out the chocolate (with help) and break into small pieces in a bowl.
ADULT: Melt the chocolate in the microwave or in a bowl over a saucepan of simmering water.
CHILD: Weigh out the crisped rice and tip it into the melted chocolate. Stir until the cereal is well coated with chocolate. Set out about 12 paper cases and spoon the mixture into them. Stand to cool and store in an airtight container. Keep in the fridge if it is a hot day. *Makes 12 servings*

361 strawberry jelly
V ⊗ ⊗ ⊗

Children love to pick their own fruit and making jelly with it afterward gives them a great sense of achievement. Jelly made from fresh fruit contains plenty of immune-boosting flavonoids.

PREPARATION
50 minutes

STORAGE
Keeps for up to
6 months; once
opened store
in the fridge

2lb 4oz strawberries that you have picked
2lb 4oz sugar
juice of 1 lemon

CHILD: Wash the fruit and put it on sheets of paper towel to dry. Hull the strawberries and put them in a large saucepan. With help, cover them with water. Weigh out the sugar. Wash out 2 jelly jars and dry them.
ADULT: Put the jelly jars in the oven on the lowest heat to warm. Put a small plate in the freezer for testing when the jelly is set. Cut any large strawberries into pieces. Bring them to the boil very slowly over a gentle heat. Add the sugar, stir with a wooden spoon, and boil rapidly for 15 minutes. Add the lemon juice and boil for a further 5 minutes. With the wooden spoon put a drop or two of the jelly on the cold plate.
CHILD: Watch to see if a skin forms as the drops cool.
ADULT: If no skin forms keep boiling for a further 5 minutes and check again. When a skin does form, pour the jam into the warm, dry jars. Allow to cool a little, but put the lid or cover on while still warm. If you are going to store the jelly for some time, make sure that the jars are full to the top, to reduce the possibility of a mold forming. *Makes 2 jars*

362 mini trifles *(above)*

Ⓥ Ⓞ Ⓣ

Making this traditional pudding will be great fun for your child. Use whatever soft fruit is in season or fruit canned in juice.

PREPARATION
20 minutes

STORAGE
Keeps for up
to 24 hours in
the fridge

4 sponge drops (recipe 363, p.204)/
  2 slices jelly roll
2 tbsp orange juice
1 ripe peach, sliced
12 strawberries, rinsed and hulled

⅔ cup custard
2 tsp whipped cream (optional)
colored sugar strands (to decorate
  —optional)

CHILD: Put 2 sponge drops or 1 slice of jelly roll in each of 2 small ramekin dishes. Spoon a tablespoonful of orange juice over each. Cover with the peach slices and strawberries. Spoon the custard over. Top with the whipped cream and sprinkle with the colored sugar strands (if using).
Makes 2 mini trifles

363 sponge drops *(below)*

 V 🎭 O

For variation, melt a little chocolate and let your child dip one end in the chocolate, allow to cool, and serve with fruit as a pudding or a snack.

PREPARATION
30 minutes

STORAGE
Keeps for up
to 2 days in an
airtight container

1 large egg
3 tbsp superfine sugar
4 tbsp all-purpose flour
1–2 tsp confectioner's sugar

ADULT: Preheat the oven to 200°C/400°F/gas mark 6. Lightly grease 2 baking pans.
CHILD: Crack the egg (with help) into a mixing bowl. Measure out the sugar and put in the bowl.
ADULT AND CHILD TOGETHER: Hold an electric whisk and whisk the egg and sugar together to form a thick, creamy mixture. This takes a few minutes so you may have to finish this without your child.
CHILD: Measure the flour and sift over the mixture, half at a time. Fold in using a metal spoon (show your child how to fold rather than stir in the flour as it is important to keep air in the mixture). Drop spoonfuls of the mixture onto a greased baking pan, leaving room for the drops to spread.
ADULT: Place in the oven and bake for 7–10 minutes until golden and spongy. Remove from the oven, allow to cool for a few seconds, and then transfer onto a wire cooling rack.
CHILD: Using a small sieve, sprinkle with confectioner's sugar.
These are delicious eaten slightly warm. *Makes 10–12 sponge drops*

364　chocolate baked bananas

This treat contains lots of vitamin B6, as well as potassium.

PREPARATION
35 minutes

STORAGE
Best served
immediately

2 large bananas, unpeeled
2oz milk/dark chocolate, broken into small segments

ADULT: Preheat the oven to 180°C/350°F/gas mark 4. Trim the ends of the bananas, but do not peel. Lay them in a baking pan on a piece of kitchen foil. Make a slit lengthwise in each banana, going through the upper skin and into the fruit.
CHILD: Press chocolate pieces into the slits and wrap the bananas in foil.
ADULT: Place in the oven and bake for 25 minutes. Allow to cool and remove the foil. Peel back the skins and scoop out the contents into bowls to serve. These are delicious with fresh cream. *Makes 2–4 servings*

365　cherry melting moments

V O

Always popular with children, these are easy to make and delicious warm. Try cutting the cherries into pieces and making faces with them.

PREPARATION
50 minutes

STORAGE
Keep for up
to 2 days in an
airtight container

4oz butter	1 cup self-rising flour
⅓ cup superfine sugar	1 small bowl of crushed cornflakes
1 egg yolk	10–12 glacé cherries, halved
a few drops of vanilla extract	

ADULT: Preheat the oven to 190°C/375°F/gas mark 5.
CHILD: Measure out the ingredients (with help). Grease 2 baking pans.
ADULT AND CHILD TOGETHER: Using an electric whisk, cream the butter and sugar. Add in the egg yolk and vanilla extract. Stir in the flour and mix to a stiff dough.
ADULT: Divide the mixture into 20–24 portions.
CHILD: Roll each portion into a ball and dip and roll it in the cornflakes. Place in a baking pan. Press half a cherry onto the top of each.
ADULT: Bake in the oven for 15–20 minutes. Cool in the other baking pan for a few minutes.
CHILD: Transfer the cookies from the baking pan to a wire cooling rack.
Makes 20–24 cookies

part five

meal planners

Children thrive on routine from an early age, so it is important to establish a feeding pattern that fits in with your child's sleeping and activity habits, ensuring that she does not become too tired or too hungry to eat. To be sustainable this feeding pattern also needs to fit in with the rest of the family's eating habits.

Meals needn't be elaborate, but always offer your child two courses to provide her with a greater variety of nutrients and to give her a second opportunity for eating if she eats little of the first course.

In this section you will find meal planners for each age-group to help you devise healthy menus for your child, based on the recipes in this book. We have also included useful information on store cupboard essentials and basic food hygiene.

USING MEAL PLANNERS

Each meal planner consists of three meals. In general, the main meal is given at lunchtime for babies (up to 12 months), and at dinnertime for toddlers and young children, in order to fit in with the rest of the family's eating patterns. However, you may decide to alter this pattern depending on the particular habits of your family, your baby's individual sleeping patterns, and other daily activities.

The first weaning stage introduces your baby to a limited selection of grains, vegetables, and fruits. As a result the menus for this stage are entirely vegetarian. In subsequent weaning stages, your baby or toddler will be ready for meat, fish, or pulses. The menus for these stages therefore include meat or fish dishes most days with one or two vegetarian days. If you are bringing up your baby or toddler as a vegetarian, use the vegetarian meals as the basis for creating menus for the rest of the week. For 3 to 6 year olds we have included one menu for meat and fish eaters and a separate one for vegetarians.

The menus for each of the weaning stages are geared to the needs of babies, with a selection of purées, mashes, and soft foods. The menus for 1 to 2 year olds include lots of finger foods to encourage toddlers to feed themselves. The main meals for this age group and for 3 to 6 year olds can be enjoyed by the whole family, and also provide opportunities for young children to learn to use cutlery.

From 7 months onward children also need snacks and drinks in between the main meals listed in the planners (see p.217 for snack suggestions). Use these snacks as a way to ensure that your child receives three servings of dairy products and five servings of fruit and vegetables each day.

Meal planner for first solids

These meals are suitable for babies who have started on puréed solids before 6 months and are now ready for three small meals a day. The amounts your baby eats will depend on her needs and appetite, and will vary from day to day and meal to meal. The main thing is to offer her a variety of tastes. In addition, continue giving your baby breast or formula feeds at other times of day to ensure that you fulfil all her nutritional needs.

	BREAKFAST	MAIN MEAL	LIGHT MEAL
DAY 1	First rice flakes *(p.33)*; breast or formula feed	Carrot and potato purée *(p.34)*; breast or formula feed	Apple purée *(p.37)*; breast or formula feed
DAY 2	First ground rice *(p.33)*; breast or formula feed	Sweet potato and cauliflower purée *(p.35)*; breast or formula feed	Avocado purée *(p.36)*; breast or formula feed
DAY 3	Millet porridge *(p.33)*; breast or formula feed	Pea and potato purée *(p.34)*; breast or formula feed	Peach and mango purée *(p.37)*; breast or formula feed
DAY 4	First ground rice (p.31) with Apple purée (p.37); breast or formula feed	Parsnip purée *(p.35, using broccoli as well as parsnip)*; breast or formula feed	Apple purée *(p.37, using pear instead of apple)*; breast or formula feed
DAY 5	First rice flakes *(p.31)*; breast or formula feed	Carrot and potato purée *(p.34, using zucchini instead of carrot)*; breast or formula feed	Pear and apple purée *(p.37)*; breast or formula feed
DAY 6	Millet porridge *(p.31)* with Apple purée *(p.37, using pear instead of apple)*; breast or formula feed	Sweet potato and cauliflower purée *(p.33, using broccoli instead of cauliflower)*; breast or formula feed	Peach and mango purée *(p.37, using apricot instead of mango)*; breast or formula feed
DAY 7	Packet baby rice made with breast or formula milk, with Apple purée *(p.37, using peach instead of apple)*; breast or formula feed	Carrot and potato purée *(p.34, using parsnip instead of potato)*; breast or formula feed	Peach and mango purée *(p.37, using apple instead of peach)*; breast or formula feed

Meal planner for 6 month olds

At 6 months babies are ready for a greater variety of tastes, and require more nutritious solids. Although these menus still consist of puréed foods, they are richer in protein, iron, and calories, which are particularly important at this age. Favorites from the earlier section in the book can also still be used. In addition, continue giving your baby breast or formula feeds at other times of day: at this age babies usually require a minimum of four breast or formula feeds every 24 hours.

	BREAKFAST	MAIN MEAL	LIGHT MEAL
DAY 1	Creamy first porridge (p.39); breast or formula feed	Lamb with spinach and sweet potato (p.41); breast or formula feed	Fruity milk pudding (p.42); breast or formula feed
DAY 2	First ground rice (p.33) with Pear and apple purée (p.37); breast or formula feed	Beef with zucchini and red bell pepper (p.41); breast or formula feed	Avocado and banana yogurt (p.42); breast or formula feed
Ⓥ DAY 3	Porridge with puréed fruit (p.39); breast or formula feed	Creamy tofu and parsnip (p.40); breast or formula feed	Creamy egg custard (p.42) with Peach and mango purée (p.37); breast or formula feed
DAY 4	¼–½ breakfast wheat cake with warm milk; breast or formula feed	Poached haddock with vegetables (p.40); breast or formula feed	Avocado purée (p.36, using mango instead of avocado) with yogurt; breast or formula feed
DAY 5	Creamy first porridge (p.39) with Apple purée (p.37); breast or formula feed	Chicken with rice and leeks (p.40); breast or formula feed	Fruity milk pudding (p.42) with Apple purée (p.37, using pear instead of apple); breast or formula feed
Ⓥ DAY 6	First ground rice (p.31) with Peach and mango purée (p.37); breast or formula feed	Lentils with carrot and coriander (p.39); breast or formula feed	Creamy egg custard (p.42) with Avocado purée (p.36, using melon instead of avocado); breast or formula feed
DAY 7	First ground rice (p.31) with Apple purée (p.37, using peach instead of apple); breast or formula feed	Pork with apple, parsnip, and swede (p.41); breast or formula feed	Fresh peach yogurt (p.43, using nectarine instead of peach); breast or formula feed

Meal planner for 6½–9 month olds

Between 6½ and 9 months old, babies are ready for some stronger flavors, a wider range of textures, and soft finger foods, which allow them to start feeding themselves. Mid-morning or mid-afternoon snacks offer them a good opportunity to practise with finger foods. In addition to meals, you still need to give breast or formula feeds. A minimum of three such feeds is usual at this age—on waking in the morning, at bedtime, and at another point during the day.

	BREAKFAST	LUNCH	DINNER
DAY 1	Scrambled egg *(p.45)* with toast fingers; breast or formula feed	Lamb casserole with tomatoes and potatoes *(p.50)* with soft-cooked cauliflower florets as finger food; Fresh peach yogurt *(p.43)*; cup of water	Fish kedgeree *(p.49)* with soft-cooked carrot sticks as finger food; 1–2 pieces of ripe kiwi fruit as finger food; breast or formula feed
DAY 2	Banana porridge *(p.45)*; 1–2 slices of banana as finger food; breast or formula feed	Chicken with leeks *(p.51)* and soft-cooked pieces of potato as finger food; Creamy egg custard *(p.42)*; 1–2 slices of ripe peach as finger food; cup of water	Poached haddock with vegetables *(p.40, mashed rather than puréed)* and soft-cooked broccoli florets as finger food; mashed ripe melon with 2–3 pieces of melon as finger food; breast or formula feed
♥ **DAY 3**	Scrambled egg *(p.45)* with toast fingers; breast or formula feed	Spinach dhal *(p.46)* with soft-cooked slices of red bell pepper as finger food; Fruity milk pudding *(p.42)*; cup of water	Macaroni cheese *(p.53, well-mashed)* with soft-cooked carrot sticks as finger food; Soft summer fruit sticks *(p.47)*; breast or formula feed
♥ **DAY 4**	Breakfast wheat cake with warm milk and mashed banana; 1–2 slices of banana as finger food; breast or formula feed	Sweet potato, chickpea, and cauliflower mash *(p.46)* with soft-cooked sweet potato sticks as finger food; Creamy egg custard *(p.42)*; cup of water	Creamy tofu and parsnip *(p.40, mashed rather than puréed)* with Soft vegetable fingers *(p.47)* as finger food; mashed ripe peach with slices of peach as finger food; breast or formula feed
DAY 5	Porridge with apple *(p.45)*; rice cake as finger food; breast or formula feed	First spaghetti bolognaise *(p.49)*; Fresh peach yogurt *(p.43, using mango instead of peach)*; 1–2 slices of mango as finger food; cup of water	Fish kedgeree *(p.49)* with soft-cooked carrot sticks as finger food; mashed banana with slices of banana as finger food; breast or formula feed
DAY 6	Porridge with apple *(p.45, using pear instead of apple)*; slice of ripe pear as finger food; breast or formula feed	Mackerel and vegetable mash *(p.50)*; Fresh peach yogurt *(p.43)*; 1–2 slices of peach slices as finger food; cup of water	Lentils with carrot and coriander *(p.39, mashed rather than puréed)*; slices of banana and ripe pear as finger food; breast or formula feed
DAY 7	Breakfast wheat cake with warm milk; Pear and apple purée *(p.37)*; 1–2 slices of ripe pear as finger food; breast or formula feed	Beef stew *(p.51)* with soft-cooked carrot sticks as finger food; Fruity milk pudding *(p.42)*; cup of water	Pasta with sweet pepper sauce *(p.48)* with slices of soft-cooked bell pepper as finger food; Pear and apple purée *(p.37, mashed rather than puréed)*; breast or formula feed

Meal planner for 9 month–1 year olds

Between 9 months and 1 year old, babies are ready to begin eating chopped foods. You can start to phase out bottle-feeding and offer formula milk in a cup instead. If you are breastfeeding, you may continue with early-morning and bedtime feeds, and possibly one or two at other times of day. However, at mealtimes your baby will need to take water from a cup. Always finish meals by offering your baby either a milky dessert or a breast or formula feed.

	BREAKFAST	LUNCH	DINNER
DAY 1	First muesli (p.53); slices of banana as finger food; breast feed or cup of formula milk	Chicken and vegetable stir-fry (p.57) with steamed/boiled rice; small yogurt with grapes and clementine segments as finger food; cup of water	Scrambled egg (p.45) with toast fingers, carrot and celery sticks; slices of ripe peach as finger food; cup of water; breast feed or cup of formula milk
DAY 2	Breakfast wheat cake with milk; slices of kiwi as finger food; breast feed or cup of formula milk	First spaghetti bolognaise (p 49) with soft-cooked broccoli florets as finger food; Fruity rice pudding with cinnamon (p.58); cup of water	Mackerel and vegetable mash (p.50, serve without mashing); slices of ripe pear as finger food; cup of water; breast feed or cup of formula milk
❤ DAY 3	Multigrain hoop cereal with milk; extra hoops and slices of soft fruits as finger food; breast feed or cup of formula milk	Zucchini, cauliflower, and chickpea curry (p.55) with steamed/boiled rice; First chocolate pudding with fruit fingers (p.59); cup of water	Spinach dhal (p.46, serve without mashing); strawberries with a small yogurt; cup of water; breast feed or cup of formula milk
❤ DAY 4	Eggy toast fingers (p.53); slices of kiwi as finger food; breast feed or cup of formula milk	Pasta with lentils (p.55) and slices of red and green bell peppers; Fruity milk pudding (p.42); cup of water	Macaroni cheese (p.53) with boiled peas; Ready-to-go fruit fingers (p.58); cup of water; breast feed or cup of formula milk
DAY 5	First muesli (p.53) with natural bio-yogurt; slices of pear as finger food; breast feed or cup of formula milk	Moroccan lamb with couscous (p.57), steamed carrot sticks and broccoli florets; Creamy egg custard (p.42) with slices of banana; cup of water	Pasta with sweet pepper sauce (p.48) and slices of red bell pepper as finger food; Ready-to-go fruit fingers (p.58); cup of water; breast feed or cup of formula milk
DAY 6	Breakfast wheat cake with milk; slices of peach as finger food; breast feed or cup of formula milk	Beef stew (p.51, serve without mashing) with Roasted vegetable sticks (p.54); Sponge drops (p.204) with Fresh peach yogurt (p.43); cup of water	Fish kedgeree (p.49) with steamed green beans; segments of orange (with seeds removed); cup of water; breast feed or cup of formula milk
DAY 7	Mini blueberry pancakes (p.81); blueberries as finger food; breast feed or cup of formula milk	Pork with apples (p.56) with steamed broccoli florets; fromage frais with fruit fingers (p.59) cup of water	Cream cheese sandwiches (cut into small fingers); slices of avocado as finger food; pear slices; cup of water; breast feed or cup of formula milk

Meal planner for 1–2 year olds

This planner shows the main meals of the day, but to balance your child's diet (see pp.12–13) you will also need to add some nutritious snacks. Most children in this age group will need one or two snacks per day (see p.217 for suggestions). We have also included a drink with each meal, but your toddler will require additional snacks and drinks, such as more water, diluted fruit juice, or whole milk (to make up the recommended three servings of milk per day).

	BREAKFAST	LUNCH	DINNER
DAY 1	First muesli (p.53) with milk; cup of diluted fruit juice	Crackers with cream cheese and pineapple (p.63) and cherry tomatoes; slices of fresh peach; cup of water	Mini meatballs (p.71) with Tomato and bell pepper sauce (p.71), pasta shapes and cooked broccoli florets; Lemon self-saucing dessert (p.165); cup of water
DAY 2	Vanilla honey French toast shapes (p.84); slices of kiwi fruit; cup of milk	Houmous and red bell pepper triangles (p.53) with baby corn; Banana custard (p.75); cup of water	Glazed chicken drumsticks (p.70) with Basic sweet potato mash (p.135) and cooked cauliflower florets and peas; Strawberry and apple crumble (p.164) with ice cream/custard; cup of water
♥ DAY 3	Creamy first porridge (p.39) with milk; Soft summer fruit sticks (p.47); cup of diluted fruit juice	Creamy leek and potato soup (p.152, made with vegetable stock) with croutons (p.155); Toddlers' tortilla (p.67); dried apricots/dates; cup of water	Mini falafels (p.66) with Mint and cucumber yogurt dip (p.147) and pasta shapes with Tomato and bell pepper sauce (p.71); Warming winter fruit salad (p.73); cup of water
DAY 4	Banana oat muffins (p.83); cup of milk	Fishy toast fingers (p.65) with cucumber and celery sticks; yogurt with slices of mango; cup of water	First chicken nuggets (p.70) with Traditional oven fries (p.137) and Roasted vegetable sticks (p.54); grapes; cup of water
DAY 5	Breakfast cereal with milk; cup of diluted fruit juice	Toast fingers with chicken liver pâté (p.65); Fresh beet salad (p.144); fromage frais with clementine segments; cup of water	Mini monkfish kebabs (p.68) with boiled rice and Honey-glazed mini corn cobs (p.72); Mini apple and pear strudels (p.169); cup of water
DAY 6	Mini blueberry pancakes (p.81); cup of milk	Mini pitta pizzas (p.71) with carrot and cucumber sticks; Tropical fruit salad (p.56); cup of water	Baby fish cakes (p.69) with Tomato and avocado salsa (p.146); yogurt and pieces of melon; cup of water
DAY 7	Scrambled eggs with smoked salmon (p.87) with toast fingers; cup of hot chocolate	Tuna pasta salad (p.107); Mixed fruit jello (p.75); cup of water	Roast chicken (p.119) with Garlicky roast potatoes (p.137) and Roasted autumn vegetables (p.138); Chocolate baked bananas (p.205) with ice cream; cup of water

Meal planner for 3–6 year olds

This planner is based on meals that meet the nutritional requirements of 3–6 year olds, but they can be enjoyed by the whole family. Bear in mind that portion sizes will vary according to family members' ages, sizes, and activity levels. Snacks are important for children of this age who need two or three snacks a day (see p.217 for suggestions). Allow about two hours between meals and snacks so that your child has time to regain her appetite.

	BREAKFAST	LUNCH	DINNER
DAY 1	Tropical muesli (p.79) with milk; glass of apple juice	Sandwich with potted chicken spread (p.100), cucumber slices and celery sticks; Brownie (p.183); with strawberries; glass of milk	Mini meatballs (p.112) with spaghetti and Sesame green beans; (p.142); Apple, lychee, and clementine fruit salad (p.160); glass of water
DAY 2	Cinnamon French toast fingers (p.84); slices of banana; cup of hot chocolate	Tuna mayonnaise pitta pockets (p.104) with celery and carrot sticks; Fruit and fromage frais (p.180); glass of water	Sesame chicken fingers and Honey mustard dipping sauce (p.115) with Warm vegetable couscous (p.148) and Baby spinach and radish salad (p.143); Lemon self-saucing dessert (p.165); glass of water
DAY 3	Corn and bacon muffins (p.86); glass of diluted orange juice	New York-style pastrami on rye (p.103) with cherry tomatoes; banana; Carrot cake (p.185); glass of water	Cod fish fingers (p.129) with Paprika potato wedges (p.138) and Oven-roasted tomatoes (p.140); Apple sponge dessert (p.166) with custard; glass of water
DAY 4	Breakfast in a glass (p.80); wholewheat toast with Plum fruit spread (p.189)	Cream cheese and ham pinwheel sandwiches (p.105) with red and green bell pepper sticks; Fruit kebab (p.180); fruit yogurt; glass of water	Lamb hotpot (p.121) with Roasted pumpkin (p.140) and Stir-fried fresh spinach (p.143); Rhubarb muesli crumble (p.163) with ice cream; glass of water
DAY 5	Microwaved porridge with apricots (p.79); glass of milk	Minted beef samosa (p.108) with Mint and cucumber yogurt dip (p.147) and carrot sticks; Chocolate muffin (p.184); apple; carton of flavored milk	Teriyaki orange salmon parcels (p.129) with Traditional oven fries (p.137) and Stir-fried mixed vegetables (p.142); Crêpes with tropical salsa (p.163); glass of water
DAY 6	Mini blueberry pancakes (p.81); glass of milk	Tomato and bacon soup (p.155); Beefburger in a bun (p.113); clementine; glass of water	Chicken fajitas (p.119) with soft tortillas, Spicy tomato salsa (p.147), and Guacamole (p.99); Sweet couscous with raisins and yogurt (p.170); glass of water
DAY 7	Tomato and basil omelet (p.87); wholewheat toast; glass of Carrot and apple juice (p.176)	Roast lamb with spiced yogurt crust (p.121) and Roasted winter vegetables with potatoes (p.139); Mini trifle (p.203); glass of water	French bread pizza (p.96) with Mixed leaf and herb salad (p.143); Crispy fruit fritters (p.170); glass of water

Vegetarian menu planner

This menu plan is suitable for vegetarians who eat eggs and milk. It is based around foods containing plenty of iron, zinc, and B-vitamins—nutrients that poorly planned vegetarian diets can sometimes lack. The menus for each day provide 2–3 servings of foods that are rich in protein and iron—sometimes as part of the savory course, sometimes as part of a dessert. In addition to these meals, offer your child protein- and iron-rich snacks, such as breakfast cereals and milk.

	BREAKFAST	LUNCH	DINNER
DAY 1	Soy yogurt shake (p.80); granary toast with butter and Strawberry jelly (p.202); glass of grape juice	Spinach and feta triangles (p.108); Mint and cucumber yogurt dip (p.147); banana; Crispy chocolate rice cake (p.202); glass of water	Chickpeas with cumin and potatoes (p.133); Nutty celery and carrot salad (p.144); Crêpes with sweet tropical salsa (p.163); glass of water
DAY 2	English muffin; Breakfast pizza (p.85); Tropical pear juice (p.177)	Pink pasta and bean salad (p.106); cheese and crackers; Almond and date spiral (p.181); mango slices; glass of water	Tofu stir-fry (p.131) with plain noodles and Sesame green beans (p.142); Plum and almond crumble (p.164); glass of water
DAY 3	Tropical muesli (p.79) with milk; glass of pure orange juice	Houmous and alfalfa pitta pockets (p.104) with celery and carrot sticks; small yogurt; Chocolate almond cake (p.183); glass of water	Rice and peas (p.133) with Fresh beet salad (p.144); Baked cheesecake (p.168) with Red berry coulis (p.169); glass of water
DAY 4	Fruity English scones (p.85) with Plum fruit spread (p.189); glass of milk	Toasted peanut butter and banana sandwich (p.102) with red and green bell pepper sticks; Date and walnut loaf (p.186); slices of apple; carton of flavored milk	Pasta with Quick tomato sauce (p.111) and grated cheese; Crunchy salad with honey mustard dressing (p.145); Orange almond dessert (p.166) with ice cream or natural bio-yogurt; glass of water
DAY 5	Apple and oat muffin (p.83); Banana and honey milk shake (p.175)	Sandwich filled with Black-eye pea spread (p.98) and slices of cucumber with cherry tomatoes; Chocolate muffin (p.184); grapes; glass of water	Baked potato with cauliflower cheese (p.89) and Multicolored corn (p.141); Raspberry mango smoothie (p.173); glass of water
DAY 6	Mixed grain pecan pancakes (p.82) with mixed berries; cup of hot chocolate	Spicy carrot, lentil, and coriander soup (p.153); Corn fritters (p.93); Elderflower apples with yogurt (p.159); glass of water	Vegetable chili (p.126) with boiled/steamed rice; Brioche pudding (p.167); glass of water
DAY 7	Mushroom omelet (p.81) with toast; glass of milk	Lentil moussaka (p.132) with Roasted pumpkin (p.140) and steamed broccoli florets; Speedy frozen strawberry yogurt (p.159); carton of flavored milk	Minestrone (p.153) with Breadsticks (p.200); Spinach and ricotta pancakes (p.95); Winter dried fruit salad (p.160); glass of water

NUTRITIOUS SNACKS

These snacks will provide your child with additional nutrients and help to sustain her energy during the day. We have not specified portion sizes as these depend on the age, size, and appetite of your child.

7–9 months
- Soft summer fruit sticks *(p.47)*
- breadstick/rusk/rice cake
- kiwi slices/clementine segments (skin and seeds removed)

9–12 months
- fruit slices (apple/pear/banana) with cup of formula milk
- berries with a small yogurt and cup of water
- mini breadsticks with small cubes of cheese and a cup of formula milk
- rice cakes with Guacamole *(p.99)*/ Houmous *(p.98)*/Spicy plum fruit spread *(p.189)*; and a cup of water

1+ years
- breakfast cereal with milk
- milk shake/smoothie
- glass of milk with fruit slices
- fruit yogurt with berries
- glass of water/milk/diluted fruit juice combined with any snack from pp.179–189
- vegetable/fruit sticks with yogurt dip
- glass of milk/diluted fruit juice with Cheese and onion straws *(p.187)*/Breadsticks *(p.200)*
- Bagel chips *(p.188)* with salsa

- Pitta bread chips *(p.187)* with Houmous *(p.98)*/Black-eye pea spread *(p.98)*
- cheese cubes with a rice cake and slices of apple
- small sandwich filled with cheese and tomato/peanut butter and banana/potted meat and cucumber

Quick finger foods
- sandwich filled with meat slices/meat spread/bean spread, with vegetable sticks and cherry tomatoes; yogurt; fruit; and a glass of water
- Meat platter: selection of sliced meats, cheese cubes, vegetable and fruit slices; toast/pitta bread triangles; and a glass of milk/ diluted juice
- Vegetarian platter: selection of cheese cubes, Houmous *(p.98)*, Falafels *(p.66)*, vegetables and fruit slices; toast/pitta bread triangles; and a glass of milk/diluted juice
- Dipping plate: Houmous *(p.98)*, Black-eye pea spread *(p.98)*, and salsa with vegetable and fruit sticks; Pitta bread chips *(p.187)*, crackers, and Cheese and onion straws *(p.187)*; and a glass of milk

STORE CUPBOARD ESSENTIALS

A well-stocked store cupboard will enable you to prepare quick nutritious meals for your children using recipes from this book.

the cupboard

- Tinned tomatoes
- Tomato passata
- Tomato paste
- Tinned fruit in juice or light syrup
- Dried fruit
- Lentils – red and green
- Tinned chickpeas
- Tinned red kidney beans
- Ground and chopped nuts, such as almonds and walnuts
- Tinned tuna in water or oil
- Tinned salmon in water or oil
- Pasta
- Rice
- Couscous
- Oats
- Fortified breakfast cereals
- Breadcrumbs
- Flour – plain and self-raising
- Sugar – white and soft brown
- Maple syrup
- Honey
- Baking powder
- Baking soda
- Selection of herbs and spices including oregano, bay leaves, cinnamon, ground ginger, ground cumin, ground coriander, saffron, and turmeric

- Vanilla extract
- Soy sauce
- Tahini
- Selection of oils for cooking – rapeseed, soy, olive, other vegetable oils, such as sunflower
- Selection of oils for flavor and salads – walnut, olive, toasted sesame, toasted pumpkin
- Onions
- Garlic
- Potatoes

the fridge

- Selection of soft cuts of meat
- Selection of fresh vegetables
- Selection of fresh fruits
- Lemons or limes
- Ginger
- Butter or margarine
- Eggs
- Milk
- Cheese

the freezer

- Peas
- Corn
- Spinach
- Chicken breasts or thighs
- Frozen fish fillets and shrimps
- Ice cream

FOOD SAFETY AND HYGIENE

Reported cases of food poisoning have increased in recent years and young children are particularly at risk because their immune systems are not yet fully developed. Hygiene in the kitchen is very important. Here are some tips for food preparation to help protect you and your family from infection.

- Always wash hands thoroughly before preparing food.
- Use separate chopping boards for meat, fish, and poultry. Never cut bread, vegetables, fruit, or cooked food on the same board.
- Always store cooked and raw food separately in the fridge. Store cooked food above raw meats to ensure that the meats cannot drip onto the cooked food.
- Always cover foods for storage.
- Defrost meats, chicken, and fish thoroughly in the fridge before cooking.
- Reheated food should be heated to piping hot before being cooled for children.
- Make sure all meat, poultry, fish, and eggs are cooked thoroughly. For meat, this is indicated by the juices running clear when you put a knife into the thickest part of the meat.
- Wash fruits and vegetables if being eaten raw.
- Eat any leftovers within 2 days and do not reheat food more than once.
- Keep the temperature of your fridge at 4°C/40°F and your freezer at or below −18°C/0°F.
- Do not refreeze food which was frozen and has been partially or completely thawed.
- Never give your family food past its "use by" date.
- Keep dried food in sealed containers and frozen food in airtight containers.
- Don't leave foods in the freezer for too long. Use them in rotation and check the freezer manual to see how long each food can safely be frozen.
- Make sure everyone washes their hands before eating.

For weaning foods
Any leftover food served to your baby must be discarded at the end of a meal as the bacteria from your baby's saliva will be mixed into the food from the weaning spoon, and will grow in stored food.

GOOD INFORMATION GUIDE

Breastfeeding support groups:

National Childbirth Trust

Tel: 0870 444 8707

www.nctpregnancyandbabycare.com

www.nct.org.uk

www.nct-online.org

Association of Breastfeeding Mothers

Tel: 0844 412 2949

www.abm.me.uk

La Lèche League

Tel: 0845 456 1855

www.lalecheleague.org

The Breastfeeding Network

Tel: 0870 900 8787

www.breastfeeding.co.uk

The United States Breastfeeding Committee

www.usbreastfeeding.org

Food scares:

The Food Standards Agency

www.food.gov.uk

The United States National Agricultural Library

www.nal.usda.gov/foodsafety

Nutrition information:

The British Dietetic Association

www.bda.uk.com

The Food Standards Agency

www.food.gov.uk

The American Dietetic Association

www.fda.gov

Preterm babies:

BLISS—the premature baby charity

www.bliss.org.uk

Parents of Premature Babies Inc.

www.preemie-L.org

Coping with allergies:

www.coeliac.co.uk

www.csaceliacs.org

www.gluten.net

www.allergyuk.org

www.foodallergy.org

www.foodallergynetwork.com

Organic food and farming:

Soil Association

www.soilassociation.org

The United States National Agricultural Library

www.nal.usda.gov

The Vegetarian Society

www.vegsoc.org

The Vegetarian Resource Group

www.vrg.org

INDEX

ACKNOWLEDGMENTS

The Authors would like to thank their family and friends for inspiration, support, and encouragement in writing this book. We are indebted to our colleagues and our patients and their parents who have all contributed to our knowledge and understanding of the complex issues involved in feeding children. And finally, we would like to thank the many children who have, knowingly or unknowingly, tested our recipes and given their reactions.

The Publishers would like to thank all the child models.

Joshua Shaer

Eden Bakker

Toby Cross

Holly Clarke

James Woollerson

Luke Richards

Rebecca Clarke

Joel Cross

Isabel Richards